ECONOMIC ANALYSIS OF TORT LAW

This book looks at the negligence concept of tort law and studies the efficiency issue arising from the determination of negligence. It does so by scrutinizing actual court decisions from three common law jurisdictions – Britain, India and the United States of America.

This volume fills a very significant gap, scrutinizing 52 landmark judgments from these three countries, by focussing on the negligent affliction of economic loss determined by common law courts and how these findings relate to the existing theoretical literature. By doing so, it examines the formalization of legal concepts in theory, primarily the question of negligence determination and liability, and their centrality in theories concerning tort law.

This book will be very helpful for students, professors and practitioners of law, jurisprudence and legal theory. It will additionally be of use to researchers and academics interested in law and economics, procedure and legal history.

Malabika Pal is Associate Professor of Economics at Miranda House, University of Delhi. She has worked as Associate Professor of Law and Legal Studies at the School of Law, Governance and Citizenship, Ambedkar University, New Delhi. Her research interests are in the fields of law and economics and international finance. She is a recipient of the National Scholarship and the Ford Foundation Scholarship.

"This study of tort cases from three jurisdictions from the perspective of negligence determination is an important contribution to the law and economics literature. The in-depth and scholarly analysis carried out in the book makes it clear that from the perspective of economic efficiency it is of utmost importance to differentiate between the two ways of determining negligence. The value of the book lies in bringing to the fore an aspect of the tort law that is of great importance from the efficiency perspective. This eminently readable text, therefore, should be of interest not only to those interested in the sub-discipline of law and economics but to judges and lawyers concerned with tort law as well."

– **Satish K. Jain,** *Retired Professor in Economics, Centre for Economic Studies and Planning, Jawaharlal Nehru University, New Delhi, India*

"The book makes an important contribution to the literature on economic analysis of liability rules. The primary focus of the book is on determination of negligence/non-negligence in actual judicial decision making. The exercise is undertaken through careful analysis of adjudicated cases from three legal jurisdictions of India, the United Kingdom and the United States. The work demonstrates that determination of negligence standards by courts has implications for the distribution of accident loss between and among the parties involved. More importantly, it has implications for efficiency properties of liability rules as predicted by the standard economic models."

– **Ram Singh,** *Professor in Economics, Delhi School of Economics, India*

"The discipline of law and economics is as yet a young and emerging area of research in India. The book makes an important contribution to this very area. The book is very well-written, and it was a pleasure to study a work such as this."

– **Naresh Kumar Sharma,** *Professor in Economics, University of Hyderabad, India*

"In my opinion, the overall impact and reach of the book is likely to go beyond the exact topic because it tries to relate a formal theory in the law and economics literature to its actual empirical context in a way which has largely been missing so far. The book is going to be a significant contribution to the very thin literature on the economic analysis of judgments from the Indian courts. In my opinion, the book tries to present the author's very competent, scholarly and relevant research in a cogent manner."

– **Rajendra P. Kundu,** *Former Professor in Economics, Ambedkar University, Delhi, India*

ECONOMIC ANALYSIS OF TORT LAW

The Negligence Determination

Malabika Pal

LONDON AND NEW YORK

First published 2020
by Routledge
2 Park Square, Milton Park, Abingdon, Oxon OX14 4RN

and by Routledge
52 Vanderbilt Avenue, New York, NY 10017

Routledge is an imprint of the Taylor & Francis Group, an informa business

© 2020 Malabika Pal

The right of Malabika Pal to be identified as author of this work has been asserted by them in accordance with sections 77 and 78 of the Copyright, Designs and Patents Act 1988.

All rights reserved. No part of this book may be reprinted or reproduced or utilised in any form or by any electronic, mechanical, or other means, now known or hereafter invented, including photocopying and recording, or in any information storage or retrieval system, without permission in writing from the publishers.

Trademark notice: Product or corporate names may be trademarks or registered trademarks, and are used only for identification and explanation without intent to infringe.

British Library Cataloguing-in-Publication Data
A catalogue record for this book is available from the British Library

Library of Congress Cataloging-in-Publication Data
Names: Pal, Malabika, author.
Title: Economic analysis of tort law : the negligence determination / Malabika Pal.
Description: Abingdon, Oxon ; New York, NY : Routledge, 2020. | Based on author's thesis (doctoral - Jawaharlal Nehru University, 2012). | Includes bibliographical references and index.
Identifiers: LCCN 2019021395 | ISBN 9781138386709 (hardback : alk. paper) | ISBN 9780367348311 (pbk. : alk. paper) | ISBN 9780429327858 (e-book)
Subjects: LCSH: Torts—Economic aspects. | Negligence—Economic aspects. | Negligence—United States—Cases. | Negligence—Great Britain—Cases. | Negligence—India—Cases.
Classification: LCC K923 .P348 2020 | DDC 346.03—dc23
LC record available at https://lccn.loc.gov/2019021395

ISBN: 978-1-138-38670-9 (hbk)
ISBN: 978-0-367-34831-1 (pbk)
ISBN: 978-0-429-32785-8 (ebk)

Typeset in Bembo
by Apex CoVantage, LLC
Printed and bound by CPI Group (UK) Ltd, Croydon CR0 4YY

CONTENTS

List of tables   *vi*
Foreword   *vii*

1	Introduction	1
2	Economic analysis of select British cases	43
3	Economic analysis of select Indian cases	104
4	Economic analysis of select American cases	155
5	Conclusion	207

Bibliography   *212*
Index   *219*

TABLES

2.A Schematic representation of the 17 cases analyzed   103
3.A Schematic representation of the 20 Indian cases analyzed   154
4.A Schematic representation of the 15 cases analyzed   206

FOREWORD

One of the most fundamental ideas of the tort law is that of "negligence." Often, whether the injurer would be held liable, and to what extent, is decided on the basis of whether the injurer is deemed to be negligent or non-negligent in the way he or she acted. Sometimes, the negligence or otherwise of the victim is taken into account, either in isolation or in conjunction with the negligence or otherwise of the injurer. There are several ways in which courts make determinations regarding negligence. One method for determining negligence or otherwise of a party is to compare the actual level of care taken by the party in conducting its activity with some standard level of care that is expected from the party. If the actual level of care is less than what is deemed to be the due care level, the party in question is found to have been negligent; and in case the actual level of care is greater than or equal to the due care level, the party is found to be non-negligent. Another way to determine the negligence question is to look for some precaution that the party in question could have taken but did not take that would have resulted in some net decrease in the social cost of harm. If such a precaution can be found, then the party who failed to take that precaution is deemed to be negligent; and if no such precaution can be found then the party is deemed to be non-negligent. There are, of course, other ways by which courts determine the negligence question, but these two ways are the most important ones. In all the cases that Malabika Pal has analyzed in this book, the negligence determination is done in these two ways only.

In this book, cases from three jurisdictions are analyzed: the USA, the UK, and India. The remarkable fact is that in all three jurisdictions both methods of negligence determination are used. This seems to indicate that courts possibly do not attach much significance to the difference between these two ways of deciding upon the negligence question. Economic analysis of these two ways of determining negligence shows that in terms of efficiency implications, these two methods are profoundly different. If negligence is decided upon by comparing the actual level with some fixed due care level, and if the due care level is chosen appropriately, then under most of the rules that are used in practice, there would be incentive for the parties to take efficient levels of care, i.e., care levels that would minimize social costs of accidents. On the other hand, if the negligence determination is done on the basis of the existence or otherwise of some untaken precaution that would have cost less than the reduction in harm that its taking would have brought about, then regardless of which rule the courts use, the incentives of the parties would not invariably be directed towards taking efficient levels of care.

This study of tort cases from three jurisdictions from the perspective of negligence determination is an important contribution to the law and economics literature. The in-depth and scholarly analysis carried out in the book makes it clear that from the perspective of economic efficiency, it is of utmost importance to differentiate between the two ways of determining negligence. The value of the book lies in bringing to the fore an aspect of the tort law that is of great importance from the efficiency perspective. This eminently readable text, therefore, should be of interest not only to those interested in the sub-discipline of law and economics but also to judges and lawyers concerned with tort law.

Satish K. Jain

1

INTRODUCTION

Negligence is a central concept in tort law. It has been widely accepted that as a matter of doctrine, the expansion of liability in modern tort law took place within the framework of the concept of negligence. Broadly, "negligence" refers to the failure of an actor to take reasonable care to prevent harm caused by the actor's conduct.[1] One close contender for being the fundamental tort principle is strict liability. It refers to liability imposed on an actor for harm the actor causes, whether or not the actor is negligent.[2] The concept of "fault" includes negligence and intentional wrongful infliction of harm on others. With respect to only unintentional torts, with which this study is concerned, the concept of fault becomes synonymous with negligence. According to the Restatement (Third) of Torts, the overarching and unifying normative principle of American tort law is fault. Although pockets of strict liability exist, unlike negligence, no overarching principle unifies them in an effective and coherent whole.[3]

The rule of negligence with the defense of contributory negligence was the dominant rule of tort law not only in America but also in most common law jurisdictions since its inception into English law in the case of *Butterfield v Forrester*[4] in 1809 and its espousal in the leading American case of *Brown v Kendall*.[5] In the latter case, the defendant took up a stick to separate fighting dogs belonging to the plaintiff and the defendant and during the attempt accidently hit the plaintiff in the eye, injuring him severely. Chief Justice Shaw laid down the rule:

> if both plaintiff and defendant at the time of the blow were using ordinary care, or if at that time, the defendant was using ordinary care, and the plaintiff was not, or if at that time, both the defendant and the plaintiff were not using ordinary care, then the plaintiff could not recover.[6]

This rule was, however, considered very harsh, and disenchantment with it led to the softening doctrine of "last clear chance," enunciated by the prominent case of

Davies v Mann.⁷ According to this, the plaintiff could recover despite being guilty of contributory negligence, if the defendant had a sufficiently good opportunity to avoid the accident at a point when the plaintiff did not. There were many who advocated the apportionment of loss; despite that, the rule of contributory negligence continued to dominate well into the middle of the twentieth century.

One of the leading tort scholars, Gary T. Schwartz, had traced the history of tort law in the United States and found that negligence, not strict liability, was at the core of tort law. In an important article, he argued that American courts and legislatures undertook to dismantle a number of formal obstacles that had previously impeded the achievement of the negligence principle's full potential.⁸ He argued that between 1900 and 1950s, American tort law remained generally stable, with tort opinions only sharpening and clarifying tort doctrines that had previously been presented in a relatively crude manner. This stability provided the backdrop for those tort changes after 1960 that demonstrated the vitality of negligence. He argued:

> These changes included the abolition of immunities for charities, governments and family – abolitions that rendered such defendants liable under the standards of negligence. Auto-guest statutes and guest doctrines were eliminated, thereby enlarging the liability of motorists for harms caused by their negligence. Many courts established a general negligence principle to cover the liability of landowners, thereby rejecting rules of limited liability that had been tied to the plaintiff's status as a land tenant. The locality doctrine in medical malpractice cases was withdrawn, thereby permitting a fuller consideration of the question of the doctor's malpractice. New affirmative duties were recognized, as in Tarasoff v Regents of University of California – duties which defendants violate if, but only if, they behave negligently. Also, new causes of action were created for the negligent affliction of economic loss and the negligent affliction of emotional distress. The traditional defense of contributory negligence was replaced by the doctrine of comparative negligence, which by apportioning liability in accordance with fault could be seen as an elaboration of the basic idea of fault liability. As well, many courts 'merged' the defense of assumption of risk into the doctrine of comparative fault, thereby confirming that negligence is the only feature of the plaintiff's conduct that merits the law's attention.
>
> *(Schwartz (1992) pp. 605–606)*

In Britain too, apportionment of loss between the plaintiff and defendant became possible in cases of maritime collision under the Maritime Conventions Act, 1911. The Law Reform (Contributory Negligence) Act, 1945, applied the principle on which the Maritime Conventions Act, 1911, was based to contributory negligence on land.⁹ Most common law jurisdictions have moved to one form or the other of comparative negligence.¹⁰ In America, although until 1968 only seven states had recognized apportionment by the mid-1970s, it had become the majority rule due to a sudden spurt in support for comparative negligence, and at present almost all states have moved to comparative negligence.[11] India has also moved towards apportionment following the change in Britain, without bringing about any corresponding enactment. Although a late entrant in this shift, Australia has also moved towards apportionment.

Since the whole issue of apportionment depends on negligence determination, what constitutes negligence is crucial for the judgments. It turns out that it is crucial for the economic analysis of law as well. This is because one of the central issues that legal scholars and economists analyzing law are concerned with is the efficiency of tort law doctrines. An analysis of the literature on the economic analysis reveals that the efficiency question hinges crucially on the conceptualization of negligence. In what follows, we first explore the issue of negligence determination as conceptualized in the economic analysis of law to bring out its efficiency implications. That section is followed by a review of the legal literature in an attempt to compare the alternative conceptualizations with that assumed by the economic model. This is followed by a section on the basis of selection of a set of negligence cases from three common law countries to examine which notion of negligence is used in actual cases litigated in court. A final section will briefly outline the chapterization.

1.1 Economic analysis of law

The origin of the economic analysis of law is often traced to the publication of the seminal article, "The Problem of Social Cost," by Ronald Coase in 1960. However, some works such as Rowley (1998) and Posner (2005) have argued that this perspective ignores the important contributions of the great political philosophers and economists of the Scottish Enlightenment and those of Jeremy Bentham, who wrote almost two centuries prior to Coase.[12] Richard Posner concentrates on the inspiration provided by the works of Bentham, particularly his *Introduction to the Principles of Morals and Legislation*.[13] Posner emphasizes that this influence is discernable in two respects: first, with respect to the explicit use of economic logic in the analysis of crime and punishment, and second, as an early proponent of non-market economics.

Regarding the first aspect, Posner writes:

> Bentham has made a number of important economic points in the Introduction: a person commits a crime only if the pleasure he anticipates from the crime exceeds the expected cost. To deter crime, therefore, the punishment must impose sufficient pain that when added to any other pain anticipated by the criminal will exceed the pleasure that he anticipates from the crime; punishment greater than this should not be imposed, because the result would be to create pain (to the undeterrable criminal) not offset by pleasure (benefits) to the potential victims of crime; the schedule of punishments must be calibrated in such a way that if the criminal has a choice of crimes, he

commits the least serious; fines are a more efficient method of punishment than imprisonment because they confer a benefit as well as impose a detriment; the less likely the criminal is to be caught, the heavier the punishment must be, to maintain the expected cost great enough to deter.

Posner argues that these points formed the basis of the economic theory of crime and punishment revived later by Gary Becker.

Posner, however, argues that just because Bentham confined his economic approach (as far as law was concerned) to criminal law, it does not follow that his influence on the economic analysis of law is necessarily confined to the area of crime. In fact, Bentham's insistence on the universality of utility calculations in human decisions can be considered to be the foundation of the economics of non-market behaviour, which is to say, "the investigation by economists of behaviour that occurs other than in explicit markets." Posner writes:

> A good deal of the economic analysis of law is an application of that economics, because law is primarily a non-market institution and one that regulates non-market as well as market behavior − the behaviour of criminals, prosecutors, accident victims, divorcing couples, testators, polluters, religious believers, speakers and so forth, as well as businessmen, workers and consumers engaged in their conventional activities (an important qualification since businessmen for example, can be polluters or criminals as well as buyers and sellers).... Bentham may be taken to have invented non-market economics.

Bentham's promise of the universality of the economic model of human behaviour was resurrected by Gary Becker in the 1950s in his doctoral dissertation on the economic analysis of racial discrimination. In his collection of essays, *The Economic Approach to Human Behavior*, Becker has used the economic approach in attempting to understand human behaviour in a variety of contexts and situations. In the first chapter he elaborates on what constitutes this "economic approach" and argues that what most distinguishes economics as a discipline from other disciplines in the social sciences is not the subject matter, as has often been projected, but its approach. Summarizing the economic approach, he argues: "all human behavior can be viewed as involving participants who maximize their utility from a stable set of preferences and accumulate an optimal amount of information and other inputs in a variety of markets." He concludes by saying that "the economic approach provides a valuable unified framework for understanding all human behavior."[14]

In the field of law, until the 1960s economic analysis was virtually synonymous with anti-trust economics. That was due to the influence of Aaron Director in the Chicago Law School. He was joined later by Ronald Coase in editing the *Journal of Law and Economics*, which Posner describes as a landmark development in the law and economics movement. Coase's "The Problem of Social Cost" undoubtedly had a revolutionary impact on the way the legal world thought about the effects of liability rules. His demonstration of the lack of effect of a legal rule on the allocation of resources where transaction costs are zero came to be known as the Coase theorem.[15] Priest (2005) argues that the roles of Coase and Director in law and economics are essentially similar, although the Coasean approach has application to a much broader range of legal rules than the Director approach. Neither had an interest in law or the development of law; both of them attempted to explain social behaviour alone.[16]

Priest distinguishes between two strands of analysis: one concerned with the explanation of behaviour and the influence of law on behaviour exemplified by the Director-Coase type of work; and another concerned with the explanation of law itself – shown by the work of Guido Calabresi and Richard Posner. According to Priest, the sudden intellectual rise of law and economics and its impact on American legal thought can be attributed to the publication of Calabresi's 1970 book, *The Cost of Accidents* and Posner's *The Economic Analysis of Law*, soon after. The former applies economic analysis, not to practices that led to legal disputes in the manner of Director and Coase, but to the accident law system in its entirety. The framework of the book was considered sufficiently general to implicate a range of other legal fields as well. However, it was Posner's *Economic Analysis of Law*, in which he proposed a theory that the central unifying feature of the common law is that its rules are defined to achieve efficiency, that had a greater impact and compelled the legal world to give greater attention to law and economics.

The reason why Posner's analysis had such widespread impact compared to Calabresi's[17] was his focus on one single central principle – efficiency, underlying all of common law. Priest emphasizes that Posner's theory of the law is simple:

> that common law rules are efficient, that common law judges define a legal rule as if they consciously weigh the relative costs to the disputants of avoiding the dispute and then consciously determine how to optimize future behaviour. Judges, of course, draft opinions incorporating legal terms and concepts, but the analysis of the central rules of common law shows that these rules achieve effects identical to those that would result where cost-benefit calculations were express.

According to Priest, Posner achieved for the law Einstein's dream for physics: a unified theory. He argues that the advantage of Posner's definition of a unidimensional scientific theory was that it allowed a scholar to discuss the legal system in a sophisticated way without having to defend any value judgment implicit in the discussion.

However, his theory was criticized on the grounds that it failed to identify the mechanism that made the common law rules efficient. In 1979, Posner provided an explanation through his theory of wealth maximization, which in turn was subject to strong criticism, prominently by Dworkin (1980), Coleman (1988), Weinrib (1980) and Kronman (1995). In Landes and Posner (1981), the claim that efficiency was the only value explaining the common law rules was modified and replaced by the argument that it was the single *dominant* value. In their landmark work, *The Economic Structure of Tort Law*, they reiterated:

> throughout the history of the common law efficiency has been the dominant value embodied in tort law, but not the only value. Distributive and other nonefficiency concerns, which have shaped legislative interventions in safety questions from workmen's compensation through no-fault automobile accident compensation, have also influenced the courts in common law cases. Thus if a rule of tort law cannot be explained on efficiency grounds, this is not a contradiction of the theory, because it is consistent with the proposition that most rather than all tort doctrines are efficient.[18]

In Posner (1995) a detailed elaboration of the theory of wealth maximization can be found. He explains:

> The concept of efficiency implicit in the use of the criterion of wealth maximization is what is called "Kaldor-Hicks efficiency," or sometimes "potential Pareto efficiency." It differs from Pareto efficiency in not requiring that persons harmed by a change be compensated. It thus lacks the aspect of unanimity that makes Pareto efficiency so attractive an ethical principle.[19]

In economics, although several different but closely related notions of efficiency are used, the most important is that of Pareto optimality, which is based on the Pareto criterion.[20] Jain (2010a) provides a lucid discussion of the efficiency criteria used in the economic analysis of law. A social alternative x is defined to be Pareto-superior to another social alternative y if and only if every individual in the society considers x to be at least as good as y and at least one individual considers x to be better than y. According to the Pareto-criterion, alternative x is considered to be socially better than alternative y if x is Pareto-superior to y. A social alternative is defined to be Pareto-optimal or Pareto-efficient if and only if there is no feasible alternative that is Pareto-superior to it. That is to say, an alternative is Pareto-efficient if and only if it is not possible to make some individual better-off without making some other individual worse off.[21]

The scope of the Pareto-criterion is limited because under it only some pairs of alternatives can be compared. If there is a person in the collective who prefers alternative x to alternative y and another who prefers alternative y to x, then under the Pareto criterion x and y cannot be compared regardless of the preferences of the remaining individuals. Thus, in many contexts, the notion of efficiency used is that which is based on the Kaldor-Hicks criterion rather than the Pareto criterion. Under the Kaldor-Hicks criterion, a change is considered better if gainers can compensate the losers and still be better-off. There is no need, however, to actually compensate the losers. One can infer from the Kaldor principle that if the gainers can compensate the losers and still be better-off then the total wealth after the change must be larger than that before the change. Since actual compensation is not paid, there is no consensual basis to the change. However, the major drawback of the Kaldor compensation principle is that it is possible that two alternatives x and y can each be better than each other, that is, the "better than" relation generated by it is not asymmetric. Under it, it is possible that of the two social alternatives x and y, each is better than the other. That is, examples can be constructed such that if there is a move from alternative y to alternative x, gainers can compensate the losers and still be better-off; and also that if there is a move from alternative x to y, gainers can compensate the losers and still be better-off.

Scitovsky proposed a criterion to resolve the difficulty: under it, one can infer that "social alternative x is better than social alternative y" from the condition that

> if there is a move from social alternative y to x then the gainers can compensate the losers and still be better off; and if there is a move from x to y then it is not the case that the gainers can compensate the losers and still be better off.

In contrast to the Kaldor criterion, the Scitovsky "better than" relation is asymmetric, but as Arrow (1963) showed, it fails to satisfy transitivity. The logical difficulties with the Kaldor and Scitovsky compensation principles are examples of the Arrow paradox relating to aggregation of individual preferences into social preferences; they can also be seen as manifestations of the fact that the notion of wealth in general cannot be separated from its distribution. Despite these difficulties, the efficiency analysis of law has been mostly done using the Kaldor criterion.

If one associates inefficiency with wastage of resources, then the importance of having efficient institutions is clear. If an institution does not have the property of invariably yielding efficient outcomes then in some situations there would be wastage of resources; on the other hand, if an institution is efficient then in no situation would there be wastage of resources. One institution that allocates resources efficiently under ideal conditions is the market.[22] However, in the absence of the ideal conditions, for instance, if there are externalities, there is no guarantee that the allocation arrived at under the market mechanism would be Pareto-efficient. Externalities create divergence between private and social cost, and this leads to socially inappropriate decisions. The socially optimal level of output is that at which the price equals the sum of private marginal cost and marginal harm, but the actual amount is equal to the amount at which price equals marginal cost, leading to over-production of the externality generating good. For efficient allocation, the divergence must be eliminated. Pigou's solution of state intervention in the form of taxes (and subsidies in case of positive externalities) was widely accepted.[23] For instance, if a factory owner is made to pay taxes equal to the harm inflicted on the people living in the neighbourhood, the factory owner will take into account the taxes in addition to the costs of producing the good while deciding how much of the good to produce.

In *The Problem of Social Cost*, Coase argued that the nature of the externality problem is reciprocal. If person A's activity is inflicting harm on B then preventing

8 Introduction

A from undertaking the harmful activity so that harm to B can be avoided would harm A, as he would have to forgo the gain accruing to him from the activity. Coase argued that what was required was to avoid the more serious harm. What Coase showed through a number of examples has come to be regarded as the Coase theorem. It states that if transaction costs are zero then the allocation of resources will be efficient regardless of liability assignments. In the examples considered by Coase, the allocation of resources was also invariant with respect to liability assignments, but this is not true in general. This is because when the injurer is liable for the harm to the victim, the distribution of wealth would be in favour of the victim, and when the harm has to be borne by the victim himself, the wealth distribution would be in favour of the injurer. From the kind of examples and considerations that were used to assert the Coase theorem, it follows that if transaction costs are prohibitively high then the allocation of resources would depend on the liability assignments. The significance of the Coase theorem for the market ideology was that in contrast to Pigovian taxes and subsidies, which required acquisition of relevant information for aligning private and social costs and intervention by the government, use of liability rules merely implied assignment or re-assignment of property rights without any necessity of intervention in the functioning of free markets.

1.2 Economic analysis of tort law

The word "tort" is derived from the Latin "tortus" or "twisted" to denote conduct that is crooked, not straight. Keeton et al. (1984) note that "tort" can be found in the French language and was in common use in England as a general synonym for "wrong." However, they explain: "a wrong is called a tort only if the harm which has resulted, or is about to result from it, is capable of being compensated in an action at law for damages, although other remedies may also be available."[24] Often tort law has been regarded as that area of common law that is concerned with accidental injuries. A suit under the law of torts is generally a private suit over injuries as opposed to criminal prosecutions. In common law countries, the law of torts has developed from a large body of formerly unrelated doctrines such as conversion, trespass, nuisance, defamation, negligence, deceit etc. The civil codes require the injurer to compensate the victim, if the legal requirements are fulfilled. A rule that apportions the harm between the injurer and the victim is called a liability rule. Liability rules are distinct from property rights, which allow the owner an exclusive right to the use, control and enjoyment of some resource – that is, a right to exclude all others from the use of the resource without the consent of the owners of the right. In contrast, a liability rule creates a right not to exclude another from using a resource but only to claim damages for the injuries. The distinction is clear from the apt illustration given in Landes and Posner (1987):

> Often property rights and liability rules coexist in the same resource. This is dramatically true of the human body: a person has a property right against someone who strikes him deliberately and without justification, but

enjoys only a protection of a liability rule against someone who strikes him accidentally.[25]

Often liability rules are divided into two groups: the polar cases of strict liability and no liability, and rules based on negligence by one party or the other. While under the rule of strict liability the injurer is made liable regardless of anything, under no liability the loss invariably falls on the victim. When one party's activity results in harm for another party it would generally be the case that the probability and extent of harm can be reduced by care taken by one or both parties. A party is said to be negligent if, following an accident, a fact-finder determines that he or she did not meet the appropriate standard of care, often called due care. Most of the liability rules used in practice apportion liability on the basis of negligence or otherwise of the parties. These include rules of negligence, negligence with the defense of contributory negligence, strict liability with the defense of contributory negligence and comparative negligence.

The essence of the negligence doctrine is that a person should be subject to liability for carelessly causing harm to another. From the time negligence emerged as a distinct liability rule it was evident that a causal connection between the defendant's breach of duty and the plaintiff's harm needed to be established such that the causation was natural, probable and not too remote. Early courts and commentators while exploring the developing rule of negligence identified its various "elements" – ranging from two to five, with four being the most common division.[26] In a very influential article, Owen (2007) has endorsed the five-element formulation rather than the usual four-element division because "each of the five components is complex and conceptually distinct, and because all must co-exist or a negligence claim will fail." These are duty, breach, cause-in-fact, proximate cause and harm.

Regarding the first element, Owen argues:

> Because choices are deemed improper only if they breach a pre-existing obligation to avoid and repair carelessly inflicted harm on others, duty gives definitional coherence to the negligence inquiry. . . . Every negligence claim must pass through the 'duty portal' that bounds the scope of tort recovery for accidental harm.

The second element of the tort of negligence is the defendant's improper act or omission, normally referred to as breach of duty which presupposes the existence of a standard of proper behaviour to avoid undue risks of harm to other persons and their property. Owen elaborates:

> While the standard of care must be adjusted for special relationships, as classically was the norm, modern negligence law imposes a duty on most persons in most situations to act with reasonable care, often referred to as 'due care', for the safety of others and themselves. A person who acts carelessly – unreasonably, without due care – breaches the duty of care, and such conduct

is characterized as 'negligent'. And so, within the tort of negligence (which we might label Negligence with a capital 'N'), the second element is negligent action or inaction, often referred to simply as 'negligence' (which we might label negligence with a lower 'n').

He adds:

> To assess what type and amount of care is reasonable in particular circumstances, negligence law turns to the standard of 'a reasonable prudent person', and asks how such a person would behave in a particular situation, in pursuing his or her own objective, to avoid harming others in the process.

Owen argues that the five-element approach permits the division of the conventional two-pronged element of "causation" into its separate components – cause-in-fact and proximate cause, recognizing the "distinctness and complexity of issues embraced by each." To prove causation, it is not enough for the plaintiff to show that the defendant's conduct caused the harm; the plaintiff must further link his or her damage to the defendant's negligence, the aspect of conduct that breached a duty to the plaintiff. The usual test for cause-in-fact is the "but-for" test: if the plaintiff's harm would not have occurred but for the defendant's negligence, the defendant's negligence is a cause-in-fact of the plaintiff's harm. However, even if a defendant's negligence is a cause-in-fact of harm, he can still escape liability if the relationship between his act and the resulting harm is in some sense "too remote." The prominent early test for proximate cause was whether a harmful result was "a direct consequence" of the defendant's negligence; this was abandoned in favour of reasonable foreseeability.[27] Under this test, the responsibility of an actor for the consequences of wrongful action is limited by the principles of reasonable foreseeability – that is, they will not be responsible for consequences that fall outside the scope of their wrong doing.

Finally, the most important element of a tort claim is harm – the damage a plaintiff suffers as a proximate result of a defendant's breach of duty. The underlying deterrent objective of the negligence cause of action is to compensate the plaintiff for harm improperly inflicted by the defendant. The interest that is usually protected by the law of negligence is freedom from improperly inflicted physical harm, including physical injury, death and property damage. Negligence law does not protect plaintiffs against the risk of "pure" economic loss (such as lost wages, lost contract or lost profits) where the plaintiff does not also suffer physical harm. However, the law of negligence allows accident victims to recover damages for their secondary losses proximately following from a physical injury, including lost earnings and earning power, pain and suffering, emotional distress and, in some cases, lost enjoyment in life.

The economic analysis of tort law is essentially concerned with the incentives that various liability rules create for individuals to take precautions against accidents. In what follows, we will attempt to show how the elements discussed earlier have been incorporated in the analysis and the main results that have been derived from the standard framework. In the literature dealing with the question of the efficiency of liability rules, the problem has been considered within the framework of accidents resulting from the interaction of two risk neutral parties, the victim (the plaintiff) and the injurer (the defendant). The social goal is taken to be the minimization of total social costs – the sum of the costs of care taken by the two parties and the expected accident loss. The probability of accident and the amount of loss in case of occurrence of accident are assumed to depend on the levels of care taken by the two parties. The levels of care at which total social costs are minimized are known as the socially efficient levels of care or, simply, the efficient levels of care. The incentives needed to obtain these levels of care would be reached when the decision maker internalizes the marginal cost and marginal benefits of his or her actions. That is, the party will take care up to the level at which the cost of taking one more unit of precaution equals the resulting savings in expected liability. The expected liability depends on the liability rule in operation. A liability rule is efficient if it invariably induces both parties to behave in ways that result in the socially efficient levels of care.

In the literature, it is generally assumed that cost of care and expected accident loss functions are such that there is a unique configuration of care levels of the two parties at which total social costs are minimized.[28] Regarding the harm, it is assumed that while adjudicating accident cases courts can costlessly assess the harm suffered by the victims. It is also assumed that "damages," the amount paid by a liable party under a liability rule, is assumed to equal the harm caused in the accident. These assumptions are very crucial for the efficiency of a liability rule. Depending on the liability rule in operation, there could be legally binding due care levels for both the parties, for only the injurer, for only the victim or for neither party. It is assumed that whenever a liability rule specifies the legally binding due care level for a party, it is set at the level at which total social costs are minimized. A party is called nonnegligent if its care level is at least equal to the due care level; otherwise it is called negligent. Under the rule of negligence, the injurer is liable only if he or she is negligent; that is, his or her care falls short of the due care level. However, in this case the victim would get compensation even if he or she were at fault, if the injurer was negligent. Thus, the defense of contributory negligence was brought in. Under the latter rule, the injurer is liable only when he or she is negligent, and the victim is nonnegligent. Under the rule of strict liability with the defense of contributory negligence, the injurer is liable as long as the victim is nonnegligent. Thus, the defense of contributory negligence completely bars the victim from recovery if he or she is negligent. Under comparative negligence, the victim and the injurer share the costs of an accident when both fail to exercise due care.

The starting point of the economic analysis of negligence was the publication of Posner's article, "A Theory of Negligence," in 1972. However, it was the first formal analysis of the efficiency aspects of important tort liability rules in Brown (1973) that gave rise to the now voluminous work on the economic analysis of negligence.[29] He showed that, in the context of his model, the rule of negligence,

negligence with the defense of contributory negligence and strict liability with the defense of contributory negligence all have the property of invariably inducing both the victim and the injurer to take levels of care that are appropriate from the perspective of minimization of total social costs. He also showed that the rules of strict liability and no liability do not possess this property. For most of the liability rules that are commonly used, the question of efficiency was settled by Brown's contribution. Jain and Singh (2002) considered the totality of liability rules that can be conceived theoretically and obtained a general characterization of efficient liability rules. It was shown that a liability rule is efficient for all applications if and only if it satisfies the condition of negligence liability. The condition of negligence liability requires that: (i) whenever the injurer is nonnegligent and the victim is negligent, the entire loss in case of occurrence of accident must be borne by the victim; and (ii) whenever the victim is nonnegligent and the injurer is negligent, the entire loss in case of occurrence of accident must be borne by the injurer.

In some situations, the parties to potential accidents control not only the level of precaution that they take but also the amount of the potentially dangerous activity, as well. For instance, one can choose how carefully to drive and how much to drive. Just as decisions about care should take into account the risks imposed on others, so should decisions about the amount of the risky activity to be undertaken. However, Shavell (1980a) has shown that if activity levels can be varied in addition to care levels, then no liability rule would invariably give rise to efficient outcomes. In Brown's model and in the subsequent literature on the efficiency of liability rules, it is assumed that the activity levels of both parties are fixed. Another issue that affects the efficiency properties of liability rules is uncertainty about the outcome of the courts. Parties can be uncertain about the level of care actually taken because of momentary lapses in care or attention. Courts can improperly identify the level of care actually taken because of evidentiary difficulties. Courts can also incorrectly identify the standard of care because they do not correctly consider all the costs and benefits of precautions. These, and other uncertainties, have been widely studied in the literature, in particular by Diamond (1974), Green (1976) and Calfee and Craswell (1984). Many of these results show that uncertainty will lead parties to take more than the appropriate level of care.

We note that the previous results are with respect to only one injurer and one victim. In this case, the problem of characterizing efficient liability rules has been completely solved. However, for the case where there are multiple injurers or multiple victims only partial results are available. Landes and Posner (1980) examined the case of multiple injurers and one victim and showed that the rule of negligence gives efficient results in all cases; but the rule of strict liability with the defense of contributory negligence does not. Jain and Kundu (2006) examined a particular subclass of liability rules, namely simple liability rules, in which the liability assignments depend only on the negligence or otherwise of parties and not on the extent of negligence. With the exception of comparative negligence, most liability rules used in practice including strict liability, no liability, negligence, negligence with the defense of contributory negligence and strict liability with the defense of contributory negligence are all simple liability rules. They show that a simple liability rule with multiple injurers and one victim is efficient if and only if it satisfies the condition of collective negligence liability. This condition requires that whenever some individuals are negligent, no nonnegligent individual bears any loss in case of occurrence of accident. The condition of collective negligence liability, in fact, can be shown to be sufficient for efficiency of any liability rule, not just any simple liability rule. However, since the question of whether the condition is necessary for the efficiency of any liability rule has not been settled, the problem of complete characterization of efficient liability rules when there are multiple injurers and one victim remains unresolved. Jain (2007) examined the case of multiple victims and one injurer and found that in such situations there does not exist any liability rule that invariably gives rise to efficient outcomes. From this it follows that when there are both multiple injurers and multiple victims, no liability rule can possibly be efficient for all applications.

In the economic analysis of tort law, there have been attempts to analyze the issues of causation and harm as well. These include Calabresi (1975), Shavell (1980b, 1987) and Landes and Posner (1987), among others. It is shown that under strict liability, if injurers are held liable for the harm that their activity causes, but not for other harm, then their incentives to take care and to engage in harmful activities will be optimal. Under the negligence rule, it has been shown that injurers will be led to take due care, if they are held liable only if they caused harm and pay damages equal to harm. With respect to damages, it has been established that under strict liability, if the magnitude of liability equals harm, then incentives to take care will be optimal in the unilateral model of accidents. In the bilateral context, damages equal to harm is optimal under the rule of strict liability with the defense of contributory negligence, if a victim's activity level is taken to be fixed. If, however, a victim's activity is variable, then optimal damages may be less than harm, for then some part of losses will be borne by victims and will moderate their level of activity. Under the negligence rule, damages can be somewhat less than harm and optimal care will be induced. However, if there is uncertainty regarding negligence determination, then damages equal to harm will not induce optimal care. When an injurer's behaviour departs substantially from what is appropriate, damages in excess of harm, called punitive damages, may be imposed. Important works include Cooter (1989), Diamond (2002) and Polinsky and Shavell (1998), among others.

Further, there is a possibility that injurers may not be able to pay in full for the harm they cause, giving rise to what is known as the judgment-proof problem. Summers (1983) and Shavell (1986) studied the problem and it was shown that under strict liability, if care is non-monetary then the injurer is induced to take lower than optimal care; if care is monetary, a theoretical possibility arises that gives rise to excessive care. Under the negligence rule, the judgment-proof problem does not lead to inadequate care unless assets are sufficiently less than the harm. Another aspect of the standard framework is that it assumes that the entire harm, to begin with, falls on one party. The question of efficiency in contexts where both parties to an accident suffer harm was studied by Leong (1989) and Arlen (1990).

While Leong argued that none of the liability rules used in practice can induce both parties to take efficient levels of care, Arlen shows that the rules of negligence, negligence with the defense of contributory negligence and strict liability with the defense of contributory negligence induce efficient care levels, but strict liability does not. The difference in the results arises from the assumption that Leong makes that victims can sue injurers, but the injurer cannot sue the victim; Arlen assumed that when both suffer losses neither party can be designated as purely an injurer or a victim.

Although the primary concern of economic analysis of law is efficiency, distributional considerations have also been brought into the analysis. In Jain and Kundu (2011) it is shown that the efficiency requirement does not preclude altogether a role for distributive considerations. They argue that part of the accident loss can be assigned between the parties purely on non-efficiency considerations without affecting the efficiency property. In order to systematically study the issue, the notion of negligence rule has been generalized so that all possible decompositions of accident loss can be considered, and the precise constraint imposed by the efficiency requirement identified. They use the term "optimal loss" to denote the loss that takes place in case of occurrence of accident when both parties are taking total social cost minimizing care levels. They show that in providing correct incentives to the parties, part of the optimal loss adjusted to take into account differing probabilities of accident with different care levels, plays no role and therefore can be apportioned between the two parties independently of their care levels. It is the apportionment of the accident loss over and above the adjusted optimal loss that turns out to be crucial from the point of view of providing correct incentives to the parties. They conclude that the requirements imposed by efficiency considerations can be quite mild depending on the context.

1.3 The two conceptualizations of negligence in the economic analysis of law

One important assumption that is made in the law and economics literature pertaining to liability rules is that the due care levels, which are specified by the courts, are appropriate from the perspective of minimization of total social costs. A party is defined to be negligent if his care level is below a certain specified level called due care level; and nonnegligent otherwise. This mainstream conceptualization of negligence, "the due care approach," has been questioned by Mark F. Grady on the grounds that "framing the inquiry in this fashion does implicit violence to the way lawyers and judges, in fact, try and decide negligence cases."[30] He pioneered an alternative notion of negligence in terms of cost-justified untaken precautions. A party is called negligent if there exists a precaution which the party could have taken but did not, and which would have cost less than the reduction in expected harm; and nonnegligent otherwise. This Grady calls the "untaken precaution approach" to negligence determination. He has consistently and cogently put forth his alternative view in a series of papers, Grady (1983, 1984, 1988, 1989).

Grady (1988) elaborates on the untaken precaution approach by comparing it with the Brown-Landes and Posner approach of due care. Grady argues that Landes and Posner (1987) have literally accepted Oliver Wendall Holmes's theory of negligence adjudication, which is in effect "a two-step process: first, courts establish the standard of care for the accident at hand; second, they measure the actual conduct against it." Grady argues that:

> In Holmes' adjudication theory, the standard of conduct had a radical meaning: it was nothing less than the set of actual precautions that must be taken in different accident situations. Holmes knew that courts and juries could not identify all these precautions in individual negligence cases, but he suggested that the experience of trial judges and the growth of precedent would go a long way toward solving the problem.

Grady quoted from Holmes's view in *The Common Law*:

> the featureless generality, that the defendant was bound to use such care as a prudent man would do under the circumstances, ought to be continually giving place to the specific one, that he was bound to use this or that precaution under these or those circumstances.[31]

Grady goes on to argue:

> If we understand Brown's equations as a translation of Holmes's theory into economic terms, once we add cause-in-fact, 'liability for everything that due care would prevent' becomes 'liability for everything that the most efficient precautions would prevent.' Under this reinterpretation of Brown's equations, Landes and Posner cannot be right that courts can decide cases without knowing the efficient precautions. Courts would not know how to conduct cause-in-fact analysis, because, as we have seen, cause-in-fact analysis asks whether the untaken precautions upon which breach of duty has been established would have prevented the particular accident that occurred.

Grady argues that in many accident situations plaintiffs do not argue that a particular set of precautions was most efficient; they argue that one or more untaken precautions, usually in the alternative, would have been reasonable on a utilitarian calculus. Grady reasons that

> assessing the costs and benefits of discrete untaken precautions is different from 'marginal analysis', which is the crux of Brown's equations and which Landes and Posner adopt. Marginal analysis asks where two schedules cross: at what precaution level the marginal cost of precaution equals the marginal reduction in risk . . . assessing costs and benefits of discrete untaken precautions provides no guarantee that the ones found cost beneficial will be

precautions that are in the efficient set, that is, the set of precautions defined by the point where the two schedules cross.

Grady re-examines the analysis of *Hendricks v Peabody Coal Co.*[32] in Landes and Posner (1987) to elucidate the prior reasoning. In that case, the plaintiff was a 16-year-old boy who, with a group of other teenagers, travelled some distance to the defendant's abandoned strip mine, which was regularly used as a swimming hole. The plaintiff was injured when he dived into a concealed sand shelf. The court listed six different precautions that the defendant did not take: posting warning signs around the property, putting up a fence, putting up road barricades, employing full time security guards or a life guard, or providing life preservers. The court singled out the defendant's failure to erect a "six foot high steel chain link fence with steel posts set in concrete surrounding the entire pit," observing that the cost of doing so was slight relative to the risk that it would have eliminated. Grady argues that "the mere fact that this precaution might have cost less than its benefit in the form of reduced risk does not mean that taking it would minimize social costs." He put hypothetical costs figures on the different precautions and the corresponding risk reduction and showed that warning signs and not a chain link fence would minimize social cost. Nevertheless, the fence was within the plaintiff's reach under a cost-benefit analysis.

The essence of the argument is, as Grady put it:

> Whenever a plaintiff is allowed to add a lump of untaken precaution to the defendant's suboptimal care level, he can show that marginal benefits exceed costs when the lump extends somewhat beyond due care. Of course, liability does not extend indefinitely beyond the due care level. The reason it is possible to get past due care at all in a cost-benefit proof is that the social surplus in the movement up to due care can offset some social deficit for the part of the movement that extends beyond due care.

He argues that Holmes's theory and Brown's equations both predict that the Hendricks court would ask what precaution level would minimize social cost. Grady's hypothetical cost-calculations show that this precaution level would be actual precaution plus warning signs. Grady emphasizes:

> The point is not whether signs were actually the most efficient precautions, but that some precaution level beyond what is efficient can easily appear desirable based on the kind of cost-benefit analysis that the Hendricks court performed and that is typical of such cases. Recall, however, that precautions beyond the efficient level only appear cost-beneficial when the defendant has been negligent.... If the defendant had actually placed warning signs around the swimming hole (assuming that signs are the efficient precaution level), no untaken precaution could appear cost-beneficial.

Grady argues that it is the cause-in-fact doctrine that prompts plaintiffs to reach as far as they can beyond the due care level for high precaution levels. The plaintiff could have successfully made several distinct proofs of the defendant's breach of duty: no fence, no barricades, or no signs. The plaintiff, however, chose the "six-foot-high steel chain link fence with steel posts set in concrete surrounding the entire pit" as the untaken precaution. Grady argues that the reason for this "ambitious proof" was the cause-in-fact issue. He argues that the theory that he describes,

> views the courts as making plaintiffs pass through the same untaken precaution through two different rings of fire, just as the actual negligence doctrine requires. For the first, the question is whether the untaken precaution had greater benefits than the costs, given the defendant's actual level of precaution. If so, the second question asks whether the accident would have occurred but for the same untaken precaution. It may at first seem impossible for the two questions to yield different answers, but of course they routinely do. There is in many cases a breach of duty but no cause-in-fact (and vice-versa). One reason for the divergence is that an untaken precaution can be cost-justified in that it tends to prevent a related type of accident but still does not prevent the plaintiff's harm.

We note that courts may attempt to locate the due care level by searching for untaken precautions that are cost-justified. A party's due care level is arrived at by assuming that the other party is taking due care. However, when one party is taking less than due care, there may exist untaken precautions beyond the due care level of the other party which are cost-justified. Therefore, in examining the issue of negligence determination by courts, just a cost-benefit analysis by courts would not be sufficient to establish that a particular approach is being used, we need to take into account what the other party in question assumes or is entitled to assume about the opposite party – that he is taking due care or not.

As mentioned earlier, the mainstream literature on the economic analysis of liability rules followed frameworks similar to those used by Brown. The analysis is based on the due care approach and it has been shown that the results on the efficiency of liability rules depend crucially on this notion of negligence. Jain (2006) proves that if the untaken precaution approach is used, for instance, if negligence is determined on the basis of existence of cost-justified untaken precaution, then no liability rule is efficient. He argues that when negligence is defined in terms of untaken precautions it introduces strategic manipulability in the system. In Jain (2015) the reason for this is explained clearly. He says now whether one is negligent or not depends not only on one's own care level but also on the care level of the other party. If the total social cost is minimized at a unique configuration of care levels of the two parties and both the victim and the injurer take those levels of care, then there would not exist any cost-justified untaken precaution and hence both would be nonnegligent. In a situation where the cares of the two parties are substitutes for each other, it may happen that when the injurer takes less than the total social cost minimizing care level, there would exist a cost-justified untaken precaution for the victim. Thus, the possibility exists that by taking less than the total social cost minimizing care level, the injurer can render the victim negligent although the victim is taking the socially optimal level of care.[33]

Grady (1988) had noted that in the Brown-Landes and Posner model an injurer using just a little less precaution than due care faces a large expected liability that abruptly disappears when the injurer achieves due care. Thus, in this model, a defendant is liable for harm that due care would have prevented and also those harms that due care would *not* have prevented – which the law calls "unavoidable accident." Grady argues that the untaken precaution approach takes care of this problem because courts would examine the desirability of each untaken precaution and when one is found that is cost-beneficial the court would deny liability for any harm that this precaution would not have prevented. In Jain (2010b) a clear distinction is made between the different versions of the negligence rule discussed in the law and economics literature. These versions are: (i) injurer is liable for the entire loss if negligent and not liable if nonnegligent and negligence is defined according to the due care approach; (ii) injurer is liable for the incremental loss, i.e. that amount of loss which can be attributed to his or her negligence, and negligence is defined according to the due care approach; (iii) injurer is liable for the incremental loss and negligence is defined according to the untaken precaution approach. Grady (1988) was referring to the third category in his espousal of the untaken precaution approach.

Jain (2010b) holds that although the literature has taken all three versions of negligence rule as efficient, a careful analysis reveals that version (iii) is not efficient. He shows that this version is not efficient even in the unilateral case. As we saw earlier, efficiency of version (i) was established in Brown (1973). Efficiency of version (ii) was established in the unilateral case by Kahan (1989) and in the bilateral case by Jain (2010b). As the efficiency implications of the two different ways of defining negligence are quite different, it is important to know how often one or other of these notions is employed by the courts for negligence determination; and what implications determination of negligence according to one conceptualization has for the other. As we will elaborate later, this study is concerned with the first of these issues.

Jain (2012b) explores the second of these issues and derives certain propositions regarding the logical relationship between these two notions. It is shown that in general the two notions of negligence are logically completely independent of each other. In the literature on the efficiency of liability rules the following three assumptions are usually made: (i) successive units of care are non-increasing in their effectiveness in reducing expected loss, the other party's care level being fixed, (ii) the effectiveness of care does not increase with the care level of the other party, and (iii) there is a unique care-configuration at which the total social costs are minimized. The complete logical independence between the two notions continues to hold even if some or all of these three assumptions are made. In the special case of unilateral interactions, the complete logical independence between the two notions continues to hold even if (i) or (iii) or both hold. Also, the complete logical independence between the two notions continues to hold even if (ii) or (iii) or both hold. However, in the context of unilateral care interactions, the two notions are logically interdependent if it is assumed that both (i) and (ii) hold. Given that both (i) and (ii) hold, in the context of unilateral (injurer care) interactions, the injurer's negligence in the sense of existence of a cost-justified untaken precaution implies the injurer's negligence in the sense of shortfall from due care. It is, however, possible for the victim to be negligent in the sense of existence of a cost-justified untaken precaution, notwithstanding that in a unilateral care (injurer care) case the victim can never be negligent in the sense of shortfall from due care.

Similarly, given that both (i) and (ii) hold, in the context of unilateral care (victim care) interactions, the victim's negligence in the sense of existence of a cost-justified untaken precaution implies the victim's negligence in the sense of shortfall from due care. It is, however, possible for the injurer to be negligent in the sense of existence of a cost-justified untaken precaution, notwithstanding that in unilateral care (victim care) case the injurer can never be negligent in the sense of shortfall from due care. It is argued in the note that in the context of real cases the assumption of uniqueness of care-configuration at which total social costs are minimized is not particularly restrictive; it will rarely be the case that they are minimized at more than one care configuration. Also, in the kind of cases that are actually litigated, it is highly unlikely that one of the two parties' actual care levels will be in excess of the level at which total social costs are minimized. While in the context of litigated cases complementarities in the cares of the parties cannot be ruled out, one expects that in most instances the assumption of effectiveness of care not increasing with the care level of the other party will be satisfied. It is, therefore, argued that if in a litigated case one party has been found to be negligent in the sense of shortfall from due care then in all likelihood the party will be negligent in the sense of existence of a cost-justified untaken precaution as well.

Actual court judgments can be divided into four categories: (i) judgments where a party has been found to be negligent because of the failure to take at least the due care; (ii) judgments where a party has been found to be nonnegligent because of the party's actual care level is adjudged to be greater than or equal to due care; (iii) judgments where a party has been found to be negligent because of existence of a cost-justified untaken precaution; and (iv) judgments where a party has been found to be nonnegligent because of failure to find any cost-justified untaken precaution. It is argued that under the assumption that courts use liability rules satisfying the conditions of negligence liability and that the due care levels are chosen appropriately from the perspective of total social costs minimization, court decisions will be efficient in cases (i) and (ii). In view of the propositions stated prior, in most cases of category (iv) court decisions are likely to be efficient. With respect to category (iii) cases, it is not possible to make any inference regarding the efficiency of tort decisions. Jain (2012b) holds that it is possible for a verdict of negligence decided on the basis of existence of a cost-justified untaken precaution to be inefficient. In fact, inefficiency is quite likely in cases where the cares of the two parties are substitutes for each other.

In the paper, some special cases are considered in which all four categories of court decisions will be efficient. These are unilateral care interactions in which successive units of care are non-increasing in their effectiveness in reducing expected loss, the other party's care level being fixed; effectiveness of care does not increase with the care level of the other party; and there is a unique care-configuration at which the total social costs are minimized; then given that the victim is taking no care, the injurer would be negligent in the sense of not having taken at least the due care if he or she would be negligent in the sense of not having taken some cost-justified precaution. Similarly, under the same assumptions, in unilateral (victim care) interactions, given that the injurer is taking no care, the victim would be negligent in the sense of not having taken at least the due care if he or she would be negligent in the sense of not having taken some cost-justified precaution. It is, however, noted that these special cases do not have much value, as most litigated cases tend to be of the bilateral type.

With respect to efficiency of court decisions, Jain (2012b) reaches the following broad conclusion:

> In cases where court uses a liability rule satisfying negligence liability, negligence is defined in terms of a shortfall from due care, and due care is chosen appropriately from the perspective of total social cost minimization; the court decisions will be efficient. Given that a liability rule satisfying negligence liability is used, the court cases where verdict of non-negligence is reached using the untaken precaution approach are likely to be efficient. In other cases, there is no reason to presume that court decisions will be efficient.

1.4 Competing conceptualizations of negligence determination in the legal literature

The economic analysis of law and the legal literature recognize that injurers and victims are not identical. However, taking account of this would imply that an efficient negligence rule should set a different due standard of care for all injurers, depending on their individual cost of taking care. Landes and Posner (1987) argue that the use of a single standard makes sense in view of the high costs of information that would be required if courts had to inquire into the ability of each individual to avoid accidents. They hold that tort law's assumption of the reasonable man as the standard by which to judge individual conformity with due care shows its sensitivity to this information problem.[34] In fact, Landes and Posner (1987) equate the reasonable person with "the average man (or woman)." In their words:

> An individual whose ability to take care is below average, perhaps because he has poor reflexes, is not excused on that account, and an individual who is above average in his ability to take care – perhaps because of exceptionally

good reflexes – generally is not held to a higher standard than an average person would be.[35]

In the legal literature, however, there are various interpretations given to the "reasonable person," with innumerable attempts at unravelling the attributes of this fictitious person.[36] Gilles (1994) argues that Landes and Posner's treatment of the reasonable person standard as merely an "average-man rule" for determining the costs under the Hand Formula is not entirely correct from a legal point of view. He says:

> As a descriptive matter, however, that account is a long stretch from the conventional instructions, which present the reasonable person standard as an open-ended invitation to imagine how a nonnegligent person might have behaved, while making no mention of the Hand Formula. Consequently, a positive economic account of negligence law as presented to the jury must contemplate a much broader role for the reasonable person standard than Landes and Posner allow.[37]

What this broader role would be, in the absence of explicit jury instructions,[38] has been the subject of controversy, making negligence determination a central issue in torts scholarship.

In a landmark article, Terry (1915) described what he called the "standard man" whose conduct or judgment constituted the test of reasonableness:

> A standard man does not mean an ideal or perfect man, but an ordinary member of the community. He is usually spoken of as an ordinary reasonable, careful and prudent man. That definition is not exactly correct, because in certain cases other qualities than reasonableness, carefulness, or prudence, e.g. courage, may be important; but it will do for our purpose. It is because the jury is supposed to consist of standard men, and therefore to know of their knowledge how such a man would act in a given situation, that questions of reasonableness and negligence are usually left to the jury.

Keeton et al. (1984) in their detailed analysis of the reasonable man,[39] state:

> The courts have gone to unusual pains to emphasize the abstract and hypothetical character of this mythical person. He is not to be identified with any ordinary individual, who might occasionally do unreasonable things; he is a prudent and careful person, who is always up to standard. Nor is it proper to identify him with any member of the very jury which is to apply the standard; he is rather a personification of a community ideal of reasonable behavior, determined by the jury's social judgment.

Although there are many scholars who have examined the meaning of negligence, from the perspective of our study, we select a few. Gilles (1994) makes an attempt to break what he describes as "the impasse that seems to characterize recent debate over the positive meaning of negligence."[40] He argues that:

> The increasingly common claim that the Hand Formula and the reasonable person standard represent mutually exclusive conceptions of negligence is descriptively false and conceptually confused. (And so is the counterclaim that the reasonable person standard is merely a rule about how the Hand Formula should be applied.). While it is true that the reasonable person standard appeals to community norms and values, the suggestion that Hand Formula negligence displaces community norms and values is mistaken. The Hand Formula itself constitutes a community norm, and its implementation requires an imaginative inquiry into the values of the average person.[41]

At the outset of his analysis, Gilles clarifies that an accurate account of existing practices must "begin with an observation that modern negligence law endorses both the Hand Formula and the reasonable person standard but (design defect cases aside) instructs the jury in only the latter."[42] He argues that no one thinks that cost-benefit analysis in negligence law is, or could be, a rigorous quantitative inquiry into continuous increments of marginal care. Rather he thinks that Grady's untaken precaution paradigm "captures the more modest aspirations of cost-benefit analysis in a functioning tort system – the actual conduct of actors is evaluated under the Hand Formula, in terms of particular precautions they could have taken to avoid the accident in question."[43] Gilles attempts to unravel the relationship between Grady's "simplified, intuitive" version of the cost-benefit analysis and the reasonable person standard. He employs the utilitarian approach of employing the single criterion of "utility" as a means of making costs and benefits comparable. Average value functions would indicate how much an average person would attach to the loss that would arise if precaution is not taken and to avoid the accident risk. Since there are no explicit markets to enable the determination of these values, it is through the reasonable person heuristic that the fact-finder is urged to use experience and knowledge of the average community member's valuation of precaution and safety risks.

Gilles argues that this exercise has a major problem in that one expects the average person to assign a lower value to the lives, safety, inconveniences and expenses of others than to his or her own.[44] This problem can be surmounted by considering the potential injurer and potential victim as the same person, the "single owner" version of the reasonable person standard. Gilles argues:

> Reasonable care can be redefined as the care that an average reasonable person takes of his or her own person and property. . . . Thus we might ask whether a reasonable person with average values in matters of safety and precaution costs – and who values the interests of others on a par with his or her own equivalent interests – would have taken the precaution at issue.

For this reason, Gilles calls this the "altruistic reasonable person standard.[45]

Gilles argues that there are two quite different arguments that support the contention that juries instructed in an undefined reasonable person standard will reach results consistent with the Hand Formula. One argument involves the empirical claim that the ordinary person subject to liability under the negligence standard will behave roughly in accordance with the Hand Formula norm. The hypothesis, in this case, is that some combination of social, reputational and legal incentives induces the average person to take approximately optimal care. Another argument is that jurors hear phrases like "reasonably prudent" or "reasonably careful" as invocations of their own intuitive notions of reasonable care, and that these notions will generally lead them to results consistent with the Hand Formula. This argument is controversial because jurors may interpret reasonable care in various ways; reasonable care could mean all possible care. However, Gilles thinks concern over juror confusion or juror nullification explains why they are not given explicit Hand Formula, single-owner instructions in order to elaborate on the reasonable person standard. Confusion could arise because devising effective instructions is a little understood art, and it could also lead to nullification – since jurors are not required to give reasons for their verdicts, any jury that is so inclined can reject the Hand Formula norm subject only to deferential appellate review.

He concludes that although more than 20 years have passed since Posner first argued that Hand Formula was not a novel interpretation of negligence, but merely "an attempt to make explicit the standard that the courts had long applied," pattern jury instructions have not made the Hand Formula explicit, or even tried to use a proxy such as the single-owner heuristic to gloss the reasonable person standard. Gilles, however, argues that it is the dominant meaning of negligence at the level of what he calls practical legal theory – what courts and treatise-writers say to explain the law. He says that the

> Hand Formula posits that a reasonable person balances costs and benefits in light of prevailing values in matters of safety and safety costs. The case law and the pattern jury instructions that ignore the Hand Formula do not reject this understanding in favor of an alternative account of how a reasonable person behaves. Students of practical reason may someday persuade the courts that some other account of reasonableness is more faithful to our practices and considered intuitions than the Hand Formula. Until then, however, we can legitimately ask courts that have endorsed the Hand Formula either to enforce it, or to offer some better justification than inertia for their failure to do so. An invisible Hand Formula is better than no Hand Formula at all. A visible Hand Formula presented to juries as law and methodically applied on review by appellate courts, would be better still.[46]

A somewhat explicit Hand Formula instruction was given by the Restatement (Third) of Torts (2005). It defined negligence as follows:

> A person acts with negligence if the person does not exercise reasonable care under all circumstances. Primary factors to consider in ascertaining whether the person's conduct lacks reasonable care are the foreseeable likelihood that it will result in harm, the foreseeable severity of the harm that may ensue, and the burden of precautions to eliminate or reduce the risk of harm.[47]

Wright (2002a) noted that the Restatement (Third) considers the three Hand Formula factors as primary rather than exclusive. He argues that the comment e sets forth explicitly an unlimited and unqualified cost-benefit analysis:

> The balancing approach rests on and expresses a simple idea. Conduct is negligent if its disadvantages outweigh its advantages, while conduct is not negligent if its advantages outweigh its disadvantages. The disadvantage in question is the magnitude of the risk that the conduct occasions: as noted, the phrase 'magnitude of risk' includes both the foreseeable likelihood of harm and the foreseeable severity of harm should an incident ensue. The 'advantages' of the conduct relate to the burdens of risk prevention that are avoided when the actor declines to incorporate some precaution.

The discussion draft of the Restatement (Third) was subject to enormous scrutiny and the issue of negligence determination dominated most discussions. A symposium organized to shed light on the concept of negligent conduct that prevails in actual practice in the courts attracted contributions from eminent scholars.[48] Gilles (2002) opted to analyze English negligence cases to investigate the concept of negligence because English law has figured prominently in the descriptive debate between scholars like Posner and Landes, who believe that the Hand Formula constitutes the meaning of negligence in Anglo-American tort law and Weinrib and Wright who think the concept of negligence makes relatively little use of cost-benefit balancing and mostly relies on corrective justice. Gilles argues that an analysis of the English Cases reveals three competing accounts of how a reasonable person behaves: first, the substantial reasonably foreseeable risk approach; second, the cost-benefit balancing approach; and third, the disproportionate cost approach.

Under the reasonably foreseeable risk approach, an actor is seen to be negligent for imposing a risk on others that a reasonable person would have foreseen, without regard to the difficulty of guarding against the risk. This approach yields an almost unlimited obligation on the part of the actor to guard against reasonably foreseeable risks. There is a further qualification, however, which serves to dampen the strictness of this approach by specifying that the unlimited obligation applies only to reasonably foreseeable risks that are "substantial." That is why Gilles terms this the "substantial risk" approach. We note that this is inconsistent with the economic approach because it only gives weight to the expected harm and does not take into account the burden of precautions when the risks are substantial. Gilles argues that although some scholars like Grey (2001) have suggested that this approach was the dominant conception of negligence in Anglo-American law until well into the twentieth century, his "limited research" on English law in the period 1860–1930 shows that there were some cases in which courts balanced precaution costs and some in which they refused to do so. Gilles concludes that during this period:

> The impression one is left with is that there was no clear doctrinal answer to the question how, if at all, the difficulty of avoiding an accident affected the determination of negligence. The meaning of negligence seems to have been

supplied primarily by the reasonable man standard and by reliance on custom and practices, safety statutes, and judicial rules of thumb about care in certain recurring circumstances.

The second approach called the cost-benefit balancing, or Hand Formula, approach fixes a finding of negligence on whether the costs of avoiding a reasonably foreseeable risk is outweighed by the benefits of doing so. This is the economic approach and limits the actor's obligation to guard against reasonably foreseeable risks compared to the "substantial risk approach." Gilles argues that in the first few decades of the twentieth century, some torts professors and lawyers began advocating for a balancing conception of negligence. Gilles attributes the gradual increase in the role of precaution costs in negligence determination in English cases to the American influence since the American Institute's First Restatement of Torts in 1934 adopted a conception of negligence as "unreasonable risk" to be determined by balancing the risk against the utility of creating the risk. Although the initial breakthrough for cost-benefit analysis in English tort law came in suits for breach of safety statutes, by 1965 it had become widespread in common law cases as well. The proviso – "so far as reasonably practicable" – provided the initial vehicle for cost-benefit balancing. Gilles's survey of English cases shows that cost-benefit balancing continued to be used in a wide variety of accident cases, without reference to whether the risk was substantial.

The disproportionate cost approach takes an intermediate position between the other two. Under this, an actor would be held negligent unless the burden of precautions to avoid the risk would have been "disproportionate" to the risk. This too is inconsistent with the economic model. Even if costs were found to be greater than benefits, the actor would be found negligent unless he or she were disproportionately greater. By this approach, many would be held negligent who would have escaped liability if the Hand Formula were used. On the whole, Gilles finds that, as in American negligence law, in England too "the reasonable person standard is the first-cut source of content for the duty of reasonable care." The balancing of costs and benefits is a derivative norm: it derives from the reasonable person standard. Gilles argues: "reasonable persons, as argument goes, consider the burdens and disadvantages of precautions when deciding how far to go in eliminating foreseeable risks to others." Since it is derivative, the balancing approach can be bypassed by a judicial finding that is stated in terms of what the reasonable person would or would not have done.

Gilles concludes:

> The upshot is that cost-benefit balancing co-exists – on the whole, remarkably peacefully – in English negligence law with what one might call the 'imaginative' use of the reasonable person as a device for determining how the defendant ought to have behaved in the circumstances.

He, therefore, argues that Landes and Posner are wrong in suggesting that cost-benefit balancing has simply supplanted the reasonable person or, alternatively, that when judges (or juries) apply the reasonable person standard, they should be presumed to engage in implicit cost-benefit analysis. On the other hand, Gilles argues that Weinrib and Wright are also wrong in their stand that cost-benefit balancing is an exceptional and marginal feature of English negligence law. This approach, Gilles holds, is "far more widespread and important than the substantial risk approach that Weinrib and (to a lesser extent) Wright endorse."

Rather than looking at the explanation given in the cases, Kelly and Wendt (2002) investigated the "pattern" jury instructions that judges in various states in the United States use to instruct the juries on the negligent conduct issue. In their view, these provide "the closest-to-the action view of judges' actual working conception of the negligent-conduct issue." They focus on the central or "focal" concept that seems to underlie all the instructions: the concept of "ordinary care" that is defined as "conduct of the reasonably careful or reasonably prudent person." They look at five different academic conceptions of negligence, of which the first two are the same as Gilles's categorization. According to them, most jury instructions do not treat the substantial foreseeable risk standard as the sole criterion, nor is there an explicit cost-benefit instruction – with the exception of Louisiana, where the pattern jury instructions contain explicit cost-benefit instruction, though optional, to be used to elaborate the basic "ordinarily prudent person."

Kelly and Wendt combine their discussion of the other three academic conceptions of negligence. The first conception, which they attribute to Catherine Wells, treats a person's conduct as negligent if it was "morally wrong according to the prevailing community moral values."[49] Another conception they take up is Heidi Feldman's "virtue ethics" theory, in which the standard of care is what a hypothetical person with the virtues of reasonableness, prudence and carefulness would have done in the circumstances.[50] The other conception is Kelly's own theory, in which the standard of care depends on the community's pre-existing safety conventions.[51] Putting all these three together, Kelly and Wendt ask whether one can say that the jury instructions are about making a moral judgment about the defendant's conduct or whether there was noncompliance with an applicable pre-existing community safety convention.

The authors argue that it is the latter interpretation that is valid. According to them, negligence liability, like tort liability overall, is a matter of objective justice or right rather than a matter of subjective virtue. Wright (2002a) critiques this conclusion on the ground that they

> go too far in claiming that neither the pattern jury instructions nor negligence liability call for any sort of moral judgment – that the standard being applied is social in nature, based simply on pre-existing community conventions, and makes no reference to fault, improper conduct, or right or wrong.

Among those who have provided conceptualizations of negligence based on moral values, Bender (1988) was one who sought to replace the reasonableness standard and its "masculine" ethic with a "feminine" ethic of care and concern for the needs and welfare of others. Responding to the criticism that the latter would only apply to women, Bender (1993) emphasized the usefulness of the "reason/care paradigm" in suggesting "reconceptualizations that make law more reflective of human experience and more responsive to concerns of justice."

Wright (1995b) had put forth another moral theory which he called the equal freedom conception of reasonableness. According to the equal freedom theory, which is the basis of the Kantian-Aristotelian theory of legal responsibility – each human being has an absolute moral worth as a free and equal member of the community. In another article Wright (1995a) had explained:

> Thus, the common good to which law and politics should be directed is not the meaningless maximization of aggregate utility or welfare of the society as a whole, as assumed by the utilitarian efficiency theory, but rather the creation of conditions that allow each person to realize his or her humanity as a self – legislating free rational being.

Under this theory, the respective weights to be given to an actor's interests and the interests of others who might be affected by that action will vary considerably depending on (among other factors) who is being put at risk, by whom, and for whose benefit. Wright elaborates:

> For example, given the Kantian requirement of treating others as ends rather than as means, it is impermissible to use someone as a means to your ends by exposing him (or his resources) to significant foreseeable unaccepted risks, regardless of how greatly the benefit to you might outweigh the risk to him. Conversely, sacrificing your interest for the benefit of someone else is regarded as morally meritorious, although not legally required, even if the risk to you greatly outweighs the expected benefit to the other person, as long as your exposing yourself to the risk does not constitute a failure to properly respect your own humanity.

Regarding the standards of care, he argues that under

> the utilitarian-efficiency theory, it is as inefficient to be above the optimal level of care as to be below it: either form of divergence therefore should be considered negligent. However, consistent with the equal freedom theory, defendants and plaintiffs are only deemed negligent for being below the required level of care, not for being above it. Only when one is below the required level of care is there any impermissible interference with the rights of others (defendant's primary negligence) or a failure properly to respect one's own humanity (plaintiff's contributory negligence).

Wright argues that the criteria of reasonableness actually differ in different situations depending on "who put whom at risk for whose benefit and by whether the person put at risk consented to such risk exposure." On that basis he distinguishes eight categories. The first category consists of "defendants' treating others as means." Wright, along with Weinrib, argues that in such cases the "substantial foreseeable risk" approach is applied. The second category consists of those where defendants are engaged in socially essential activities. Wright argues that in any society certain risks – such as those posed by properly constructed, maintained and operated electrical generation and transmission facilities, dams, trains, automobiles and planes – will be unavoidable aspects of activities essential to all persons in the society. He argues: "Under the supreme principle of Right (universalizable equal freedom), all members of society will be deemed to have accepted such activities and their unavoidable risks as being reasonable." It must be noted that the socially important activity must be operated in the most careful manner to minimize the risks to others, and the activity will be deemed reasonable only if the risks to others are not too serious and are greatly outweighed by the activity's social utility. Also, in emergency situations the defendant is held to be justified in engaging in practices, such as driving at high speeds, on the wrong side of the road and through traffic signals, that ordinarily would be held negligent, but they are required to take other steps to avoid exceeding the objectively acceptable level of risk.

The third category is the defendant occupiers' on-premises risks. One of these situations involves risks from activities or conditions to persons who come to the defendant's property. Here the standard of care varies according to whether the plaintiff was a business invitee for whom the highest objective standard of care is required, a social guest, a licensee, a child trespasser or an adult trespasser for whom the lowest, semi-subjective standard of care is required. The fourth category which Wright calls defendants' activities involving participatory plaintiffs encompasses situations in which the defendant puts the plaintiff at risk at least partially to benefit the plaintiff and the plaintiff sought to benefit directly from the defendant's risky activity, like if the plaintiffs were customers or willing spectators of the defendant's risky activity. In these situations, even if the risk is substantial, it will be deemed reasonable. The equal freedom theory would entail a comparison which may be qualitative depending on the values involved. For instance, serious risks to life or health would never be outweighed by mere economic benefits. The fifth category involves paternalistic defendants consisting of situations in which the defendant put the plaintiff at risk for what the defendant considered to be the plaintiff's best interest, but the plaintiff did not consent to or seek to benefit from the risk. Wright argues that, consistent with the equal freedom theory, defendants are not allowed to do this without the plaintiff's consent even if the expected benefits allegedly greatly outweigh the risks.

The sixth category termed plaintiff's self-interested conduct relates to contributory negligence. Wright argues that in these situations the plaintiff put him or herself at risk for his or her own benefit. According to the equal freedom theory, only risks and benefits to the plaintiff are taken into account rather than all risks and benefits to anyone who might be affected by the plaintiff's conduct. The question would be whether the plaintiff failed to properly respect his or her own humanity. The seventh category concerned the plaintiff's self-sacrificing conduct, covering situations in which the plaintiff puts him or herself at risk for some third party's benefit. Under the equal freedom theory, the plaintiff's willingness to sacrifice his or her own interests to benefit someone else is considered not only reasonable but also mutually praiseworthy, even if under a utilitarian comparison the risks to the plaintiff outweigh the expected benefit to the third party "as long as the plaintiff's conduct does not constitute lack of respect for his own humanity." We find that the last requirement does not lead to any definite method or criteria of determining contributory negligence. The last category concerned the defendant's failure to aid or rescue. Wright explains the general lack of duty to rescue using the equal freedom theory, stating that no person can be used solely as a means for the benefit of others if such an obligation requires a significant sacrifice of one's autonomy or freedom for the alleged greater good of others. Wright concludes that the equal freedom theory, therefore, explains, justifies and illuminates various aspects of the multiple standards of care in negligence law.

An attempt at deciphering the meaning of negligence based on community norms was prepared by Abraham (2001). He divided negligence cases into two categories: unbounded cases – those in which the finder of fact must in effect create a norm in order to determine whether the defendant was negligent; and bounded cases – those governed by a pre-existing, independent norm. He argues that no matter how negligence is defined in instructions to the jury or in the law applied by a judge in a bench trial, the negligence standard is abstract and general. He argues: "Within wide bounds, the finder of fact does not identify a pre-existing norm, but simultaneously determines for itself what would constitute reasonable behavior under the circumstances and then applies this norm to the situation at hand." Abraham, therefore, concludes: "given this norm creation in unbounded cases, instead of having a law of negligence that applies in such cases, we merely have (as Leon Green put it years ago) a process for deciding negligence cases."[52] Further, he argues that the process of norm creation has survived because of the presence of juries. They do not need to explain their decisions, and therefore norm creation has been masked by the "featureless generality" of the jury verdict. In bounded cases, custom, professional standards and statistics aid in removing the norm-creation function from the finder of fact.

We find most attempts are examining the reasons behind the different standards in different situations. Keeton et al. (1984) state the problem in the following way:

> The whole theory of negligence presupposes some uniform standard of behavior. Yet the infinite variety of situations which may arise makes it impossible to fix definite rules in advance for all conceivable human conduct. The utmost that can be done is to devise something in the nature of a formula, the application of which in each particular case must be left to the jury, or to the court.

Further they state:

> The application of this standard of reasonable conduct is as wide as all human behavior. There is scarcely an act which, under some conceivable circumstances, may not involve an unreasonable risk of harm. Even going to sleep

becomes negligence when it is done on a railway track, or at the wheel of an automobile.

Therefore, we find that although the "reasonable person standard" uniformly guides the negligence issue, it is in its application to a broad spectrum of situations that ambiguities arise.

There are certain common issues that arise in the application of the standard. One important issue concerns the requirement that a hypothetical reasonable person must anticipate and guard against the conduct of others.[53] In particular, they must realize that there will be a certain amount of negligence in the world. Keeton et al. (1984) state:

> In general, where the risk is relatively slight, a person is free to proceed upon the assumption that other people will exercise proper care. It would not be easy to move traffic if motorists could not assume that other cars will keep to the right, obey stop signs and stop lights and otherwise proceed with care and obey the law.

The due care approach in the economic analysis of law seems to follow this idea in all cases of negligence. Keeton et al. (1984), however, identify situations in which this may not be the correct approach:

> But when the risk becomes a serious one, either because the threatened harm is great, or because there is a special likelihood that it will occur, reasonable care may demand precautions against 'that occasional negligence which is one of the ordinary incidents of human life and therefore to be anticipated'."[54]

They quoted from *Dragotis v Kennedy*: "it is not due care to depend on the exercise of care by another when such reliance is accompanied by obvious danger."[55] This confirms Grady's untaken precaution approach.

In Keeton's tort treatise it is further argued:

> Thus an automobile driver may not proceed blindly across a railway track, upon the assumption that any approaching train will sound bell and whistle, or into an intersection in the confidence that other vehicles will yield the right of way.

They elaborate:

> The duty to take precautions against the negligence of others thus involves merely the usual process of multiplying the probability that such negligence will occur by the magnitude of the harm likely to result if it does, and weighing the result against the burden upon the defendant of exercising such care. The duty arises, in other words, only where a reasonable person would

recognize the existence of an unreasonable risk of harm to others through the intervention of such negligence.

The legal literature does recognize this problem that, for the most part, has been ignored by the standard law and economics literature.

This chapter began by noting the centrality of the concept of negligence in tort law. Over the twentieth century, the rule of comparative negligence has assumed dominance in which liability is apportioned. The chapter traced the origin of the economic analysis of law and the claim that efficiency is the single dominant value explaining common law rules. An elaboration of the concept of efficiency as used in the economic analysis of law was provided. In the literature on the economic analysis of tort law the main results establish that liability rules are efficient if and only if they satisfy the following condition: if one party is negligent and the other is not then the negligent party must bear the entire liability. The efficiency question hinges crucially on the way the notion of negligence is conceptualized – the result holds if negligence is taken as a shortfall from a due care level but does not hold if negligence is defined as the existence of some cost-justified untaken precaution. This chapter also discussed the legal literature to bring out some of the alternative conceptualizations, and in the process some vital concepts in the question of negligence determination was covered.

In this book, the objective is to look at important negligence cases to examine how the question of negligence is determined. From the foregoing analysis, it is clear that the general "reasonable person" standard is interpreted differently in different contexts. When the negligence of the other person is known, reasonable care would warrant taking of additional care. An analysis of cases would reveal how often courts use this reasoning, called the untaken precaution approach, and how often courts use the due care approach. If it is revealed that the dominant approach is the untaken precaution approach, then it would have significant implications for the efficiency thesis of the economic analysis of law.

1.5 Basis of selection of cases

The book analyzes 52 negligence cases taken from three common law jurisdictions – Britain, India and the United States. The factors that were taken into consideration while selecting the cases were the following: one, how often the case had been cited by the courts; two, whether negligence determination was the focus of discussion and the extent of elaboration on the reasoning; and three, the importance that tort literature has placed on the case in the discourse on the question of determination of negligence. Regarding the first two factors, sources such as Indlaw and LexisNexis were relied upon. For the third factor, important tort treatises and casebooks of the respective countries were relied upon. For the British cases, the widely referred book by Rogers titled *Winfield and Jolowicz – Torts* was used, along with other authoritative treatises like Heuston and Buckley's *Salmond and Heuston on the Law of Torts*, Buckley's *The Law of Negligence*, Street's *The Law of Torts*, etc.

and casebooks such as Weir's *A Casebook on Tort*, etc. In the case of India, the main reference was Justice G. P. Singh's *Ratanlal and Dhirajlal The Law of Torts* which is by far the most referred tort text in India. Supplementary references were Lakshminath and Sridhar's *Ramaswamy Iyer's The Law of Torts*, B. M. Gandhi's *Law of Torts*, etc. For the American cases, the main references were Keeton et al. *Prosser and Keeton on the Law of Torts* and Schwartz et al. *Prosser, Wade and Schwartz's Torts – Cases and Materials*. Additional references were Barnes and Stout *Cases and Materials on Law and Economics*, Grady's *Cases and Materials on Torts* and Farnsworth and Grady's *Torts – Cases and Questions*. Also, various law reviews were consulted to decide on the importance the cases occupied in the discourse on negligence determination.

The book is divided into five chapters. This introductory chapter is followed by a chapter on the examination of British cases. These are the most useful set of cases for our purposes because of the elaborate explanation of the reasoning behind the verdicts. As Gilles (2002) had aptly stated, British cases have figured prominently in the discussion on negligence determination for the precise reason that unlike American cases that are tried by the jury which "delivers a general verdict without disclosing its reasoning," in England trial judges instruct themselves on the law of negligence and apply the law as finders of fact – all in the form of opinions explaining their verdicts. Gilles argues that:

> And while English appellate courts give some deference to the fact finding of trial judges, the level of deference seems considerably lower than that extended to American civil juries. The appellate review of negligence issues in England is accordingly both freer and – because the appellate tribunal is confronted with a judge's explanatory opinion, rather than a jury's delphic verdict – better informed. There is consequently good reason to think that the study of English negligence cases can shed interesting light on how courts in common law systems actually employ the negligence standard.

Our analysis is different from Gilles's in that we look at the cases from the point of view of application of the due care approach or the untaken precaution approach and what implications that has on the efficiency question.

The third chapter takes up the Indian negligence cases. So far there has been almost no attempt to analyze the Indian cases from the law and economics point of view.[56] Although not as elaborate in its explanation, the influence of English cases is discernable in the Indian judgments. The fourth chapter covers the American cases. Although these cases have been subject to numerous analyses, they have not been looked at in the manner done in this study from the perspective of the two notions of negligence used in the economic analysis of law. The cases date from as early as 1871[57] to as late as 2013.[58] Although there are many oft-cited cases that have been left out of the set, the ones chosen encompass accidents in a number of different contexts. Not only have substantive issues like rule v flexible standard been discussed, but the major opinions of stalwarts like Holmes, Cardozo, Hand and Posner have also been included.

A concluding chapter summarizes the findings of the study and provides suggestions for further research. Schwartz (1992) had argued: "the reasoning set forth in judicial opinions contributes to the intellectual development of tort law." Attempts at studying the actual cases would not only serve to examine the claims made in the abstract models but also aid in their validation or rejection. Even Coase, while discussing his seminal article, had argued: "I referred to legal cases because they afforded examples of real situations as against the imaginary ones normally used by economists in their analysis."[59]

Notes

1 Henderson (2002). The definition often quoted by courts is that of B. Alderson in *Blyth v Birmingham Waterworks Co.* (1856) 11 Ex. 781: "Negligence is the omission to do something which the reasonable man guided upon those considerations which ordinarily regulate the conduct of human affairs, would do, or doing something which a prudent and reasonable man would not do." The concept of negligence will be elaborated upon, covering leading conceptualizations both in the legal and law and economics literature.
2 We note that scholars like George Priest have argued that it was not negligence but "enterprise liability" that was at the heart of the revolution that was witnessed by the Anglo-American legal system. Henderson (2002) describes enterprise liability as being synonymous with strict liability, except that the former phrase connotes a broader commitment to holding commercial enterprises strictly liable for the harm they cause. See Priest (1985).
3 The dominance of negligence has been widely accepted. Posner begins his landmark article on negligence by saying: "Negligence – the failure to exercise the care of an ordinarily prudent and careful man – has been the dominant standard of civil liability for accidents for the last 150 years or so, in this as in most countries of the world; and accident cases, mainly negligence cases, constitute the largest item of business on the civil side of the nation's trial courts." Posner (1972), p. 29. Many others have argued along similar lines. Prominent among them are Dobbs (2000) and Owen (2007).
4 103 Eng Rep. 926 (K.B. 1809).
5 60 Mass. (6 Cush) 292 (1850).
6 Brown (1973).
7 152 Eng Rep. 588 (Exch. 1842).
8 Schwartz (1981).
9 Section 1(1) of the Act of 1945 provides as follows: "Where any person suffers damage as a result partly of his own fault and partly of the fault of any other person or persons, a claim in respect of that damage shall not be defeated by reason of the fault of the person suffering the damage, but the damages recoverable in respect thereof shall be reduced to such an extent as the court thinks just and equitable having regard to the claimant's share in the responsibility for the damage." Rogers (2010), p. 364.
10 "Comparative negligence" is an American term denoting a regime that allows for apportionment of loss.
11 Only four states – Alabama, Maryland, North Carolina and Virginia – and the District of Columbia continue to apply contributory negligence as a complete bar to recovery.
12 Rowley (1998) gives an analysis of the influence of Hume (1739), Ferguson (1767) and Smith (1776), among others.
13 Expanded edition, 1789.
14 See also Jack Hirshleifer (1985), 'The Expanding Domain of Economics', 75 *American Economic Review*, Anniversary Issue, 53. In this context, Landes and Posner (1987) argue: "People can apply the principles of economics intuitively – and thus "'do' economics

without knowing they are doing it.... People who say judges are not economists are sometimes confused about the meaning of economics. If economics were limited to explicitly economic phenomena such as monopoly and inflation, it would indeed be odd to describe a judge deciding an accident case as engaged in economic reasoning. But if economics is defined as the science of rational choice or (equivalently) as the attempt to get the most from scarce resources, it becomes more natural to conceive of a judge in an accident case as trying to ascertain whether the injurer and the victim were behaving carefully in the sense of trying to minimize the sum of expected-accident and accident-avoidance costs" (p. 23).

15 Priest (2005) argues that it took about a decade for the article to be clearly understood. Although widely acclaimed, it has been subjected to critical examination by many. See for instance Regan (1972), Mumey (1971) and Cooter (1982). For a recent analysis, see Jain (2012a).

16 Director considered the anti-trust cases as sources of evidence for studying industrial behaviour. Coase (1993) had said about his seminal contribution: "It is generally agreed that this article has had an immense influence on legal scholarship, but this was no part of my intention. For me, 'The Problem of Social Cost' was an essay in economics. It was aimed at economists. What I wanted to do was to improve our analysis of the working of the economic system. Law came into the article because, in a regime of positive transaction costs, the character of the law becomes one of the main factors determining the performance of the economy."

17 Priest (2005) argues that even the realists such as Langdell failed to create such an impact when they attempted to discover a scientific foundation of law. Christopher Columbus Langdell was appointed the Dean of the Harvard Law School in 1870 and is credited with the promotion of the idea that law is a science, by the use of the case method in American legal education.

18 Landes and Posner (1987), pp. 23–24.

19 Posner (1995), p. 104, n.13.

20 For the efficiency criteria see Kaldor (1939), Scitovsky (1941), Arrow (1963) and Sen (1970). A critique of the efficiency criteria used in the economic analysis of law is provided by Coleman (1988).

21 Jain (2010a) notes that the notion of Pareto-efficiency is defined with respect to a particular set of social alternatives and a particular set of individuals. If the set of social alternatives changes, for instance if it contracts, then an alternative that earlier was Pareto-inefficient might become Pareto-efficient; and if the set of social alternatives expands then an alternative that was earlier Pareto-efficient might become Pareto-inefficient.

22 The fundamental theorems of welfare economics established the link between the decentralized competitive markets and economic efficiency. One of the central assumptions on which these theorems rest is the absence of externalities.

23 Pigou (1932).

24 Keeton et al. (1984) have explained in detail why an exact definition if a tort is difficult, although numerous attempts have been made to find one. See pp. 1–15.

25 Landes and Posner (1987), p. 36.

26 Galligan (1993) provides a four-fold division of the elements of the negligence doctrine after an analysis of the different decisional models and concludes that irrespective of the division adopted, there is a unified "pattern" for deciding a negligence case.

27 In the two cases of *Wagon Mound* that are discussed in section 2.1 of this study.

28 We note that Jain and Singh (2002) do not impose this restriction. No assumptions are made on the cost of care, and expected loss functions apart from assuming the existence of a pair of levels of care that minimize total social costs. That is, unlike the standard framework, they allow the possibility of the existence of more than one configuration of care levels at which total social costs are minimized.

29 Some of the important contributions are Cooter (1985), Shavell (1980a, 1987), Landes and Posner (1987), Polinsky (2003), Posner (2007), Miceli (1997, 2004), Cooter and Ulen (2004) and Kaplow and Shavell (1996, 1999), among others.

30 Grady (1989), p. 139.

31 Holmes, O.W. (1881), *The Common Law*, p. 111.
32 115 Ill. App. 2d 35, 253 N.E. 2d 56 (1969).
33 *Baltimore and Ohio Railroad Co. v Goodman* was one such case; discussed in Chapter 4, section 4.1.
34 Lord Macmillan had famously argued in *Glasgow Corporation v Muir* [1943] A.C. 448: "The standard of foresight of the reasonable man is in one sense an impersonal test. It eliminates the personal equation and is independent of the idiosyncrasies of the particular person whose conduct is in question. Some persons are by nature unduly timorous and imagine every path beset with lions; others, of more robust temperament, fail to foresee or nonchalantly disregard even the most obvious dangers. The reasonable man is presumed to be free from both over-appreciation and from over-confidence."
35 Landes and Posner (1987), p. 126. In *Vaughan v Menlove* [1837, 3 Bing. N.C. 468, 132 Eng. Rep. 490], Tindal C.J. had held: "Instead, therefore, of saying that the liability for negligence should be co-extensive with the judgment of each individual, which would be as variable as the length of the foot of each individual, we ought rather to adhere to the rule which requires in all cases a regard to caution such as a man of ordinary prudence would observe."
36 The oft-quoted description of the reasonable man is from Herbert (1930): "He is an ideal, a standard, the embodiment of all those qualities which we demand of the good citizen★★★He is one who invariably looks where he is going, and is careful to examine the immediate foreground before he executes a leap or a bound; who neither star-gazes nor is lost in meditation when approaching trapdoors or the margin of a dock; ★★★who never mounts a moving omnibus and does not alight from any car while the train is in motion★★★and will inform himself of the history and habits of a dog before administering a caress; ★★★ who never drives his ball until those in front of him have definitely vacated the putting-green which is his own objective; who never from one year's end to another makes an excessive demand upon his wife, his neighbors, his servants, his ox, or his ass; ★★★who never swears, gambles or loses his temper, who uses nothing except moderation, and even while he flogs his child is meditating only on the golden mean." Quoted from Keeton et al. (1984), pp. 174–175, n.9.
37 Gilles (1994), pp. 1027–1028.
38 Gilles (2002) states: "Most American negligence cases are tried to a jury that receives only a general instruction equating negligence with failure to behave like a reasonably prudent person."
39 Keeton et al. (1984), pp. 173–193.
40 Gilles (1994), p. 1052.
41 Ibid., p. 1052.
42 Ibid., p. 1023.
43 Ibid., pp. 1028–1029.
44 Wright (2002a) has argued in this context: "Although a number of justice-oriented scholars once argued that the aggregate-risk-utility test is consistent with and indeed required for the attainment of justice, they now almost universally agree that it is inconsistent with the principles of justice. This should be clear with only a little reflection. It is not properly respectful of the equal dignity and autonomy of others, and hence not just, for you to impose substantial unaccepted risks of injury or loss upon them merely for your own personal benefit, even if your gain will exceed their loss. Indeed, corporations and individuals who are thought to have done so are at great risk of being held liable for punitive damages."
45 Gilles argues that the altruistic single-owner version played at least a modest part in nineteenth-century negligence law, but judging by pattern jury instructions it has largely disappeared in modern American practice.
46 Gilles (1994), pp. 1053–1054.
47 In the Restatement of Torts 291 (1) (1934) and Restatement (Second) of Torts 291 (1965), the corresponding definition was: "When an act is one which a reasonable man would recognize as involving risk of harm to another, the risk is unreasonable and the act is negligent if the risk is of such magnitude as to outweigh what the law regards as the utility of the act or of the particular manner in which it is done."

48 Wright, Richard W. (2002a).
49 Wells (1990).
50 Feldman (2000).
51 Kelly (1990).
52 Leon Green (1930), 'Judge and Jury', 67.
53 Custom, emergency and shifting responsibility are some of the other issues.
54 Keeton et al. (1984), p. 198.
55 This case is discussed in Chapter 4, section 4.1.
56 Singh (2004), in an article on motor vehicle accidents in India, looked at how damage awards varied in similar cases, but there was no analysis of individual cases as to the logic used.
57 *Eckert v Long Island Railroad* [43 N.Y. 502; 1871 N.Y.].
58 *Parmasivan v Wicks* [2013] EWCA Civ.262. Although not part of the set of 52 cases, a more recent case, *Scott v Gavigan* [2016] ECWA Civ.544, has been discussed briefly in section 2.2, to elaborate on the application of the untaken precaution approach in the determination of negligence in actual cases.
59 Coase (1993).

References

Abraham, Kenneth S. (2001), 'The Trouble with Negligence', 54 *Vanderbilt Law Review*, 1187.
Arlen, J. (1990), 'Re-Examining Liability Rules When Injurers as Well as Victims Suffer Losses', 10 *International Review of Law and Economics*, 233–239.
Arrow, Kenneth J. (1963), *Social Choice and Individual Values*, 2nd ed., New York, Wiley.
Babu, P.G. et al. (2010), *Economic Analysis of Law in India: Theory and Application*, New Delhi, Oxford University Press.
Baird, Douglas G. et al. (1994), *Game Theory and the Law*, Cambridge (MA), Harvard University Press.
Bar-Gill, Oren and Omri Ben-Shahar (2003), 'The Uneasy Case for Comparative Negligence', 5 *American Law and Economic Review*, 433–469.
Barnes, David W. and Lynn A. Stout (1992), *Cases and Materials on Law and Economics*, St. Paul, Minnesota, West Publishing Co.
Becker, G. (1968), 'Crime and Punishment: An Economic Approach', 76 *Journal of Political Economy*, 169.
Becker, Gary (1971), *The Economics of Discrimination*, Chicago, Chicago University Press.
Becker, Gary (1976), *The Economic Approach to Human Behavior*, Chicago, Chicago University Press.
Becker, Gary (1993), 'Nobel Lecture: The Economic Way of Looking at Behaviour', 101 (3), *Journal of Political Economy*, 385–409. [Reprinted in Francesco Parisi and Charles K. Rowley (eds.), *The Origins of Law and Economics: Essays by the Founding Fathers*, Cheltenham (UK), Edward Elgar.]
Bender, Leslie (1988), 'A Lawyers Primer on Feminist Theory and Tort', 38 *Journal of Legal Education*, 3.
Bender, Leslie (1993), 'An Overview of Feminist Torts Scholarship', 78 *Cornell Law Review*, 575.
Bernstein, Anita (2002), 'Symposium on Negligence in the Courts: The Actual Practice: The Communities that Make Standards of Care Possible', 77 *Chicago-Kent Law Review*, 735.
Brown, John P. (1973), 'Towards an Economic Theory of Liability', 2 *Journal of Legal Studies*, 323–350.
Buckley, Richard A. (2007), *Buckley: The Law of Negligence*, United Kingdom, LexisNexis Butterworths.
Burrows, P. (1999), 'A Deferential Role of Efficiency Theory in Analyzing Causation-Based Tort Law', 8 *European Journal of Law and Economics*, 29–49.

Burrows, P. and Cento G. Veljanovski (1981), 'Introduction: Economic Approach to Law', in P. Burrows and Cento G. Veljanovski (eds.), *The Economic Approach to Law*, London, Butterworths, 1–33.
Calabresi, Guido (1961), 'Some Thoughts on Risk Distribution and the Law of Torts', 70 *Yale Law Journal*, 499–553.
Calabresi, Guido (1970), *The Cost of Accidents: A Legal and Economic Analysis*, New Haven, Yale University Press.
Calabresi, Guido (1975), 'Concerning Cause and the Law of Torts', 43 *University of Chicago Law Review*, 69–108.
Calabresi, Guido (1980), 'About Law and Economics: A Letter to Ronald Dworkin', 8 *Hofstra Law Review*, 553–562.
Calabresi, G. and J. Hirshoff (1972), 'Towards a Test for Strict Liability in Tort', 81, *Yale Law Journal*, 1055–1092.
Calabresi, Guido and D. Melamed (1972), 'Property Rules, Liability Rules and Inalienability: One view of the Cathedral', 85 *Harvard Law Review*, 1089.
Calabresi, Guido and Jeffrey Cooper (1996), 'New Directions in Tort Law', 30 *Valparaiso University Law Review*, 859–884.
Calfee, J. and R. Craswell (1984), 'Some Effects of Uncertainty on Compliance with Legal Standards', 70 *Virginia Law Review*, 965–1003.
Chung, Tai-Yeong (1993), 'Efficiency of Comparative Negligence: A Game Theoretic Analysis', 22 *Journal of Legal Studies*, 395–404.
Coase, Ronald H. (1960), 'The Problem of Social Cost', 3 *Journal of Law and Economics*, 1–44.
Coase, Ronald H. (1993), 'Law and Economics at Chicago', 3 *Journal of Law and Economics*, 1–44.
Coleman, Jules L. (1988), *Markets, Morals and the Law*, Cambridge, Cambridge University Press.
Cooter, Robert D. (1982), 'The Cost of Coase', 11 *Journal of Legal Studies*, 1.
Cooter, Robert D. (1985), 'Unity in Torts, Contracts and Property: The Model of Precaution', 73 *California Law Review*, 1–51.
Cooter, Robert D. (1989), 'Punitive Damages for deterrence: When and how much?' 40 *Alabama Law Review*, 1143–1196.
Cooter, Robert D. (1991), 'Economic Theories of Legal Liability', 5 *Journal of Economic Perspectives*, 11–30.
Cooter, Robert D. and Thomas Ulen (2004), *Law and Economics*, 4th ed., Delhi, Pearson.
Craswell, R. and J. Calfee (1986), 'Deterrence and Uncertain Legal Standards', 2 *Journal of Law, Economics and Organization*, 279–303.
Cunningham, Lawrence A. (2010), 'Traditional versus Economic Analysis: Evidence from Cardozo and Posner Torts Opinions', 62 *Florida Law Review*, 667.
Dari Mattiacci, G. (2002), 'Tort Law and Economics', in A. Hatzis (ed.), *Economic Analysis of Law: A European Perspective*, Cheltenham (UK), Edward Elgar.
Demsetz, Harold (1972), 'When does the Rule of Liability Matter?' 1 *Journal of Legal Studies*, 13.
Demsetz, Harold (1997), 'The Primacy of Economics: An Explanation of the Comparative Success of Economics in the Social Sciences', 35 *Economic Inquiry* 1.
Dharmapala, Dhammika and Sandra Hoffman (2005), 'Bilateral Accident with Intrinsically Interdependent Costs of Precaution', 34 *Journal of Legal Studies*, 239–272.
Diamond, P. (1974), 'Single Activity Accidents', 3 *Journal of Legal Studies*, 107–164.
Diamond, P. (2002), 'Integrating Punishment and Efficiency Concerns in Punitive Damages for Reckless Disregard of Risks to Others', 18 *Journal of Law, Economics and Organization*, 117–139.
Dobbs, Dan B. (2000), *The Law of Torts*, St. Paul, Minnesota, West Publishing Co.
Dworkin, Ronald (1980), 'Is Wealth a Value', 9 *Journal of Legal Studies*, 323–356.
Dworkin, Ronald (1986), *Law's Empire*, Oxford (UK), Hart Publishing.

Englard, Izhak (1991), 'Law and Economics in American Tort Cases: A Critical Assessment of the Theory's Impact on Courts', 41 *University of Toronto Law Journal*, 359.

Farnsworth, Ward and Mark F. Grady (2009), *Torts – Cases and Questions*, 2nd ed., New York, Aspen Publishers.

Feldman, Heidi Li (2000), 'Prudence, Benevolence, and Negligence: Virtue Ethics and Tort Law', 74 *Chicago-Kent Law Review*, 1431.

Feldman, Allan M. and John M. Frost (1998), 'A Simple Model of Efficient Tort Liability Rules', 18 *International Review of Law and Economics*, 201–215.

Ferguson, Adam (1767), *An Essay on the History of Civil Society*, edited by L. Schneider, New Brunswick (NJ), Transaction Publishers, 1980.

Galligan, Thomas C., Jr (1993), 'A Primer on the Patterns of Negligence', 53 *Louisiana Law Review*, 1509.

Galligan, Thomas C., Jr (1997a), 'Cats or Gardens: Which Metaphor Explains Negligence? Or, Is Simplicity Simpler than Flexibility?' 58, *Louisiana Law Review*, 35.

Galligan, Thomas C., Jr (1997b), 'Revisiting the Patterns of Negligence: Some Ramblings Inspired by Robertson', 37 *Louisiana Law Review*, 1119.

Gandhi, B.M. (2006), *Law of Torts*, 3rd ed., Lucknow, Eastern Book Company.

Geistfeld, Mark (2001), 'Economics, Moral Philosophy, and the Positive Analysis of Tort Law', in Gerald J. Postema (ed.), *Philosophy and the Law of Torts*, 250–275, Cambridge, Cambridge University Press.

Gilles, Stephen G. (1992), 'Negligence, Strict Liability and the Cheapest Cost: Avoider', 78 *Virginia Law Review*, 1291.

Gilles, Stephen G. (1994), 'The Invisible Hand Formula', 80 *Virginia Law Review*, 1015–1054.

Gilles, Stephen G. (2001), 'On Determining Negligence: Hand Formula Balancing, the Reasonable Person Standard, and the Jury', 54 *Vanderbilt Law Review*, 813.

Gilles, Stephen G. (2002), 'Symposium on Negligence in Courts: The Actual Practice: The Emergence of Cost-Benefit Balancing in English Negligence Law', 77 *Chicago-Kent Law Review*, 489.

Goodman, John C. (1978), 'An Economic Theory of Evolution of the Common Law', *Journal of Legal Studies*, 393–406.

Grady, Mark F. (1983), 'A New Positive Theory of Negligence', 92 *Yale Law Journal*, 799–829.

Grady, Mark F. (1984), 'Proximate Cause and the Law of Negligence', 69 *Iowa Law Review*, 363–449.

Grady, Mark F. (1988), 'Discontinuities and Information Burdens: A Review of the Economic Structure of Tort Law by William M. Landes and Richard A. Posner', 56 *George Washington Law Review*, 658–678.

Grady, Mark F. (1989), 'Untaken Precautions', 18 *Journal of Legal Studies*, 139–156.

Grady, Mark F. (1994), *Cases and Materials on Torts*, St. Paul, Minnesota, West Publishing Co.

Green, J. (1976), 'On the Optimal Structure of Liability Laws', 7 *Bell Journal of Economics*, 553–574.

Green, Michael D. (1997), 'W. Page Keeton Symposium on Tort Law: Negligence = Economic Efficiency: Doubts', 75 *Texas Law Review*, 1605.

Grey, Thomas C. (2001), 'Accidental Torts', 54 *Vanderbilt Law Review*, 1225.

Haddock, D. and C. Curran (1985), 'An Economic Theory of Comparative Negligence', 14 *Journal of Legal Studies*, 49–72.

Harrington, Matthew (1998), 'The Admiralty Origins of Law and Economics', 7 *George Mason Law Review*, 105.

Hart, H.L.A. (1961), *The Concept of Law*, London, Oxford University Press.

Henderson, James A. (2002), 'Why Negligence Dominates Tort', 50 *UCLA Law Review*, 377.

Hepple, B.A. and M.H. Matthews (1974), *Tort: Cases and Materials*, London, Butterworths.
Herbert, A.P. (1930), *Misleading Cases in the Common Law*, 12–16.
Hetchner, Steven (2001), 'Non-Utilitarian Negligence Norms and the Reasonable Person Standard', 54 *Vanderbilt Law Review*, 863.
Heuston, R.F.V. and R.A. Buckley (1992), *Salmond and Heuston on the Law of Torts*, 20th ed., London, Sweet and Maxwell.
Hume, David (1739), *A Treatise on Human Nature*, edited by P.H. Nidditch, New York, Oxford University Press, 1978.
Hurd, Heidi M. (1996), 'Symposium: The Deontology of Negligence', 76, *Boston University Law Review*, 249.
Jain, Satish (2011), 'Uncertainty Regarding Interpretation of the "Negligence Rule" and Its Implications for the Efficiency of Outcomes', Unpublished Manuscript, Centre for Economic Studies and Planning, Jawaharlal Nehru University, New Delhi.
Jain, Satish (2012a), 'The Coasian Analysis of Externalities: Some Conceptual Difficulties', Unpublished Manuscript, Centre for Economic Studies and Planning, Jawaharlal Nehru University, New Delhi.
Jain, Satish (2012b), 'A Note on the Logical Relationship between Different Notions of Negligence', Unpublished Manuscript, Centre for Economic Studies and Planning, Jawaharlal Nehru University, New Delhi.
Jain, Satish K. (2006), 'Efficiency of Liability Rules: A Reconsideration', 15 *The Journal of International Trade and Economic Development*, 359–373.
Jain, Satish K. (2007), 'Efficiency of Liability Rules with Multiple Victims', 14 *Pacific Economic Review*, 119–134.
Jain, Satish K. (ed.) (2010a), *Law and Economics*, New Delhi, Oxford University Press.
Jain, Satish K. (2010b), 'On the Efficiency of the Negligence Rule', 14, *Journal of Economic Policy Reform*, 343–359.
Jain, Satish K. (2015), *Economic Analysis of Liability Rules*, New Delhi, Springer.
Jain, Satish K. and Ram Singh (2002), 'Efficient Liability Rules: Complete Characterization', 75 *Journal of Economics*, 105–124.
Jain, Satish K. and Rajendra P. Kundu (2006), 'Characterization of Efficient Simple Liability Rules with Multiple Tortfeasors', 26 *International Review of Law and Economics*, 410–427.
Jain, Satish K. and Rajendra P. Kundu (2011), 'Decomposition of Accident Loss and Efficiency of Negligence Rule', in Krishnendu Ghosh Dostidar et al. (eds.), *Dimensions of Economic Theory and Policy: Essays for Anjan Mukherji*, New Delhi, Oxford University Press.
Johnston, Jason Scott (1991), 'Uncertainty, Chaos and the Torts Process: An Economic Analysis of Legal Form', 76 *Cornell Law Review*, 341.
Kahan, Marcel (1989), 'Causation and Incentives to Take Care under the Negligence Rule', 18 *Journal of Legal Studies*, 427–447.
Kaldor, Nicholas (1939), 'Welfare Propositions of Economics and Interpersonal Comparisons of Utility', 49 *Economic Journal*, 549–552.
Kaplow, Louis and Steven Shavell (1996), 'Property Rules versus Liability Rules', 109 *Harvard Law Review*, 713–790.
Kaplow, Louis and Steven Shavell (1999), 'The Conflict between Notions of Fairness and the Pareto Principle', 1 *American Law and Economics Review*, 63–77.
Keating, Gregory C. (1996), 'Reasonableness and Rationality in Negligence Theory', 48 *Stanford Law Review*, 311.
Keeton, W. Page et al. (1984), *Prosser and Keeton on the Law of Torts*, 5th ed., St. Paul, Minnesota, West Publishing Co.

Kelly, Patrick J. (1990), 'Who Decides? Community Safety Conventions at the Heart of Tort Liability,' 38 *Clev. St. L. Rev.*, 315.
Kelly, Patrick J. (2001), 'Teaching Torts: The Carroll Towing Company Case and the Teaching of Tort Law', 45 *Saint Louis University Law Journal*, 731.
Kelly, Patrick J. and Laurel A. Wendt (2002), 'Symposium on Negligence in the Courts: The Actual Practice: What Judges Tell Juries About Negligence: A Review of Pattern Jury Instructions', 77 *Chicago-Kent Law Review*, 587.
Kidner, Richard (2002), *Casebook on Torts*, 7th ed., New Delhi, Oxford University Press.
Kornhauser, L. and R. Revesz (1989), 'Sharing Damages among Multiple Tortfeasors', 98 *Yale Law Journal*, 831–890.
Kronman, A. (1995), 'Remarks at the Second Driker Forum for Excellence in the Law', 42 *Wayne Law Review*, 115.
Lakshminath, A. and M. Sridhar (2007), *Ramaswamy Iyer's: The Law of Torts*, 10th ed., Nagpur, LexisNexis Butterworths Wadhwa.
Landes, William M. and Richard A. Posner (1980), 'Joint and Multiple Tortfeasors: An Economic Analysis', 9, *Journal of Legal Studies*, 517–556.
Landes, William M. and Richard A. Posner (1981), 'The Positive Economic Theory of Tort Law', 15 *Georgia Law Review*, 851.
Landes, William M. and Richard A. Posner (1987), *The Economic Structure of Tort Law*, Cambridge (MA), Harvard University Press.
Leong, A.K. (1989), 'Liability Rules When Injurers as Well as Victims Suffer Losses', 9 *International Review of Law and Economics*, 105–111.
Lyons, Edward C. (2005), 'Balancing Acts: Intending Good and Foreseeing Harm: The Principle of Double Effect in the Law of Negligence', 3 *Georgetown Journal of Law and Public Policy*, 453.
Marshall, Jared (2010), 'Note: On the Idea of Understanding Weinrib: Weinrib and Keating on Bipolarity, Duty and the Nature of Negligence', 19, *Southern California Interdisciplinary Law Journal*, 385.
Medema, Steven G. (1999), 'The Place of the Coase Theorem in Law and Economics', 15 *Law and Philosophy*, 209–233.
Miceli, Thomas J. (1997), *Economics of the Law: Torts, Contracts, Property, Litigation*, New York, Oxford University Press.
Miceli, Thomas J. (2004), *The Economic Approach to Law*, California, Stanford University Press.
More, Daniel (2003), 'The Boundaries of Negligence', 4 *Theoretical Inquiries in Law*, 339.
Mumey, Glen A. (1971), 'The "Coase Theorem": A Re-Examination', 85 *Quarterly Journal of Economics*, 718–723.
Noah, Lars (2000), 'General Tort Principles: The Role of Statutes in Common Law Adjudication: Statutes and Regulations: If Noncompliance Establishes Negligence per se, Shouldn't Compliance Count for Something?' 10 *Kansas Journal of Law and Public Policy*, 162.
Owen, David G. (2007), 'The Five Elements of Negligence', 35 *Hofstra Law Review*, 1671.
Perry, Stephen (2001), 'Symposium: Cost – Benefit Analysis and the Negligence Standard', 54 *Vanderbilt Law Review*, 893.
Pigou, A.C. (1932), *The Economics of Welfare*, 4th ed., London, Macmillan.
Polinsky, A. Mitchell (2003), *An Introduction to Law and Economics*, 3rd ed., New York, Aspen Publishers.
Polinsky, A. Mitchell and Steven Shavell (1998), 'Punitive Damages: An Economic Analysis', 111 *Harvard Law Review*, 869–962.
Porat, Ariel (2003), 'The Many Faces of Negligence', 4 *Theoretical Inquiries in Law*, 105.
Posner, Richard A. (1972), 'A Theory of Negligence', 1 *Journal of Legal Studies*, 29.

Posner, Richard (1995), 'Wealth Maximization and Tort Law: A Philosophical Inquiry', in David G. Owen (ed.), *Philosophical Foundations of Tort Law*, New York, Oxford University Press.

Posner, Richard (2005), 'The Law and Economics Movement: From Bentham to Becker', in Francesco Parisi and Charles K. Rowley (eds.), *The Origins of Law and Economics: Essays by the Founding Fathers*, Cheltenham (UK), Edward Elgar.

Posner, Richard A. (2007), *Economic Analysis of Law*, 7th ed., New York: Aspen Publishers.

Priest, George L. (1977), 'The Common Law Process and the Selection of Efficient Rules', 6 *Journal of Legal Studies*, 65.

Priest, George L. (1985), 'The Invention of Enterprise Liability: A Critical History of the Intellectual Foundations of Modern Tort Law', 15 *Journal of Legal Studies*, 461.

Priest, George L. (2005), 'The Rise of Law and Economics: A Memoir of the Early Years', in Francesco Parisi and Charles K. Rowley (eds.), *The Origins of Law and Economics: Essays by the Founding Fathers*, Cheltenham (UK), Edward Elgar.

Rabin, Robert L. (2011), 'The Pervasive Role of Uncertainty in Tort Law: Rights and Remedies', 60 *DePaul Law Review*, 431.

Regan, Donald H. (1972), 'The Problem of Social Cost Revisited', 15 *Journal of Law and Economics*, 427–437.

Rogers, W.V.H. (2010), *Winfield and Jolowicz on Tort*, 18th ed., London, Sweet and Maxwell.

Rose-Ackerman, Susan (1986), 'The Simple Economics of Tort Law: An Organizing Framework', 2 *European Journal of Political Economy*, 91–98.

Rowley, Charles K. (1998), 'Law and Economics from the Perspective of Economics', in Peter Newman (ed.), *The New Palgrave Dictionary of Economics and the Law*, Vol. 2, New York, Macmillan.

Schwartz, Gary T. (1978), 'Contributory and Comparative Negligence: A Reappraisal', 87 *Yale Law Journal*, 697–727.

Schwartz, Gary T. (1981), 'Tort Law and the Economy in Nineteenth-Century America: A Re-Interpretation', 90 *Yale Law Journal*, 1717.

Schwartz, Warren F. (1989), 'Objective and Subjective Standards of Negligence: Defining the Reasonable Person to Induce Optimal Care and Optimal Populations of Injurers and Victims', 78 *Georgetown Law Journal*, 241.

Schwartz, Gary T. (1992), 'The Beginning and the Possible End of the Rise of Modern Tort Law', 26 *Georgia Law Review*, 601.

Schwartz, Gary T. (1999), 'Cardozo as Lawmaker', 49 *DePaul Law Review*, 305.

Schwartz, Victor E., Katherine Kelly and David F. Partlett (2010), *Prosser, Wade and Schwartz's Torts – Cases and Materials*, 12th ed., New York, Thompson Reuters Foundation Press.

Scitovsky, Tibor (1941), 'A Note on Welfare Propositions in Economics', 9 *Review of Economic Studies*, 77–88.

Sen, Amarya K. (1970), *Collective Choice and Social Welfare*, San Francisco, Holden-Day.

Shavell, Steven (1980a), 'Strict Liability versus Negligence', 9 *Journal of Legal Studies*, 1–25.

Shavell, Steven (1980b), 'An Analysis of Causation and the Scope of Liability in the Law of Torts', 9 *Journal of Legal Studies*, 463–516.

Shavell, Steven (1981), 'A Note on Efficiency v Distributional Equity In Legal Rulemaking: Should Distributional Equity Matter Given Optimal Income Taxation?' 71 *American Economic Review*, 414–418.

Shavell, Steven (1986), 'The Judgment Proof Problem', 6 *International Review of Law and Economics*, 45–58.

Shavell, Steven (1987), *Economic Analysis of Accident Law*, Cambridge (MA), Harvard University Press.

Shavell, Steven (2004), *Foundations of Economic Analysis of Law*, Cambridge (MA), Harvard University Press.
Shavell, Steven (2007), 'Liability for Accidents', in A. Mitchell Polinsky and Steven Shavell (eds.), *Handbook of Law and Economics*, Vol. 1, Oxford (UK), North-Holland.
Singh, Ram (2003), 'Efficiency of "Simple" Liability Rules When Courts Make Erroneous Estimation of the Damage', 16 *European Journal of Law and Economics*, 39–58.
Singh, Ram (2004), 'Economics of Judicial Decision-Making in Indian Tort Law. Motor Accident Cases', *Economic and Political Weekly*, June 19, 2613–2616.
Singh, Ram (2007), 'Causation-Consistent Liability, Economic Efficiency and the Law of Torts', 27 *International Review of Law and Economics*, 179–203.
Singh, G.P. (2010), *Ratanlal and Dhirajlal The Law of Torts*, 26th ed., Nagpur, LexisNexis Butterworths Wadhwa.
Smith, Adam (1776), *The Wealth of Nations*, Vol. 2, edited by E. Cannan, London: Metheun and Co, 1904; repr. 1961.
Street, Harry (1972), *The Law of Torts*, 5th ed., London, Butterworths.
Summers, J. (1983), 'The Case of the Disappearing Defendant: An Economic Analysis', 132 *University of Pennsylvania Law Review*, 145–185.
Terry, Henry T. (1915), 'Negligence', 29 *Harvard Law Review*, 40–54.
Weinrib, Ernest J. (1980), 'The Case for a Duty to Rescue', 90 *Yale Law Journal*, 247.
Weinrib, Ernest J. (2007), 'Can Law Survive Legal Education', 60 *Vanderbilt Law Review*, 401.
Weir, Tony (2004), *A Casebook on Tort*, 10th ed., London, Sweet and Maxwell.
Wells, Catherine (1990), 'Tort Law as Corrective Justice: A Pragmatic Justification for Jury Adjudication', 88 *Michigan Law Review*, 2348.
Wright, Richard W. (1987), 'The Efficiency Theory of Causation and Responsibility: Unscientific Formalism and False Semantics', 63 *Chicago-Kent Law Review*, 553.
Wright, Richard W. (1995a), 'Right, Justice and Tort Law', in David G. Owen (ed.), *Philosophical Foundations of Tort Law*, New York, Oxford University Press.
Wright, Richard W. (1995b), 'The Standards of Care in Negligence Law', in David G. Owen (ed.), *Philosophical Foundations of Tort Law*, New York, Oxford University Press.
Wright, Richard W. (2002a), 'Symposium on Negligence in Courts: The Actual Practice: The Emergence of Cost-Benefit Balancing in English Negligence Law', 77 *Chicago-Kent Law Review*, 489.
Wright, Richard W. (2002b), 'Justice and Reasonable Care in Negligence Law', 47 *American Journal of Jurisprudence*, 143.
Wright, Richard W. (2003), 'Hand, Posner and the Myth of the Hand Formula', 4 *Theoretical Inquiries in Law*, 145–274.

2
ECONOMIC ANALYSIS OF SELECT BRITISH CASES

In this chapter we conduct an analysis of English cases, many of which are considered landmark decisions having an impact on the development of tort law in the United Kingdom and by precedent in other common law countries as well. The cases are divided into six categories depending on whether the injurer is held negligent or nonnegligent by the mainstream due care approach, the alternative untaken precaution approach or both approaches.[1] The categorization is based on the final verdict in the litigation process, although the arguments and findings at all stages will be discussed. Although the focus is on the injurer's negligence or otherwise, the approach taken in the determination of negligence of the plaintiff, wherever applicable, will be noted.

2.1 Cases in which the injurer is declared negligent by considerations which point towards use of due care approach

An important case in this category is *Home Office v Dorset Yacht Company Limited*.[2] In September 1962, ten boys from the Portland Borstal Institution, a "closed borstal," were sent for a training exercise to Brownsea Island in Poole Harbour. One night seven of them escaped, boarded a yacht, the Diligence of Marston, which was moored off Brownsea Island and collided with another one, Silver Mist, and damaged it. They later boarded it and caused further damage. The three officers in charge of the boys were sleeping, contrary to instructions. The owners of the damaged yacht, the Dorset Yacht Co. Ltd., recovered the damage from their insurers who, in turn, decided to recoup that from the Home Office. Speaking in the name of the owners of the yacht, the insurance company alleged in their action that there was no proper supervision of the boys. It was quite clear that these boys, being in borstal, had previous criminal records, including breaking and entering houses, for larceny and taking away vehicles without consent. Five of them had even escaped before and had been recaptured, and therefore, the three officers should have taken precautions to prevent their escaping; they were negligent in not doing so, and the Home Office, being responsible for these officers, ought to pay for the damage done.

There was a preliminary trial of a question of law whether on the facts of the case, any duty of care capable of giving rise to a liability in damages was owed to the plaintiffs by the defendants, their servants or agents. An affirmative answer was given by the trial court judge J. Thesiger and by the Court of Appeal. The Home Office appealed to the House of Lords, which dismissed the appeal. It was quite obvious that the boys might try to escape and, in that case, would try to use the yacht, with the consequent likelihood of damaging it. In both the Court of Appeal and the House of Lords it was held that in that situation a duty of care was owed by the officers to the owners of the nearby yacht. The principle expressed in Lord Atkin's classic words in his speech in *Donoghue v Stevenson*[3] was found to be directly applicable:

> You must take reasonable care to avoid acts or omissions which you can reasonably foresee would be likely to injure your neighbor. Who, then, in law is my neighbor? The answer seems to be – persons who are so closely and directly affected by my act that I ought reasonably to have them in contemplation . . . when I am directing my mind to the acts or omissions which are called in question.[4]

The owners of the yachts were persons so closely and directly affected by what the officers did or failed to do that they ought reasonably to have them in contemplation of the officers. In the Court of Appeal, Lord Denning argued:

> I think that the officers of the borstal institutions should be liable for negligence. And the reason I say this is because of the people who live in the neighbourhood. When the authorities open a borstal institution, those living nearby are surely entitled to expect that reasonable care will be taken to protect them.

The breach of duty question was taken up explicitly by Lord Pearson who clarified:

> It may be artificial and unhelpful to consider the question as to the existence of a duty of care in isolation from the elements of breach and damage. The actual damage alleged to have been suffered by the respondents may be an example of a kind or range of potential damage which was foreseeable, and if the act or omission by which the damage was caused is identifiable, it may put one on the trail of a possible duty of care of which the act or omission would be a breach. In short, it may be illuminating to start with the damage and work back through the cause of it to the possible duty which may have been broken.

In terms of the economic model, this is translatable as calculating due care from expected loss. He put forth the facts alleged or inferred regarding the breach: (i) the three officers of the Home Office who had charge of the boys failed to keep any watch or exercise any control over them at the material time but retired to bed leaving them to their own devices; (ii) none of those three officers was on duty at the material time; (iii) they failed to make any effective arrangements for keeping the boys under control at night; and (iv) knowing that there were craft such as the Silver Mist offshore and that there was no or effective barrier in the way of the boys gaining access to such craft, they failed to take any adequate steps to check the movement of the boys.

The complaint was of injurious interference by the borstal boys with boats moored off Brownsea Island. It was alleged that since these boys were under detention for compulsory training and the boats being easily accessible constituted a natural temptation, it was eminently foreseeable that there would be interference unless the Home Office's officers took precautions to prevent it. Lord Pearson argued:

> If the Home Office had any duty to take care for the safety of the boats, then on the facts alleged in the statement of claim it would seem that there was a breach of the duty causing damage of which the respondents complain. What would be the nature of the duty owed by the Home Office to the respondents if it existed?

He was of the opinion that the Home Office did not owe the respondents a general duty to keep the borstal boys under detention. He reasoned:

> If the Home Office had, in the exercise of its discretion, released some of these boys, taking them on shore and putting them on trains or buses with tickets to their homes, there would have been no prospect of damage to the respondents as boatowners and the respondents would not have been concerned and would have had nothing to complain of. Again the boys might have escaped in such a way that no damage could be caused to the respondents as boatowners; for instance, they might have escaped by swimming ashore or by going ashore in a boat belonging to or hired by the borstal authorities or by having their friends bring a rescue boat from outside and carry them off to a refuge in the Isle of Wight or Portsmouth or elsewhere. On the other hand the boys might interfere with the boats from motives of curiosity and desire for amusement without having any intention to escape from borstal detention.

Working back from damage to the duty question he argued: "the essential feature of this case was not the 'escape' but the interference with the boats. The duty of care would be simply a duty to take reasonable care to prevent such interference." Although physical detention could be an aspect of the duty, there were other means such as supervision, keeping watch, dissuasion or deterrence.

46 Economic analysis of select British cases

Regarding the question of existence of such a duty, like Lord Reid, he too quoted Dixon J from *Smith v Leurs*[5]: "The general rule is that one man is under no duty of controlling another to prevent his doing damage to a third. There are, however, special relations which are the source of a duty of this nature." In Lord Pearson's opinion:

> This case falls under the exception and not the rule, because there was a special relation. The borstal boys were under the control of the Home Office's officers, and control imports responsibility. The boy's interference with the boats appears to have been a direct result of the Home Office's officers' failure to exercise proper control and supervision.

Moreover, the claim was not based on a breach of statutory duty but on common law negligence. He quoted Lord Blackburn from *Geddis v Proprietors of Barn Reservoir*[6]:

> For I take it, without citing cases, that it is now thoroughly well established that no action will lie for doing that which the legislature has authorized, if it be done without negligence, although it does occasion damage to anyone; but an action does lie for doing that which the legislature has authorized, if it is done negligently. And I think that if by a reasonable exercise of powers, either given by statute to the promoters, or which they have at common law, the damage could be prevented it is, within this rule, 'negligence' not to make such reasonable exercise of their powers.

There was no breach of duty in bringing the boys to Brownsea Island but in their "failure to properly exercise their powers of supervision and control for the purpose of preventing damage to the respondents as 'neighbours.'"

Also, the fact that one method of borstal training is to give the boys some measure of freedom, making the risk of escape and damage not wholly avoidable, does not rule out the existence of duty of care. It would affect the content or standard that would require the exercise of "such care for the protection of the neighbours and their property as is consistent with the due carrying out of the borstal system of training." He, therefore, concluded that in answer to the preliminary question of law he would say that

> the Home Office owed no duty to respondents with regard to the detention of the borstal boys (except perhaps incidentally as an element in supervision and control) nor with regard to the treatment or employment of them, but the Home Office did owe to the respondents a duty of care, capable of giving rise to a liability in damages, with respect to the manner in which the borstal boys were disciplined, controlled and supervised.

Lord Diplock, while dismissing the appeal argued:

> The risk of sustaining damage from the tortuous acts of criminals is shared by the public at large ... what distinguishes a borstal trainee who has escaped

from one who has been duly released from custody, is his liability to recapture, and the distinctive added risk which is a reasonably foreseeable consequence of a failure to exercise due care in preventing him from escaping is the likelihood that in order to elude pursuit immediately on the discovery of his absence the escaping trainee may steal or appropriate and damage property which is situated in the vicinity of the place of detention from which he has escaped.

He further went on to argue:

I should, therefore, hold that any duty of a borstal officer to use reasonable care to prevent a borstal trainee from escaping from his custody was owed only to persons whom he could reasonably foresee had property situate in the vicinity of the place of detention of the detainee which the detainee was likely to steal or to appropriate and damage in the course of eluding immediate pursuit and recapture.

He concluded:

If therefore it can be established at the trial of this action: (1) that the borstal officers in failing to take precautions to prevent the trainees from escaping were acting in breach of their instructions and not in bona fide exercise of a discretion delegated to them by the Home Office as to the degree of control to be adopted: and (2) that it was reasonably foreseeable by the officers that if these particular trainees did escape they would be likely to appropriate a boat moored in the vicinity of Brownsea Island for the purpose of eluding immediate pursuit and to cause damage to it, the borstal officers would be in breach of a duty of care owed to the respondents and the respondents would, in my view, have a cause of action against the Home Office as vicariously liable for the 'negligence' of the borstal officers.

It is clear from the reasoning that it was a failure of the borstal officers to take what constituted due care in the circumstances, that is, "given the previous criminal and escaping record of the individual trainee concerned and the nature of the place from which he escaped," that constituted negligence. The untaken precaution of failure to take steps to prevent the youths from escaping their custody and control was cost-justified since both the probability and extent of harm were high; thus, expected harm was high. It was implicit that the aforesaid untaken precaution was also a cause-in-fact since if the officers had taken reasonable care, they could have prevented the escape and the damage.

Two cases – commonly referred to as *Wagon Mound (1)*[7] and *Wagon Mound (2)*,[8] which arose out of the same accident, have become landmark decisions for laying down explicitly certain principles in the determination of negligence. Although our concern is with the second, we discuss the first one to provide the background. The *S. S. Wagon Mound*, a ship under the control of the defendants, Overseas Tankship

(UK), was moored at Caltex Wharf, Sydney Harbour, for the purpose of discharging gasoline products and taking in bunkering oil. On October 30, 1951, a large quantity of bunkering oil was carelessly allowed to spill which spread over a considerable part of the bay. The *Wagon Mound* then headed to sea and the defendants made no attempts to disperse the oil. About 600 feet away on Sheerlings Wharf, owned by the plaintiffs, Morts Dock, a ship Corrimal was being repaired, using electric and oxyacetylene welding equipment. When the plaintiff's works manager became aware of the situation, he stopped work, and asked the manager of the Caltex Oil Co. whether it was safe to continue welding. He was assured that the oil could not be ignited when spread on water and gave instructions accordingly for the welding to continue. Two days later, however, a spark from the welding ignited the oil, and the resulting fire spread rapidly over the surface of the oil and severely damaged the plaintiff's timber wharf and the ships moored there, including the Corrimal. In the first case, *Wagon Mound (1)*, Morts Dock brought an action in negligence against Overseas Tankship (UK) in the Supreme Court of New South Wales.

The trial judge found that the fire started when molten metal fell from the plaintiff's wharf onto a rag or some other inflammable material floating on the water and burned for a sufficient time to act as a wick to ignite the oil. He made a critical finding:

> The *raison d'etre* of furnace oil is, of course, that it shall burn, but I find that the defendant did not know, and could not reasonably be expected to have known, that it was capable of being set on fire when spread on water.

In this multiple-risk case the same precautions, that is, preventing the discharge of oil, would have prevented both the risk of muck on the spillways as well as the risk of fire. Following *Re Polemis*,[9] the trial court held that the defendants were liable for the muck on the spillway, which was clearly a foreseeable risk, as well as the destruction of the wharf by fire, which was a direct but unforeseeable consequence of the carelessness of the defendants. The defendants appealed to the Privy Council. While upholding the judgment regarding liability for muck on the spillway, the Privy Council overruled the principle laid down in *Re Polemis*, stating that it was against all notions of justice and morality, that "for an act of negligence, however slight or venial, which results in some trivial foreseeable damage, the actor should be liable for all consequences, however unforeseeable and however grave, so long as they can be said to be 'direct'." We note here that this case is not about due care or untaken precaution but about foreseeability of damage and that the latter need not have a cost-benefit dimension. In this case, there was no comparison of costs and benefits but only a discussion of the extent of harm and what elements would be considered while calculating it.

In *Wagon Mound (2)*, Miller Steamships Co., the owners of the two ships, the Corrimal and Audrey D, that were docked at Sheerlegs Wharf and were damaged by the fire brought an action against Overseas Tankship (UK), the defendants in *Wagon Mound (1)*. In this action, the trial judge made significantly different findings of fact; the court found that "the officers of the *Wagon Mound* 'would regard furnace oil as very difficult to ignite upon water' – not that they would regard this as impossible"; and that they probably would have considered such fire "rare" but not unheard of.[10] In an attempt to find out whether these differences would result in different results in law, Lord Reid distinguished between what was "foreseeable" and "reasonably foreseeable." He referred to *Bolton v Stone*[11] and highlighted the basic departure which *Bolton v Stone* had brought about in the determination of negligence. He argued that before that case, there could be only two classes of cases – those in which, any *ex ante* analysis would reveal that the risk was too unreal or far-fetched and any reasonable man would not pay any attention to it and those where a real and substantial risk existed, and a reasonable man would have to take steps necessary to eliminate it. In *Bolton v Stone*, it was held that although the injury was foreseeable, the risk was so small that a reasonable man would neglect it and it would be justifiable because it "would involve considerable expense to eliminate the risk. He would weigh the risk against the difficulty of eliminating it." That the injurer could be held nonnegligent even if there was a foreseeable possibility of damage is clear from Lord Reid's statement:

> In their Lordship's opinion Bolton v Stone did not alter the general principle that a person must be regarded as negligent if he does not take steps to eliminate a risk which he knows or ought to know is a real risk and not a mere possibility which would never influence the mind of a reasonable man. What that decision did was to recognize and give effect to the qualification that it is justifiable not to take steps to eliminate a real risk if it is small and if the circumstances are such that a reasonable man, careful of the safety of his neighbor, would think right to neglect it.

We note that this kind of reasoning is contrary to economic logic because here a distinction is being made between small and large expected harm. For risks that are non-small, the connection with cost-benefit calculation has not been examined.[12]

In the present case, he argued that the Privy Council was of the opinion that:

> a properly qualified and alert chief engineer would have realized there was a real risk here, and they do not understand Walsh J to deny that; but he appears to have held that, if a real risk can properly be described as remote, it must then be held to be not reasonably foreseeable. That is a possible interpretation of some of the authorities; but this is still an open question and on principle their lordships cannot accept this view.

In the opinion of the lordships:

> If a risk is one which would occur to the mind of a reasonable man in the position of the defendant's servant and which he would not brush aside as far-fetched, and if the criterion is to be what that reasonable man would have

done in the circumstances, then surely he would not neglect such a risk if action to eliminate it presented no difficulty, involved no disadvantage and required no expense.

This kind of reasoning is consistent with the untaken precaution approach. He went on to say:

the evidence shows that the discharge of so much of oil on to the water must have taken a considerable time, and a vigilant ship's engineer would have noticed it at an early stage. The findings show that he ought to have known that it is possible to ignite this kind of oil on water.

Even if he thought that this could happen only in very exceptional circumstances, "it does not mean that a reasonable man would dismiss such a risk from his mind and do nothing *when it was so easy to prevent it*" (emphasis added). This is particularly so, because damage by fire "involved considerable expense financially." In other words, if the expected harm was large compared to the "easy" way of preventing damage, the reasonable man ought to take the precaution and would be held liable if he had not taken it. Therefore, the chief engineer of *Wagon Mound* ought to have taken steps to eliminate the risk. The defendants were held liable by the Privy Council.

One famous cricket case, which although termed a negligence case had clear elements of strict liability, was *Miller v Jackson*.[13] In the village of Lintz in County Durham, cricket had been played since 1905 on a small ground leased by the National Coal Board. The Board also owned the adjacent field, which it sold to Stanley Urban District Council, who in turn sold it to Messrs Wimpey's Ltd. who built a line of semi-detached houses in 1972, one of which was bought by the Millers. The Millers' garden wall was only 102 feet from the wicket, so cricket balls kept sailing over it causing minor damage to their house in terms of chipped paintwork and broken roof tiles, but risking personal injury to the Millers, which was the main cause of panic for them. They brought an action in negligence and nuisance against the cricket club, claiming damages and an injunction to stop cricket being played on the ground. J. Reeve, who heard the case at first instance in the High Court in Nottingham, upheld their claim and granted damages and an injunction. The defendants appealed against the injunction, although they agreed to pay damages. The majority in the Court of Appeal (Lord Geoffrey Lane and Lord Cumming-Bruce) held that the playing of cricket was a nuisance and the defendants were negligent. Lord Denning dissented on both the counts. As to the question of the injunction, Lord Geoffrey Lane was of the opinion that it should be granted. However, Lord Denning and Lord Cumming-Bruce held that there should be no injunction. The appeal was allowed, and an enhanced amount of damages was granted to the plaintiffs.

At the trial it appeared that cricket could not be played on the small ground without the occasional ball going over. It was argued by the defendants that they had taken every feasible step to prevent injury. Before the cricket season opened in 1975, they increased the height of the fence from 6 feet to 15 feet by means of galvanized chain links. They could not raise it further because the wind might blow it down as had happened on one occasion earlier. They even told batsmen to hit the balls low and not hit them for six. Despite this, a few balls did get over. According to the club's estimates:

> In 1975, there were 2,221 overs, that is, 13,326 balls bowled. Of them there were 120 six hits on all sides of the ground. Of these only six went over the high protective fence and into this housing estate. In 1976 there were 2,616 overs, that is 15,696 balls. Of them there were 160 six hits. Of these only nine went over the high protective fence and into the housing estate.

The club offered to remedy all damage and pay all expenses. They offered to install unbreakable glass, louvered window shutters and a net over the garden whenever cricket was being played. Mr Jackson, the chairman of the club admitted "that there was no way in which they could stop balls going into the premises in Brackenridge from time to time ... that something like an average of eight balls a year were going to land in the vicinity of the plaintiff's house." As for the harm, apart from broken tiles, chipped paint and broken windows, there was danger of personal injury, and Mrs Craig was said to have been lucky to have avoided it. There had been no case of actual injury. Mrs Miller, however, had been in a state of panic because of the balls and exclaimed to the judge: "Have we got to wait until someone is killed before anything can be done?" Reeve argued: "I have no hesitation in reaching the conclusion that when cricket is played on this ground any reasonable person must anticipate that injury is likely to be caused to the property at 20 Brackenridge or its occupants." His reasoning was based on a high probability of harm, without any reference to the extent of harm or the burden of precautions.

In the Court of Appeal, Lord Geoffrey Lane said that it would be improper to depart from the earlier finding. Further, referring to the case of *Latimer v Aec Limited*[14] stated:

> It is true that the risk must be balanced against the measures which are necessary to eliminate it and against what the defendants can do to prevent accidents from happening.... It was held by the House of Lords that the risk of injury from the slippery floor was not sufficient to require the defendants to shut the factory.

However, he concluded:

> In the present case, far from being one incident of an unprecedented nature about which complaint is being made, this is a series of incidents, or perhaps a continuing failure to prevent incidents from happening, coupled with the certainty that they are going to happen again. The risk of injury to

persons and property is so great that on each occasion when a ball comes over the fence and causes damage to the plaintiffs, the defendants are guilty of negligence.

His conclusion on the negligence question was based on the expected harm and did not factor in the burden of precautions. This is contrary to economic logic. Regarding the question of nuisance, he reiterated: "The danger of injury is obvious and is not slight enough to be disregarded. There is here a real risk of serious injury." He was attributing a high probability as well as a high magnitude of harm. The remedy suggested – that of stopping the playing of cricket altogether seemed to be justified. Here the economic logic was being used since Lord Geoffrey Lane thought that the expected harm justified the drastic step of closing down the club. Also, he argued that he was bound by the authority in *Sturges v Bridgman*.[15]

Lord Denning, however, dissented:

> The club was entitled to use this ground for cricket in the accustomed way. It was not a nuisance, nor was it negligence of them to so run it. Nor was the batsman negligent when he hit a ball for a six. All were doing simply what they were entitled to do.

He reached this conclusion based on his observation that cricket has been played on the ground for 70 years and was "a delight to everyone." The Millers had bought one of the houses on the edge of the cricket ground, with the benefit of the open space, knowing that it was the village cricket ground, and balls would sometimes fall into their gardens. Applying modern principles to the present case, Lord Denning argued there is "a contest here between the interest of the public at large and the interest of a private individual." He concentrated on the cost of the alleged untaken precaution – that of stopping the playing of cricket. He said:

> the judge, much against his will, has felt that he must order the cricket to be stopped; with the consequences, I suppose, that the Lintz Cricket Club will disappear. The cricket ground will be turned to some other use. I expect for more houses or a factory. The young men will turn to other things instead of cricket. The whole village will be much the poorer.

He went on to argue:

> I recognise that the cricket club are under a duty to use all reasonable care consistently with the playing of the game of cricket, but I do not think the cricket club can be expected to give up the game of cricket altogether.

Keeping in mind the extent of panic among the plaintiffs, he thought one party would have to move "for peace in the future." As far as the club was concerned, he said: "I do not suppose for a moment there is any field in Lintz to which they can move." He concluded: "As between their conflicting interests, I am of the opinion that the public interest should prevail over the private interest. The cricket club should not be driven out." His argument can be interpreted as saying that the untaken precaution of stopping the game is not cost-justified once the public interest is factored in.

Lord Cumming-Bruce agreed with Lord Geoffrey Lane, that the defendants were liable in negligence and nuisance, both with regard to the reasoning and the conclusion. Further, although he too thought that the court was bound by the decision in *Sturges v Bridgman*, he did not think that injunction was the appropriate remedy in this case. He argued:

> There is authority that in considering whether to exercise a judicial discretion to grant an injunction the court is under a duty to consider the interests of the public. . . . Courts of equity will not ordinarily and without special necessity interfere by injunction where the injunction will have the effect of very materially injuring the rights of third persons not before the court.

He, therefore, disagreed with the judgment of Reeve, saying:

> He does not appear to have had regard to the interest of the inhabitants of the village as a whole. Had he done so he would in my view have been led to the conclusion that the plaintiffs having accepted the benefit of the open space marching with their land should accept the restrictions on enjoyment of their garden which they may reasonably think necessary. That is the burden which they have to bear in order that the inhabitants of the village may not be deprived of their facilities for an innocent recreation which they have so long enjoyed on this ground.

The reasoning of Cumming-Bruce can be better understood by an analysis of the landmark case *Sturges v Bridgman*. In that case, the defendant, Mr Bridgman, a confectioner, had been using the back section of his property on Wigmore Street for decades as a kitchen in which he had two large mortars to pound meat and other materials for his confectionery. No problem arose as long as the adjoining property on Wimpole Street was used as a garden because the noise did not disturb anyone. The plaintiff, Dr Sturges, a physician, had recently built a consulting room in the garden and complained that the pounding noise interfered with his practice. The court ruled in favour of the plaintiff. The reasoning used can be inferred from the statements of Lord Justice Thesiger:

> The Defendant contends that he had acquired the right *** by uninterrupted [use] for more than twenty years. *** [T]he laws governing the acquisition of easements by [use] stands thus: Consent or acquiescence of the owner of the [affected land] lies at the root of prescription. ***[A] man cannot, as a general rule, be said to consent to or acquiesce in the acquisition by his neighbor of

an easement through an enjoyment of which he has no knowledge, actual or constructive, or which he contests and endeavours to interrupt, or which he temporarily licenses.

This was the legal issue of coming to the nuisance; the court reasoned that when the doctor had no knowledge of the defendant's mortars or had no reason to object, the presumption of acquiescence was untenable, and no easement could be granted.

Lord Justice Thesiger, however, continued his reasoning in the following way:

> The case also is put of a blacksmith's forge built away from all habitations, but to which, in course of time, habitations approach. *** [T]hat is really an *idem for idem* case with the present. It would be on the one hand in a very high degree unreasonable and undesirable that there should be a right of action for acts which are not in the present condition of adjoining land, and possibly never will be any annoyance or inconvenience to either its owner or occupier; and it would be on the other hand in an equal degree unjust, and from a public point of view, inexpedient that the use and value of the adjoining land should, for all time and under all circumstances, be restricted and diminished by reason of the continuance of acts incapable of physical interruption, and which the law gives no power to prevent. The smith in the case supposed might protect himself by taking a sufficient cartilage to ensure what he does from being at any time an annoyance to his neighbor, but the neighbor himself would be powerless in the matter.

The Lord Justice concluded by giving what has been the oft-quoted and most critically analyzed part of the judgment:

> Individual cases of hardship may occur in the strict carrying out of the principle upon which we found our judgment, but the negation of the principle would lead even more to individual hardship, and would at the same time produce a prejudicial effect upon the development of land for residential purposes.

This reasoning, as famously argued in Coase (1960), pointed to an economic logic.

It has been pointed out that in the nuisance context, economic thinking as portrayed by Coase's analysis is concerned with harms and costs, whereas legal thinking is concerned with rights and remedies.[16] Coase had argued:

> The judges' view that they were settling how the land was to be used would be true only in the case in which the costs of carrying out the necessary market transactions exceeded the gain which might be achieved by any rearrangement of rights. And it would be desirable to preserve the areas (Wimpole Street or the moor) for residential or professional use (by giving non-industrial users the right to stop the noise, vibration, smoke, etc., by

injunction) only if the value of the additional residential facilities obtained was greater than the value of cakes or iron lost. But of this the judges seem to have been unaware.

The legal aspect was stressed by Weinrib (2007):

> Coase treats the court as attempting to achieve a certain economic goal (the development of residential housing) in ignorance of proper economic reasoning. If, however, one reads the judgment as a whole and views the offending sentence ['produce a prejudicial effect upon the development of land for residential purposes'] in its own light, a different picture emerges. The court was concerned not with settling how the land was to be used, but with determining the conditions under which an action by the defendant could diminish a right of the plaintiff. The court's focus was juridical, not economic.

An analysis of the present case would also point to two issues – the legal issue and the economic one. Lord Cumming-Bruce did not distinguish the two issues. An examination of his reasoning shows that as far as the legal issue of coming to the nuisance is concerned, his argument was that since the residents knew of the existence of the cricket field when they bought their land; the rights of the club should prevail. As far as the economic logic was concerned, the Lord's reasoning was based on the comparison between loss to the village of a recreation they had long enjoyed and the inconveniences faced by the plaintiffs. By this, his conclusion was that interest of the party which faced the prospect of greater loss if shifted out of the present location should predominate. Like Lord Denning, Lord Cumming-Bruce also gave importance to the "loss to society" that would result from a closing of the grounds, which Reeve had overlooked and ruled in favour of the club. The burden of precautions would be too great. He pointed to other cost-justified precautions that could be taken: "The risk of damage to the house can be dealt with in other ways, and is not such as to fortify significantly the case for an injunction stopping the play on this ground." Even Lord Geoffrey Lane had conceded: "It does not seem just that a long established activity, in itself innocuous, should be brought to an end because someone chooses to build a house nearby and so turn an innocent pastime into an actionable nuisance." We note that Lord Reid had stated in *Wagon Mound (2)* the playing of cricket is a lawful activity, and therefore the public utility must be a major consideration.

We find that in deciding the question of negligence, Reeve had only taken account of the risk of injury and did not consider the full burden of precautions. Lord Geoffrey Lane's estimate of expected harm was high enough to warrant an injunction, and Lord Denning and Lord Cumming-Bruce took account of public interest as well in calculating the burden of precautions, and they therefore reached a conclusion different from the other two as regards to the precaution in question.

Another inclusion in this category is the motorway pile-up case of *Knightley v Johns and others*[17] in which the question of negligence determination of multiple tortfeasors came up. The first defendant, Mr Johns was travelling northbound along the Queensway tunnel between Suffolk Street and Great Charles Street in Birmingham in the evening twilight in October 1974, when his car somersaulted while trying to negotiate a sharp bend. The bodies of his passengers lay injured or unconscious blocking the tunnel. Mr Williams, who was driving behind Mr Johns, stopped and used an emergency booth to report the accident to the police, but the location of the accident was not conveyed correctly. Inspector Sommerville arrived at the scene and failed to obey standing orders and close off the entrance to the tunnel. When he remembered, he instructed the plaintiff, Mr Knightley, a constable on patrol duty who had come to the scene after receiving a message on his radio, to go to the entrance and close it. This involved driving in the wrong direction, and just before reaching the entrance a motor car driven by Mr Cotton at 35–40 miles per hour struck the plaintiff, badly injuring him. The plaintiff sued Mr Cotton for causing him serious injuries, the police inspector Somerville and the Chief Constable of the West Midlands as the inspector's superior for the inspector's negligence in instructing or at the least permitting him to ride the wrong way. He, however, alleged that Mr Johns was first and foremost responsible for his injuries because it was his negligence in overturning his car in the tunnel that was the cause of all trouble.

The trial judge acquitted all others of negligence except Mr Johns. He appealed to the Court of Appeal, questioning whether his negligence caused the plaintiff's accident and whether the negligence of the other defendants, or the plaintiff himself, caused or contributed to it. The Court of Appeal held that Mr Johns was not negligent, nor was the plaintiff. The police inspector and Mr Cotton were held negligent and liable for the damages. The inspector's untaken precautions were failing to ascertain from Mr Williams precisely where the collision was, failing to close the tunnel before going into it and having failed to close it, instructing the plaintiff and another constable to go back and close it instead of using the telephone or sending them forward to radio for more assistance. The trial court judge found that these did not amount to negligence because decisions were to be taken on the spur of the moment. However, the Court of Appeal found that not taking the afore-mentioned precautions violated the police force standing instructions for road accidents and vehicle breakdowns on the Queensway tunnel. Further precautions meant for the safety of the emergency personnel, like not allowing traffic till the emergency had been cleared, posting an officer to direct traffic away from the tunnel, sending someone by foot to the scene and reporting back to the control room, were ignored. Thus, L. J. Stephenson held that the inspector "was negligent in not closing the tunnel and in ordering or allowing his subordinates to do a very dangerous thing contrary to standing orders." Mr Cotton was held negligent for driving at 35–40 miles per hour and causing injury to the plaintiff.

Regarding the question of negligence of the plaintiff, Stephenson said that he was not to blame because as a member of the West Midlands police force, he was following instructions in order to get the tunnel closed quickly. The plaintiff had got off his motorcycle with the intention of rendering first-aid, when the inspector said to him and PC Easthope, "I have forgotten to close the tunnel; you two go back and do it." He had a choice of taking the long way round by St Chad's Circus, but the detour would have taken 3 1/2 minutes and, keeping in mind the hazardous situation on the tunnel, he felt he had no alternative but to take the wrong way, although he knew that "it was a hair-raising thing to do, exposing him to very considerable risk of accident." It was noted that had he taken the longer route and an accident had ensued in the tunnel he may have been indicted for failure to follow instructions. The question therefore was what constituted reasonable conduct of Mr Knightley, in the circumstances of the case? On the one hand, there was the danger to himself and on the other his fear based on his experience in policing the motorway that "oncoming traffic would fill up the carriageway back nearly as far as the bend and further vehicles, perhaps a coach or tanker, might come round too fast and into the tailback with much more disastrous consequences." Even at the cost of being struck, he chose the option that he thought would prevent a greater expected harm. Both policemen were riding at a speed of 20 miles per hour, showing main beam lights and flashing taillights and sounding two-tone horns. The Court held that the plaintiff was not "acting unreasonably or negligently in obeying the inspector's orders and riding the wrong way" and was not responsible to any extent for his own injuries. Stephenson went on to say:

> Of those who expose themselves to the danger of being injured by the negligence of others, rescuers are of course in a special category. For they will come and rescue often by deliberate and courageous choice as by instinctive reaction.

The trial judge had found that the "the plaintiff's injury was the natural and probable result of the original negligence of Mr. Johns ... his negligence was the operative cause of the plaintiff's injury." He based his judgment on the view that "the motorist ought to foresee that if he is negligent and creates an emergency other people are likely to be put at risk," particularly police officers, fire officers and ambulance officers. Stephenson, however, held: "Mistakes and mischances are to be expected when human beings, however well trained, have to cope with a crisis; what exactly they will do cannot be predicted." He argued that the inspector's negligence was not a concurrent cause running with Mr John's negligence but a new cause disturbing the sequence of events up to the injury to the plaintiff. Exonerating Mr John and placing the blame for the injury on the inspector's negligence, the Lord argued:

> Coming as it did on top of the muddle and misunderstanding of Mr. William's telephone call and followed by the inspector's order to remedy his own negligence by the dangerous manoeuvre, it was the real cause of the plaintiff's injury and made the injury too remote from Mr. John's wrongdoing to be a consequence of it.

Highlighting the special circumstances of the case that warranted this decision, the Lord concluded:

> In my judgment, too much happened here, too much went wrong, the chapter of accidents and mistakes was too long and varied, to impose on Mr. Johns liability for what happened to the plaintiff in discharging his duty as a police officer, although it would not have happened had not Mr. Johns negligently overturned the car. The ordinary course of things took an extraordinary course. The length and the irregularities of the line leading from the first accident to the second have no parallel in the reported rescue cases, in all of which the plaintiff succeeded in establishing the original wrongdoer's liability.

He went on to state:

> The reasonable hypothetical observer would anticipate some human errors, some forms of what might be called folly, perhaps even from trained police officers, and some unusual and unexpected accidents in the course of their rescue duties. But would he anticipate such a result as this from so many errors as these, so many departures from commonsense procedures prescribed by the standing orders for just such an emergency as this?

Although there is a hint of the untaken precaution approach being followed at the trial stage, in the Court of Appeal the due care approach was used to hold two of the alleged tortfeasors negligent. Inspector Sommerville was held negligent for not following standing instructions and Mr Cotton for driving too fast. In fact, the due care approach was used to hold Mr Johns nonnegligent; it was held that though it is reasonable to anticipate folly, the nature of what happened was far beyond expectation, and the trial judge in holding that Mr Johns ought to have reasonably foreseen was setting too high a standard of care for him, and as Stephenson said, it carried "Mr. Johns's responsibility too far." Similarly, the plaintiff's nonnegligence was decided by the due care approach. Finally, it can be said that Mr Cotton would have been negligent even if the untaken precaution approach was taken because he did not keep a proper look-out and did not slow down when the policemen were sounding the horns and showing their flashlights.

2.2 Cases in which the injurer is declared negligent by considerations which point towards the untaken precaution approach

In *Lang v London Transport Executive and Another*[18] the defendant was held to be negligent for not having taken "extraordinary precautions" in view of the negligence of the plaintiff. An omnibus was being driven along Malden Road, which was a main road, when a motor cyclist came out of a side road called South Lane, disregarding the "slow" sign. A collision occurred in which the cyclist was killed.

His widow sued for damages. The Queen's Bench Division apportioned the blame as two-thirds that of the plaintiff and one-third that of the defendant. It was held that the deceased was substantially to blame for the accident because

> he did not see, or else completely disregarded, the Slow sign, and either did not see the bus at all (which he clearly ought to have done) or if he did see it he hopelessly misjudged the distance that the bus was away, and its speed.

Further, "he came out of the minor road at twenty miles per hour at a time when it was extremely dangerous to do so, and when the bus was so close that collision was inevitable, or at any rate highly probable." He was, therefore, held to be "guilty of a very high degree of negligence," and this negligence was "substantially the cause of the accident."

However, regarding the negligence of the driver of the omnibus, Lord Havers, who delivered the judgment, attempted to find whether one could reconcile the decision of the Court of Session in Scotland in *Browne v Central SMT Co.*[19] and the dicta of the House of Lords in *London Passenger Transport Board v Upson.*[20] In the former case, an accident occurred when a motorcyclist came from the side road and collided with an omnibus on the major road. It was held by the Court of Session:

> that the driver of the omnibus had not been negligent, seeing that, as a driver on a main road, he was entitled, in the absence of any indication to the contrary, to assume that the motor cyclist, a driver on a side road, would conform to the warning signal and either stop or slow down and give him the right of way.

In the same case, Lord Justice-Clerk (Lord Thompson) said this:

> the real difficulty in the case is whether it was open to a reasonable jury to take the view that the omnibus was not entitled to maintain its course or speed in view of the presence in Gallowflat Road of a motor bicycle which, in order to proceed on its way, would have to cross the omnibus line of traffic either in front of or behind the omnibus.

Since both options were open to the cyclist, was the omnibus driver justified in assuming that he would take the safe one which was to cross from behind? Lord Thomson had asked although the omnibus had a right of way, being on a major road, ought he to have exercised that right in a reasonable way by giving it up "in anticipation of possible failure on the part of the cyclist to not take the safe course?"

In the same case, Lord Mackay had given the answer:

> The driver was well entitled, keeping a position on the main road in full daylight and seeing a vehicle at least as far away as he himself was to proceed on the footing that the vehicle would obey the sign which it was bound to do.

He further argued that vehicles could rely

> on side road traffic behaving as the rules of the road desired, until it may be at the last moment some observation of a gross infringement by others calls for a special attempt to deal with it. Such duty arises only pro re nata and cannot be stated as a universally present obligation. I am prepared to agree with what [counsel for the pursuer] said, that there may be exceptional cases (as when you see a man swaying from side to side as if out of control) you may take exceptional measures.

Lord Havers, however, went on to say that this case was decided before the House of Lords announced its decision in Upson's case. In the later case, Lord Du Parcq held: "A driver is *never* entitled to assume that people will not do what his experience and common sense teach him that they are, in fact, likely to do" (emphasis added). Lord Havers concluded that he felt bound to follow the principle enunciated by Lord Dunedin, which was referred to by Lord Du Parcq in Upson that when the danger is really apparent, extraordinary precautions are warranted.[21] Lord Havers went on to enquire whether, in this case, the possibility of danger was reasonably apparent? The omnibus driver had said that "he was aware, from his experience that sometimes persons would suddenly emerge from a side road even when it was not prudent to do so." Lord Havers held that the driver was, therefore, under a duty to take precautions against the possibility that the deceased may not slow down and accordingly kept a look-out at the side road. If he had looked, the possibility of danger occurring would have been reasonably apparent to him, and he would have been able to slow down and allow the bicycle to pass. In this respect, he

> failed to take reasonable care for the safety of other traffic on the road, and was therefore negligent. He made a mistake in assuming that the deceased would not do what his experience should have taught him that persons in fact sometimes do.

The essential difficulty in reconciling the decision of the Court of Session in *Browne v Central SMT Co.* and of the House of Lords in Upson's case, was that while in the former the driver of the omnibus was held nonnegligent using the due care approach; in the latter case the driver was held negligent using the untaken precaution approach. Lord Havers adopted the reasoning of the House of Lords in the Upson case and concluded that extraordinary precautions are warranted when the other party is negligent. That he thought that the "reasonable care" required in this case was above the due care level is clear from his admission: "I have come to this conclusion very reluctantly because he was on the major road, and he was driving at a moderate speed, and especially in view of his very fine record."

Another case in which the untaken precaution approach was used to affirm the negligence of the injurer was *Belka v Prosperini*.[22] The plaintiff, who was with a companion, Mr Lanik, was on an unregulated crossing on a dual carriageway, the A193 Byker bypass in Newcastle-upon-Tyne. This is one of five roads leading into and out of a roundabout. The injurer entered the roundabout from Millers Road, which is almost opposite to the bypass. The plaintiff was struck by the defendant's taxi and thrown up on its bonnet, breaking the windscreen. Just before the accident, the defendant was driving at 25 to 30 miles per hour, which was within the speed limit.

At the trial court, H. H. J. Walton found that the defendant should have seen the two men when they were standing on the "refuge," which was halfway across the two lanes of the bypass. When Mr Lanik waited for the taxi to pass, the plaintiff ran across the road and in doing so "took a risk setting off when, unless the driver took some avoiding action, an accident was likely." The defendant said that when he was about 25 to 50 metres away he saw only one person, possibly Mr Lanik, on the refuge. The judge held that when the defendant was about 30 metres away he should have taken his foot off the accelerator as a precaution against any untoward movement by the pedestrian. He concluded that "with a better lookout, and a slight easing of speed, I am satisfied that the accident would have been avoided." This shows that although the defendant was within the speed limit, he was expected to take extra precaution of slowing down by anticipating the negligence of others. The apportionment of damage was one third for the defendant and two thirds for the plaintiff.

The plaintiff appealed to the Court of Appeal on the ground that the judge should have found that the defendant's "degree of blameworthiness" was very high and more than the plaintiff. Justice Hooper dismissed this on the ground that the plaintiff took a deliberate risk of running across the road in front of the taxi and contributed "more immediately" to the accident than anything that the respondent did or failed to do. Thus, the plaintiff was more to blame than the respondent. The apportionment of liability was upheld. Lord Justice Stanley Burnton and Lord Justice Rix agreed with the verdict.

We find that although the trial court found that the "immediate cause" of the collision was the "deliberate risk" taken by the plaintiff, the verdict that one third of the liability would still fall on the respondent was based on the view that he should have taken extra precaution. That the accident would not have happened had the plaintiff not been negligent is clear from Justice Hooper's dismissal when he said: "It is difficult to imagine how the respondent would have collided with the appellant if the appellant had been crossing the road non-negligently rather than running across the road in the path of the oncoming taxi."

In *Parmasivan v Wicks*[23] the Court of Appeal affirmed the finding of negligence on the part of the injurer but reduced his proportion of liability from 50 percent to 25 percent. The untaken precaution approach was used to decide the negligence of the injurer. He was driving at 25 miles per hour along a suburban road in Leatherhead and upcoming on his right were a row of about three or four shops, and adjoining the shops was a pavement in which a group of seven or eight boys of about 13 years of age were standing. The speed limit governing the road, which was in a normal residential area, was 30 miles per hour. It was around 9.45 p.m. at the end of July and dusk had set in and it was 25 minutes past the lighting up time. The defendant's car had sensors and the headlights had got switched on.

The plaintiff was a 13-year old in the group who suddenly threw an ice-cream at one of his friends and ran across the pavement, through the nearby parking, between the parked cars and then across the northbound carriageway into the front side of the defendant's car. The boy suffered severe head injuries, but there was no damage to the defendant's car. The defendant said that he had neither seen the plaintiff nor the group of boys. The plaintiff had not seen the approaching car because not only was he running across but was looking back over his shoulder towards his friends.

The trial court judge held the injurer negligent on the basis of two untaken precautions. First, the defendant ought to have seen the group gather on the right side. Second, 25 miles per hour was "too fast in the circumstances." He held that the defendant ought to have been travelling at 15 miles per hour once he had seen the group. Since the plaintiff ran seven and a half metres across the road, at 25 miles per hour the defendant had no time to stop, but at 15 miles per hour "he would just have been able to stop, on a balance of probabilities." On these grounds, the trial court judge apportioned the liability equally since the plaintiff was obviously negligent. We note that the defendant was required to have lowered his speed by 10 miles per hour; this can be said to be extraordinary precaution given the negligence of the plaintiff.

This finding that the defendant ought to have driven at 15 miles per hour was challenged at the Court of Appeal by the defendant's lawyer. Further, it was pointed out that the trial court judge had taken the running speed of the boy as 3.6 metres per second and that was the slowest known average speed among a sample of 13-year old males, whereas the driver who was behind the defendant had said that he saw the boy sprinting across the road. Justice Hughes in the Court of Appeal argued that if the required speed of 15 miles per hour had been a finding of primary fact, the court would have been reluctant to interfere. Since it was a question of whether it was "reasonable or unreasonable" in the circumstances of the case, Justice Hughes argued that it is "not a counsel of reasonable care, but of perfection," and thus, "unrealistic." The group of youngsters were a comparatively safe distance away from the carriageway in which the defendant was travelling; they were not infants running indiscriminately, nor did they give a signal that they were about to run across the road. They were laughing and talking, but they did not "provide any reason to require every driver passing by on the far side of the roads to reduce his speed to as low as 15 miles per hour." So Justice Hughes held that driving at 25 miles per hour was negligent.

The defendant was, however, held negligent for not keeping a look-out. Although he had just 2.1 seconds to see the claimant and 1.1 seconds to brake, these time durations "were significant in terms of moving vehicles and people." Justice Hughes agreed with the trial court judge's conclusion that the defendant ought to have seen the plaintiff and was in a breach of duty in not doing so. Since the boy was old enough to "understand roads" and created a hazard by being careless, he contributed to his injury. The additional complaint that he was travelling too fast was removed, but the defendant's fault was to "fail to respond, as he should have, in the briefest of moments." So although his portion of liability was reduced by a quarter, he was still held liable for the plaintiff's injury.

An analysis of the untaken precautions that were considered in determining negligence in the prior cases raises the issue as to the circumstances when injurers face liability for not taking extraordinary precautions and when they do not. One case in which this is clearly spelled out is that of *Scott v Gavigan*.[24] In this case, in the Court of Appeal, it was held that the circumstances of this case did not warrant extraordinary precautions. The defendant, Mr Nicholas Joseph Gavigan, was riding a motorbike on July 13, 2008, along Valley Road, Lambeth, London. It was dusk, but visibility was good because the streetlights were on. The plaintiff, Mr Darren Scott, was walking towards a pub and was on the opposite side of the road on which the defendant was travelling. The accident occurred when the defendant approached an informal pedestrian crossing with two bollards in the middle of the road, each on a small raised island with a gap in between for stopping halfway across the road. The road had a speed limit of 30 miles per hour, and at the time of the accident there were cars parked on the side of the road.

The defendant was travelling at 30 miles per hour, and when he was about 20 metres away from the first bollard he saw the plaintiff crossing the road, but when he was about 10 metres away the plaintiff ran across the road and, despite an attempt by the defendant to swerve, the plaintiff was injured on his lower leg and required a skin graft. The defendant accepted that he did not brake as he approached the pedestrian crossing, but when he saw the plaintiff he braked and blew his horn. The trial judge held that at the place where the accident took place an ordinary prudent motorcyclist would have been driving at no more than 20 miles per hour and would have braked earlier. He held that on a balance of probabilities, the collision would not have occurred if Mr Gavigan had been riding at 20 miles per hour instead of 30 miles per hour. The judge also found that the plaintiff was very drunk, and that impaired his ability to take care while crossing the road. In such a situation, even if the defendant was travelling at 20 miles per hour, he would have to take "emergency evasive action" to avoid the crash. The trial court judge concluded that the plaintiff's own conduct eclipsed the defendant's wrongdoing and constituted a *novus actus interveniens*, breaking the chain of causation and thus held the plaintiff entirely responsible for the accident.

In the Court of Appeal, the plaintiff's lawyer argued that had the defendant been travelling at 20 miles per hour he would have missed the plaintiff and that it was wrong to find that the risk confronting the defendant was not one that he should have reasonably foreseen. Referring to *Lang v London Transport Executive and Another*, he argued on behalf of the defendant that the failure to anticipate carelessness on the part of others is regarded as carelessness itself, and therefore the liability should have been apportioned.

Lord Justice Christopher Clarke, in the Court of Appeal, upheld the trial court judge's reasoning on the grounds that the plaintiff's action of crossing the road at that point without giving any indication of any intention to cross or that he could be drunk or disturbed was not a "common place" but "egregious" folly. The situation differed from *Lang v London Transport Executive and Another*, in which the bus driver was aware from his experience that sometimes people would emerge suddenly from the side road in question. In this case, the risk was not one which the defendant should have reasonably foreseen. The Court of Appeal denied any apportionment. Justice Simon and Justice Elias agreed to the verdict. We find that the Court of Appeal made a fine distinction regarding the "form" the follies take and which of them would demand extraordinary precautions.

2.3 Cases in which the injurer is declared negligent by considerations which point towards use of both the approaches

Paris v Stepney Borough Council[25] was an important negligence case in which the standard of care owed by an employer towards his workmen came under scrutiny. The plaintiff, Mr Paris, had been employed as a garage hand in the cleaning department by the Stepney Borough Council since 1942, and one of his duties was to assist in the dismantling of motor vehicles. It was only in July 1946, that his employers found out that Mr Paris was, for all practical purposes, blind in the left eye due to an injury suffered in May 1941, as a result of an air raid. The medical examination was in connection with enrolling as a member of the permanent staff and with joining its superannuation scheme. On May 16, 1947, he was given two weeks' notice (expiring on May 30) for termination of his employment. Two days before the notice was to expire, a large vehicle used for cleaning sewers and gulleys was brought into the garage to be stripped for examination. It was raised about four and a half feet from the garage floor by means of a ramp. To do this work, the plaintiff had to stand with his eyes level with or slightly below the point at which he was working. While removing a U-bolt holding the springs of an axle, he hit the U-bolt with a steel hammer, as a result of which a piece of metal flew off and entered his right eye, leaving him completely blind. The plaintiff alleged that it was the duty of the defendants "to supply him with suitable goggles for the protection of his eyes while he was engaged in such work and to require him to use them." He, therefore, claimed damages in negligence. At the trial stage, J. Lynskey held that the defendants were negligent. This was unanimously reversed by the Court of Appeal. Finally, the House of Lords re-instated the verdict of the learned judge, with two out of the five Lords dissenting.

In the evidence, a Captain Patterson had answered the learned judge that in the whole of his experience he had about a dozen times seen a man wearing goggles when he was using a hammer to knock a rusted bolt in dismantling a car, adding that that would be when working under a vehicle. Mr Parker, at the time the mechanical superintendent of the respondent's cleansing department, while emphasizing that it was not normal practice to wear goggles for the work in question, said he had seen men who were working underneath a vehicle wearing glasses, adding that he thought that could be to prevent dust from getting in the eyes. After considering the facts, particularly the known risk of metal flying when this sort of work was being done, the position of the workmen, with the plaintiff's eyes close to the bolt he was hammering and on the same level with it or below it, and the disastrous consequences of a particle of metal falling into his one good eye, Lynskey concluded that the defendants had failed in their duty. He argued:

> In this case the real question is whether the employers in adopting this system and not providing or requiring the use of goggles for the workers on this system were taking responsible care to provide a suitable system of work and provide a suitable plant.

Emphasizing the importance of the plaintiff's having, to the defendant's knowledge, only one useful eye, he concluded: "I am satisfied here that there was, so far as this particular plaintiff was concerned, a duty on the employers to provide goggles and require the use of goggles as part of their system." The reasoning seems to be consistent with the economic model, in the sense that Lynskey was stating that the greater expected harm to this particular plaintiff required that goggles be provided.

In the Court of Appeal, Lord C. J. Goddard said:

> The way that the learned Judge has decided the case and the ground on which counsel for the workman has endeavoured to uphold the judgment is that as this workman had one eye only a greater duty was owed to him than was owed to other persons because the consequences of an accident would be so much more serious.

There were two conclusions on the basis of which the Court of Appeal reversed the judgment of Lynskey: first, that there was no duty on the respondents to provide goggles to ordinary, two-eyed workmen employed in this work; and second, that there was therefore no duty towards the one-eyed man as well, since although the consequences were more serious, the risk of accident was the same for all workmen. This latter reasoning was stated clearly by L. J. Asquith:

> The disability can only be relevant to the stringency of the duty owed to the workman if it increases the risk to which the workman is exposed. A one-eyed man is no more likely to get a splinter or a chip in his eye than is a two-eyed man. The risk is no greater, but the damage is greater to a man using his only good eye than to a man using two good eyes. The quantum of damage, however, is one thing, and the scope of duty is another. The greater the risk of injury is not the same thing as the risk of greater injury, and the first thing seems to me to be relevant here.

We note that this is inconsistent with economic logic since the standard of care depends *both* on the probability of harm and the extent of harm.

In the House of Lords, Lord Macdermott emphasized the importance of this opinion of the Court of Appeal when he said: "This view of the law raises a question of far reaching importance, for if sound, it must, in my opinion pervade, if not the whole domain of negligence, at least a very large part of it." However, he went on to argue that it was not a sound proposition, even with respect to the care required of an employer towards his employees. He stated:

> I think it is enough to say that the employer's duty to take reasonable care for the safety of his workmen is directed – and, I venture to add, obviously directed – to their welfare and for that reason, if for no other, must be related to both the risk and the degree of injury.

He argued that the doctrine that "the extent of injury" is not relevant finds no support in authority. This view was endorsed by Lord Simonds. In fact, the House of Lords unanimously held that both the likelihood of an accident happening and the gravity of the consequences were important. In order to highlight that the gravity of the injury was an important factor, Lord Morton of Henryton stated:

> "if A and B who are engaged in the same work, run precisely the same risk of an accident happening, but if the results of an accident will be more serious to A than to B, precautions which are adequate in the case of B may not be adequate in the case of A, and it is a duty of the employer to take such additional precautions for the safety of A as may be reasonable.

He, therefore, refuted the contention of the Court of Appeal that the one-eyed condition of the plaintiff was an irrelevant factor in the determination of the standard of care. This argument of the House of Lords is consistent with economic logic.

However, the Lords were divided in their opinion about the negligence question. The difference of opinion arose not because of differences in logic because they all agreed that both the probability of harm and the extent of harm were important, but because their estimates of the extent of harm differed. Lord Normand argued that the standard of care would be high for all workmen, whether one-eyed or two-eyed. He emphasized:

> Even for a two-eyed man the risk of losing an eye is a very grievous risk, not to speak of the foreseeable possibility that both eyes might be simultaneously destroyed, or that the loss of one eye might have as a sequel the destruction of vision in the other. It may be said that, if it is obvious that goggles should have been supplied to a one-eyed workman, it is scarcely less obvious that they should have been supplied to all the workmen.

He criticized the judgment of Lynskey, saying: "it rests on an unreal and insufficient distinction between the gravity of the risk run by a one-eyed man and the gravity of the risk run by a two-eyed man." He argued that a high level of care, not necessarily the same level of care, was required in case of a one-eyed man as was applicable for two-eyed men and to that extent the learned judge's verdict that goggles should have been provided to the plaintiff should be restored, although he did not first consider what precautions would have been appropriate for two-eyed men and then go on to compare whether a higher level of care was needed for a one-eyed man. In terms of economic logic, Lord Normand's view can be summarized by saying that he thought that the extent of harm was substantially large for both two-eyed men and the one-eyed plaintiff, and therefore the due care level should have been set high for both; since the defendants did not take the higher levels of care they fell short of their duty to this particular plaintiff as well.

While endorsing Lord Normand's conclusion that goggles should have been provided to the plaintiff, Lord Oaksey argued:

> the question was not whether the precaution ought to have been taken with ordinary two-eyed workmen and it was not necessary, in my opinion, that Lynskey J should decide that question – nor did he purport to decide it, although it is true that he stated the question in one sentence too broadly.

However, he thought that it was for the judge at the trial

> to weigh up the risk of injury and the extent of damage and to decide whether, in all the circumstances including the fact that the workman was known to be one-eyed and might become a blind man if his eye was struck, an ordinarily prudent employer would supply such a workman with goggles. It is a simple and inexpensive precaution to take to supply goggles and a one-eyed man would not be likely, as a two-eyed man might be, to refuse to wear the goggles. Lynskey J appears to me to have weighed the extent of the risk and of the damage to a one-eyed man, and I am of opinion that his judgment should be restored.

We find that the untaken precaution approach was being used because the provision of goggles was seen to be a cost-justified precaution, which was not taken. Lord Macdermott stated that although he subscribes to the view of the Court of Appeal that the employers were under no general obligation to provide goggles to all their work-men, the additional element that the defendants knew that the appellant was a one-eyed man "made it proper to arrive at a different conclusion regarding their duty to him." He reasoned:

> His chances of being blinded were appreciably greater and blindness is an affliction in a class by itself which reasonable men will want to keep from those who work for them if there are reasonable precautions which can be taken to that end. To my mind, whatever may be said of the respondents' duty to their two-eyed employees, there was ample evidence to sustain the view that they failed in their duty to the appellant.

68 Economic analysis of select British cases

He was following the due care approach.

The dissenting opinions of Lord Simonds and Lord Morton of Henryton were based on the fact that "it was not part of the system of work to provide goggles for two-eyed men because the degree of risk did not demand that precaution in a reasonable employer." Although they thought that both the probability of harm and the extent of harm were important, they ascribed a lower probability of harm to the event, and therefore, their estimate of expected harm was lower. Based on this, they argued that the custom of not providing goggles in these situations seemed appropriate, and the employer cannot be held to be negligent for not providing them. They thus endorsed the Court of Appeal's view that the same lower standard should be applicable with respect to all workmen, but their reasoning differed.

We find that the reasoning adopted in the House of Lords to determine the negligence of the defendant indicates the use of both the due care approach and the untaken precaution approach.

An early example is the well-known case of *London Passenger Transport Board v Upson and Another*,[26] in which the defendant was held negligent by considerations that point to both approaches to negligence determination. In that case, an accident occurred at the intersection of Baker Street and Blanford Street, London, when Mrs Upson, the plaintiff, was hit by an omnibus belonging to the defendants, London Passenger Transport Board, while attempting to cross the road against the lights. There was a taxicab parked obstructing her view of the oncoming traffic; and of the omnibus as to whether anyone was already on the pedestrian crossing when the lights turned green or whether someone was trying to cross against the lights. The trial court held that the driver was negligent; the defendants appealed to the Court of Appeal, which held the driver negligent but based on a reasoning that differed from that of the trial court. The defendants appealed to the House of Lords, which dismissed the appeal.

In her action, the plaintiff alleged the following untaken precautions: failure to give the plaintiff free and uninterrupted rite of passage over the said recognized crossing; failure to keep a proper look-out; driving at an excessive speed; driving on the wrong portion of the road; failure to apply the brakes soon enough, or at all; and failure to give any, or adequate, warning. The trial court held that the failure to keep a proper look-out constituted the untaken precaution for which the defendant should be held negligent. This was based on the reasoning that the driver should have assumed that people do not in fact take due care while walking or driving across intersections but are often negligent. This is clearly brought out by the propositions on which the original finding of negligence, based on this particular untaken precaution, was articulated at the trial court by Judge Humphreys. They were:

> 1) that the driver knew from experience that a pedestrian might cross against the lights; 2) that he knew that he was not entitled to run a pedestrian down merely because he was negligent; 3) that the conductor and Mrs. Grenfall [a witness], who were inside the omnibus, saw the plaintiff hurrying across the pavement with the obvious intention of attempting to cross, and that if the driver, instead of watching the road, had turned his eyes towards the

pavement, as they did, he must have seen what they saw and drawn the inference that they did.

In the Court of Appeal,[27] the majority held that the failure of the defendant's driver to comply with the Pedestrian Crossing Places (Traffic) Regulations, 1941, constituted negligence. It was agreed that the regulations were "effective to set up a standard of care." L. J. Cohen clearly put it:

> It seems to me that, in considering whether a party has been negligent, the court is entitled to have regard to what restrictions parliament has thought it necessary to impose on motor traffic for the protection of pedestrians whether the relevant provisions are found to be in an Act of Parliament or in regulations made thereunder.

The regulation directly applicable in the present case was said to be regulation 3, which stated: "The driver of every vehicle approaching a crossing shall, unless he can see that there is no foot passenger thereon, proceed at such a speed as to be able if necessary to stop before reaching such a crossing." With respect to the case at hand, Cohen said:

> On the evidence it is plain that at all material times the presence of the stationary taxicab prevented the driver having an uninterrupted view of the whole of the crossing. That being so, it was impossible for him to see that there was no foot passenger thereon, and it was, therefore, his duty under the regulation to proceed at such a speed as to be able, if necessary, to stop before reaching the crossing. On the driver's own evidence he saw the plaintiff when she was 9 ft. away from the omnibus, and when he stopped the front wheels of the bus were on the crossing. Had he been driving at such a pace as to enable him to stop short of the crossing, it must, in my opinion, follow that he could have stopped within these 9 ft.

He therefore concluded:

> I see no reason to assume that any undue inconvenience would be caused if the law requires that a driver approaching a vehicle in such a position should comply with regulations which have been imposed to prevent such a breach leading to an accident. For these reasons (which are not the same as those given by the learned judge) I am of the opinion that his decision was right and should be affirmed.

L. J. Asquith too argued along the same lines as Cohen, and he too categorically distinguished his approach from that of Judge Humphreys by saying:

> At common law the driver of a motor vehicle is, of course, not entitled in all circumstances to assume that other users of the road will behave

unimpeachably, but neither is he bound to anticipate and provide against every eccentricity and folly, however improbable, which they may elect to commit.... I think the conduct of the plaintiff was consummately imprudent and so as no bus driver could reasonably be expected to foresee in pursuance of his common law duty of care.

However, regulation 3 could not be ignored, and the breach of duty question hinged on the failure to adhere to it. M. R. Greene, in his dissenting opinion, argued that the driver was nonnegligent because he had been driving at the perfectly reasonable speed of 15 miles per hour, and he had applied the brakes, which perhaps helped to save the life of the plaintiff. Further, the driver had the lights in his favour and therefore was "entitled to assume that the plaintiff, like other pedestrians, would conform to common-sense and ordinary care in the presence of an adverse signal, particularly in view of the provisions of the Highway Code." He argued that the accident occurred entirely due to the negligence of the plaintiff. What Judge Humphreys called "an honest miscalculation" on the part of the plaintiff, Greene regarded as "reckless disregard" of her own safety.

The defendants appealed to the House of Lords, which restored the order of Judge Humphreys and held the driver negligent at common law. In addition to the finding of negligence due to violation of regulation 3, the reasoning was also based on the "common experience" that many users of the road do not actually take reasonable care. Lord Uthwatt, dissenting from the view expressed by Greene that drivers are "entitled to drive on the assumption that other users of the road whether drivers or pedestrians would behave with reasonable care," said that it is common experience that many do not. His oft-quoted statement followed: "A driver is not, of course, bound to anticipate folly in all its forms, but he is not, in my opinion, entitled to put out of consideration the teachings of experience as to the form those follies commonly take." Affirming this line of reasoning, Lord Du Parcq further added:

> the propositions advanced by the learned Master of The Rolls do not, I think, accord with the law as it has been laid down in your Lordships' House. The correct principle was stated by Lord Dunedin in *Fardon v Harcourt-Rivington* when he said: If the possibility of the danger emerging is reasonably apparent, then to take no precautions is negligence; but if the possibility of danger emerging is only a mere possibility which would never occur to the mind of a reasonable man, then there is no negligence *in not having taken extraordinary precautions* (emphasis added).

He continued: "a prudent man will guard against all possible negligence of others when experience shows such negligence to be common." We note that it is explicitly stated here that the injurer should have taken account of the negligence of the victim and hence taken a greater level of care when experience shows that it is not a mere possibility, but quite a common occurrence.

Lord Wright agreed with Lord Du Parcq's criticism of Greene. Arguing along similar lines, Lord Merton of Henryton summed up:

> I could not accept it [the argument of Greene MR] as correct in a case as the present case, where an obstruction on a pedestrian crossing prevents the driver from seeing whether a pedestrian has begun to cross the road against the signals. In such a case, I think that a driver fails to exercise due care, apart altogether from the regulations of 1941, if he proceeds on the assumption that pedestrians will refrain from crossing the road until the lights change, and drives his vehicle in such a way that he cannot avoid an accident if a pedestrian emerges suddenly from behind the obstruction.

We can infer that the trial court judge was using only the untaken precaution approach to arrive at the negligence verdict. It was reiterated by Lord Porter that the learned judge accepted that the speed of 15 miles an hour, at which the driver was driving was a perfectly reasonably pace, the lights were in his favour, he had braked when he saw the plaintiff and eased off to the left a little and had the vehicle under perfect control. Further as, Asquith put it:

> Humphreys J decided the case on the footing that the Pedestrian Crossing Places (Traffic) Regulations, 1941, should be ignored for all practical purposes and liability determined by exclusive reference to the common law as it would have operated if no such regulations had ever been made.

In the Court of Appeal, this approach was held to be erroneous, and Greene said:

> In considering the position in which this driver was as he approached the crossing and what was the extent of his duty to take care, it is, in my view, misleading to ignore the regulations and the Highway Code which have an important bearing on the extent of that duty so far as regards pedestrians.

The due care approach was used in the Court of Appeal, by the majority to arrive at a verdict that the driver was negligent and by Greene to absolve him of negligence and liability. Greene had argued:

> if drivers were not entitled to drive on the assumption that other users of the road, whether drivers or pedestrians, would behave with reasonable care, all traffic would come to a standstill, since everyone at his peril would have to act on the hypothesis that his neighbor might at any moment put his own life in danger by behaving in a negligent manner.

We may infer that he was saying that the cost of "keeping a proper look-out" might be very high because traffic would come to a standstill. The precaution in question would, therefore, not be cost-justified.

The reasoning used in the House of Lords points to both the approaches to negligence determination. They were unanimous about the failure to adhere to regulations as being negligent, and Lord Uthwatt, Lord Du Parq and Lord Merton of Henryton used the untaken precaution approach as well. Explicit reference was made by Lord Du Parcq to taking "extraordinary precautions," implying thereby that cost-justified precautions could be identified beyond the due care level because the victim was negligent. Since the defendant did not take that precaution, he was negligent.

Although the focus of the litigation was on the negligence of the defendant and the plaintiff's negligence was admitted at some stages, her negligence was attributed to failure to take due care in the circumstances. She was held negligent "because she failed to take the precaution of looking to see whether the lights were green or red," "for not proceeding with the caution demanded both by the colour of lights and the presence of the taxicab" and for "reliance on a wild estimate of the speed of the omnibus." Greene, in fact, questioned whether "keeping a look-out" was *the* untaken precaution which could have prevented the accident. Greene MR said that the "real cause of the accident... was the negligent act of the plaintiff herself," and the evidence satisfied him that "the accident would have happened in any event." That is, according to him, it would not be a cause-in-fact, as it did not satisfy the but-for test of causation. One can argue that the untaken precaution of blowing the horn would also have been cost-justified but may not have been effective at a busy intersection.

Greene also raised a duty question when he asked:

> The fact that the driver could have seen something if he had looked is, of course, conclusive against him when he was under a duty to look. To say that he was under a duty to look because, if he had looked, he would have seen is, with respect, entirely to misunderstand the nature and foundations of the duty to keep a proper look-out.

The answer to this can be found in a later American case, *Davis v Consolidated Rail Corporation*[28] in which judge Posner argued that potential injurers may

> be required to take some care for the protection of the negligent, especially when the probability of negligence is high or costs of care very low. You cannot close your eyes while driving through an intersection, merely because you have a green light. If, as a jury could have found, Conrail could have avoided the accident by the essentially costless step of blowing the train's horn, it may have been *duty-bound* to do so even if only a careless person would have been engendered by the sudden movement of the train.

We note that what Judge Posner was saying is inconsistent with the approach adopted in the economic model for defining negligence. In the economic approach, one compares the expected harm that can be avoided with the burden of precautions.

Another important negligence case is that of *Davies v Swan Motor Company (Swansea) Limited*.[29] Mr Davies, in the course of his employment, was riding on the steps of a dustcart lorry when it collided with an omnibus belonging to the defendants. As a result of the collision Mr Davies was killed, and his wife brought an action in negligence against the driver of the omnibus. The trial court found for the plaintiff and awarded damages. The defendants appealed to the Court of Appeal and raised questions regarding the negligence of the deceased and the dustcart lorry driver as well.

The Court of Appeal affirmed the verdict of the trial court and held the omnibus driver negligent. This was based on the reasoning that "he attempted to overtake in a narrow road on a bend without warning and before receiving a signal." The dustcart lorry driver was also held negligent. This verdict was reached "because he turned suddenly across the road without making proper use of his mirror and without giving sufficient warning of his intention to do so." Lord Denning further added: "Although the dustcart driver did not actually know that he was on the step, he might have foreseen it."

Regarding the negligence of the deceased, the Court of Appeal found him negligent after an in-depth analysis. L. J. Bucknill argued:

> in standing where he did on the lorry, the deceased committed a breach of duty to the omnibus driver because by so doing he made the driver's task in passing the lorry more difficult than it would otherwise have been, and, to that extent, increased the risk of collision.[30]

This was because the position taken by the deceased "increased the width of the lorry, thereby making the passageway less broad." The deceased had disregarded repeated instructions from the Cleaning Department, warning employees from standing on the steps of motor vehicles. The court further noted that in order to establish whether the deceased was contributorily negligent, one must consider whether he could have avoided the consequences of the other party's negligence by taking reasonable care. Bucknill quoted from Charlesworth's *The Law of Negligence*[31]:

> The doctrine of contributory negligence cannot, I think, be based upon breach of duty to the negligent defendant. It is difficult to suppose that a person owes a duty to anyone to preserve his own property. *He may not recover if he could reasonably have avoided the consequences of the defendant's negligence.*[32] (emphasis added)

This way of defining negligence conforms with the untaken precaution approach and not the due care approach. It was held that on both grounds the deceased man was guilty of contributory negligence – breach of duty and failure to take reasonable care to avoid the consequences of the injurer's negligence.[33]

We find that although both approaches were used to determine the negligence of the lorry driver and that of the deceased, the due care approach was used to hold the omnibus driver negligent. However, given the facts of the case and some of the authorities that were cited, one can infer that the omnibus driver too would be negligent by both the approaches. L.J. Denning had pointed out that the omnibus driver "actually saw the deceased man standing on the steps of the dust lorry." Bucknill had argued:

> It is one thing for a vehicle to pass another vehicle with wooden or iron sides, and another thing for it to pass another vehicle with wooden or iron steps attached to its sides and a living human body standing on those steps.

Given the negligence of the other party, the omnibus driver should have taken greater care. That is, knowing that a man was standing on the steps, the care required of him was higher. To demonstrate the importance that "taking account of the negligence of the other party" plays in negligence determination, the judgment of L.J. Greer in *The Eurymedon*,[34] a case of collision between two ships, was quoted:

> I think that the law arising out of what is usually called Davies v Mann may be stated as follows: If, as I think was the cause in Davies v Mann, one of the parties in a common law action actually knows from observation the negligence of the other party, he is solely responsible if he fails to exercise reasonable care towards the negligent plaintiff.

L.J. Evershed further elaborated this with the help of Lord Shaw's speech in *Anglo-Newfoundland Development Co v Pacific Steam Navigation Co.*[35]:

> The principle does not apply to shipping law alone, but to all the law of contributory negligence, from Davies v Mann downwards. And I take the principle to be that, although there might be – which for the purpose of this point I am reckoning that there was – fault in being in a position which makes an accident possible yet, if the position is recognized by the other prior to operations which result in an accident occurring, the author of that accident is the party who, recognizing the position of the other, fails negligently to avoid an accident which with reasonable conduct on his part could have been avoided.

With respect to the negligence of the deceased, we can refer to what Denning had explicitly highlighted on this aspect in the later case of *Jones v Livox Quarries Ltd*.[36]:

> A person is guilty of contributory negligence if he ought reasonably to have foreseen that, if he did not act as a reasonable, prudent man, he might be hurt himself; *and in his reckonings he must take into account the possibility of others being careless*. (emphasis added)

This way of defining contributory negligence is based on the untaken precaution approach. We may argue that although it was wrong on the part of the deceased to stand on the steps in the first instance, once he saw the omnibus approaching he had only two options – getting inside the bus and staying where he was. It was stated:

> On the one hand, the deceased man could not get off the steps on which he was standing when the omnibus was approaching the lorry, and apparently, on the other hand, he could not get into the lorry without a great deal of difficulty.

Since the lorry driver did not know that he was on the steps, the probability of harm if he remained on the steps would be high; thus, expected harm would be high. By comparison, the burden of precautions – the "great deal of difficulty" – would be lower. Therefore, we can say that for the deceased, the precaution of getting inside the bus was cost-justified; thus, his failure to do so amounted to negligence.

Rouse v Squires and others[37] was a multiple accident case where the issue of negligence of multiple tortfeasors arose. At about 10.30 p.m. on a frosty December night, Mr Allen was driving up the north-bound carriageway of the M1 in his employer's lorry, when he lost control, skidded and got into what was called a jack-knife position obstructing the slow and centre lanes of the carriageway. An "1100" motor car driven by Mr Scattergood, travelling on the centre lane of the same carriageway, collided with the part of Mr Allen's vehicle that was on the lane, and after the collision its rear lights stayed on. Next Mr Rouse, who was driving a lorry, arrived on the scene, saw the trouble, parked his vehicle safely away from the scene of accident and went back to help. Close behind was another lorry driven by Mr Franklin, who noticed the situation and pulled up in the nearside lane of the carriageway 15 feet short of the jack-knifed lorry and left his headlights on to illuminate the scene. Finally, Mr Squires came along, and it was only when he was within 150 yards that he noticed the situation; unable to stop, he hit the rear end of Mr Franklin's lorry pushing it forward so that it knocked down Mr Rouse, who was standing somewhere near the jack-knifed lorry and caused him fatal injuries. His widow brought an action under the Fatal Injuries Acts 1846–59 against the defendant, Mr Squires.

Q. C. Judge Norman Richards, sitting as deputy High Court judge, held Mr Squires extremely negligent for: driving too fast in frosty conditions, he admitted that he was driving at 50mph; failing to observe that the vehicles ahead were stationary until he was within 150 yards of them, when he ought to have realized it from 400 yards away; failing to realize that there might have been a breakdown and reducing his speed; and failing to switch on full headlights when he saw that there was some obstruction ahead. Mr Squires had taken third party proceedings against Mr Allen and the owners of the lorry he was driving, F. V. Carroll & Sons Ltd, and he claimed against them indemnity, or contribution. The learned judge found Mr Allen negligent too but held that his negligence was not a cause of Mr Rouse's injuries. He reached this conclusion based on the following argument:

> If the first accident had occurred so that the obstruction which resulted was unlit or lit only to such an extent, due to atmospheric conditions, that the

driver keeping a proper look-out could not take avoiding action in time as was the case in Harvey v Road Haulage Executive, other considerations might apply, but here I am satisfied that the scene of the obstruction was adequately lighted to warn any driver coming along and keeping a proper look-out that there was or might be trouble ahead.

The trial court, therefore, found for the third parties. The defendants appealed.

The Court of Appeal held that both Mr Squires and Mr Allen were negligent and apportioned the blame as three-fourths and one-fourth respectively. It was explicitly stated that one cannot expect reasonable behavior from highway users. As far as the negligence of the defendant, Mr Squires, was concerned, L. J. Cairns agreed with the finding of the trial judge:

> Mr. Squires has been held by the learned judge (and I do not query this part of his finding) to have been extremely negligent in that, in addition to driving too fast, he failed to keep a proper lookout. But it can be said of him that he did not initiate the dangerous situation but failed to take adequate steps to cope with a situation that already existed. Through that failure he must be held to be the person mainly responsible for this calamity.

J. Mackenna also argued that if Mr Squires had been keeping "an intelligent look-out" he would have noticed that the vehicles ahead of him were stationary and not moving as he said he thought at the time. Besides, "he was driving at an excessive speed."

Regarding of the negligence of Mr Allen, Cairns emphasized that one ought to take account of the negligence of others. He began:

> It is not reasonable to expect that every user of the highway will use it in a reasonable manner. It is reasonable to expect that nobody will drive into a lorry parked so as to occupy only a third of a well-lighted carriageway. It would, however, be wholly unreasonable to expect that if you so mismanage a lorry that it obstructs two lanes of the carriageway on an unlighted motorway it is not going to constitute a danger to other road users.

He further went on to argue: "I think this court ought to accept that it was because the centre lane was blocked that Mr. Squires had to apply his brakes harder and that caused the fatal skid." He cited the case of *Barber v British Road Services*:

> There a large lorry was backed out into the road so as to obstruct it and the driver of another vehicle went into it. It is said in terms by Pearson LJ and was implicit in the other judgments, that a driver must not assume that other drivers will be driving at moderate speed or keeping a proper look-out.

He referred to the opinion of Lord Uthwatt in the case of *London Passenger Transport Board v Upson* discussed earlier that a driver is not entitled to put out of consideration the teachings of experience as to the forms human follies commonly take. He reasoned:

> I do not think it can be said that the negligence of which Mr. Squires was undoubtedly guilty was of such a character or degree as to take it out of the conduct which another driver ought to expect may occur on the highway

Mackenna argued that the present case was closest to the case of *The Eurymedon*:

> There the plaintiff's ship lay at anchor in a dangerous position athwart the fairway of the Thames. Her position was indicated by lights which those in charge of the defendants' ship should have identified as anchor lights in time to avoid a collision. They did not do so because they were not expecting to find a ship in this unusual position. Both ships were held responsible for the collision. The position of Mr. Allen's lorry in the present case was at least as unusual as that of the plaintiff's ship in The Eurymedon.

Buckley also affirmed that Mr Allen's negligence was a cause of the fatal injury. He said that he had culled out the "firm conclusion" that:

> Anyone who by a negligent act creates a danger on a highway to users of the highway can be liable to another user if damage results from the danger so caused. The question whether there is danger is to be determined by the ordinary test of foreseeability. But for the purpose, when considering how other road users can reasonably be expected to use the road, *you are not entitled to assume that they will exercise the proper degree of care.* (emphasis added)

As an answer to whether there was a break in the chain of causation between the prior negligent act of causing an obstruction and the immediate consequences of the latter negligent act of a driver on the highway who causes an accident, he thought there was no break. As to whether, in the present case, there was a reasonable likelihood that a driver using the north-bound carriageway at the time of the accident in question would fail to appreciate the dangerous situation which resulted from Mr Allen's negligence, he thought that it would be right to adopt the approach of Lord Birkenhead in *The Volute*:[38]

> 'somewhat broadly and upon common-sense principles as a jury would probably deal with it', and one must bear in mind that not all users of the highway will be exercising that degree of care and circumspection which constitutes a proper look-out.

To the extent that Mr Squires did not appreciate the dangerous situation, or its extent, on time, there was no break in the chain of causation, and therefore Mr Allen's negligence also contributed to the accident. There would have been a break if Mr Squires had seen and appreciated the nature and extent of the obstruction and taken evasive action.

We note that in this case the untaken precaution approach was heavily relied upon in negligence determination. The trial court judge and the judges of the Court of Appeal used both the approaches to decide the negligence of Mr Squires. As to the question of how Mr Allen lost control of his vehicle, it was noted that the "reasons were not fully explained but which admittedly involved negligence on Mr. Allen's part." The court predominantly relied upon the untaken precaution approach to determine his negligence and contribution to the damage. It was argued that Mr Allen's lorry posed a danger to all vehicles "driving at an excessive speed and not observing or interpreting correctly lights ahead." It is clear from the reasoning that the court arrived at the conclusion that both parties were to blame because both should have taken the other's negligence into account.

Another case in which the employer's liability towards his workmen came under scrutiny was *General Cleaning Contractors Limited and Others v Christmas*.[39] The case concerned a window cleaner, Mr Christmas, who was employed by General Cleaning Contractors Ltd. and sent by them to clean the windows of the Caledonian Club. While cleaning one of the large library windows from outside, he fell 29 feet into the basement below and was injured. He brought an action against his employers on the grounds that either (i) in breach of their duty to him they had failed to take reasonable care to provide a safe system of work; or (ii) they were negligent so that he sustained injury. As his employers said that it was not their fault but the fault of the club, the plaintiff added the club as defendants also. J. Jones found that both the contractors and the club were equally to blame. Each defendant appealed and the Court of Appeal held that the former were negligent but the latter was nonnegligent. The contractors appealed to the House of Lords; they were held negligent.

The plaintiff's employers had a standing contract to clean the windows of the club, and the plaintiff had frequently been one of the men sent to do this work. He was a good workman who had been in the employment of the contactors for 20 years, on piece-work terms. The learned judge accepted the evidence of Mr Harrington that the lower sash of the window on which the plaintiff was working at the time of the accident was defective and had a tendency to move suddenly because the weights were not heavy enough to provide proper balance. The involuntary closing of the window displaced the plaintiff's finger-grip and caused him to lose balance and fall. The learned judge found that this involuntary closure constituted an unusual danger, which the club ought to have known if they had exercised reasonable care in having the windows inspected from time to time and repaired when necessary. The judge found that the plaintiff's employers were in breach of duty in not taking reasonable care to provide a safe system of working and for negligence. Contributory negligence on the part of the plaintiff was negative.

The Court of Appeal held that although the finding that the window was defective must be accepted, it does not follow that the club was guilty of negligence. L. J. Denning distinguished the duties that the club owed to its members and servants and to the window cleaners. He argued that in general a householder must be concerned to see that the windows are safe for his servants to open and close, and in the present case the defect in the window presented a danger that could be considered too remote to form a basis of a charge of negligence. He elaborated:

> The duty which a householder owes to his servants is much higher than that which he owes to a window cleaner who is only an invitee. The householder employs the window cleaner as an independent contractor to clean his windows, and leaves it to him to decide how he shall do it and what safeguards he shall take, whether he shall use ladders or cradles or simply stand on the sill. The householder does not know what strains or stresses the window cleaner is going to put on the window. If the window cleaner chooses to rely on the window for his safety, then it is for him, and not for the householder, to take steps to see that it is safe for his special purposes.... Windows, which are often quite serviceable for ordinary purposes, may yet have some minor defect, such as rusty screws or worn sash cords, or ill-balanced weights, making them unsuitable for window cleaners to put their trust in.

Both L. J. Hodson and J. Lloyd-Jacob agreed with Denning that windows, though defective, could not be said to constitute an "unusual danger" for window cleaners. Llyod-Jacob argued that since no complaint had been made about that particular window by expert cleaners, who quite often complained about the other windows, to expect the club to have knowledge of it was "to impose a duty on an invitor more onerous than has yet been found appropriate for normal human relations."

Regarding the negligence of the employers, Denning held that since the plaintiff fell due to one of the dangers usual to window cleaning, the employers failed to take reasonable care to protect the plaintiff. He elaborated:

> There is a difference between a master-man and a journeyman. A master-man, working on his own account, who knows of the dangers, has a choice before him. He need not do the work if he does not wish to run the risk. But a journeyman, working for another, has no such easy choice. He has been sent to do the work and he may well feel that do it he must, even though he knows that it involves risk. If such a man has no remedy against the occupier – the Horton's case shows that he has none – then it must be the duty of his employer to take reasonable care to protect him.[40]

He specifically pointed out certain untaken precautions – provision of a ladder, inserting hooks into the brickwork so as to attach a safety belt. He was not convinced by the employer's answer that these precautions were not practicable and that it was the usual thing for the men to clean windows by standing on the sill. He argued:

> If employers employ men on this dangerous work for their own profit, they must take proper steps to protect them, even if they are expensive. If they

cannot afford to provide adequate safeguards, they should not ask them to do the task at all.

We find that Denning was saying that the risk of a fall was so great that it would outweigh the cost of any precaution, including the cost of stopping the cleaning work altogether. He agreed with the trial judge that the plaintiff was not guilty of contributory negligence. Hodson also argued that a workman asked to undertake a risky operation must be provided safeguards and since the plaintiff's employers did not provide these, they would be "liable for breach of duty and in not taking reasonable care to provide a safe system of work and for negligence." Llyod-Jacob also agreed that the contractors were negligent.

In the House of Lords, Lord Reid implicitly rejected Denning's argument and held that sufficient evidence did not exist to establish that "the ladder method or the safety belt method are as a general rule reasonably practicable alternatives." He argued further that although the ladder method may have been safe and practicable in this particular situation, it may not be practicable in a large number of cases. He was thinking of the standard as the average one as opposed to the economic concept of individualized due care. As for hooks, Lord Reid argued that even when they were provided, window cleaners often neglected to use safety belts. We find that Lord Reid was referring to the actual level of care usually taken by people in the plaintiff's position. This indicates the use of the untaken precaution approach. In fact, Lord Reid even identified a cost-justified untaken precaution that, if taken, would have averted the accident. According to him:

> a simple test would show whether a sash was loose or not and that if it moved at all easily it could be wedged or something could be placed across the window sill which would prevent the sash from closing fully.

This view was endorsed by Earl Jowitt and Lord Oaksey, who thought that employers should have instructed their workmen to examine the sashes and provide them with wedges to prevent them from closing.

Further, Lord Oaksey argued:

> Workmen are not in the position of employers. Their duties are not performed in the calm atmosphere of a boardroom with the advice of experts. They have to make their decisions on narrow window sills and other places of danger and in circumstances in which the dangers are obscured by repetition.

He was of the opinion:

> An employer must take account that workmen may have disregard for their own safety. This means that they must minimize the danger of a workman's own carelessness and take reasonable care to ensure that employees comply with necessary safety precautions.

Lord Reid also held:

> Where the practice of ignoring an obvious danger has grown up, I do not think that it is reasonable to expect an individual workman to take the initiative in devising and using precaution. It is the duty of the employer to consider the situation, to devise a suitable system, to instruct his men that they must do and to supply implements that may be required.

We find that the reasoning adopted by Jones and the Court of Appeal point towards the due care approach. The learned judge argued that both the club and the plaintiff's employers fell short of the standard of care owed to the plaintiff. In the Court of Appeal, Denning specifically argued that the club owed a lower level of care to the invitee (the plaintiff in this case) than to its members and servants. In the case of the employers, he argued that cost-justified precautions existed. Since the risk was so great, one would not be convinced by a defense based simply on cost, in terms of money, of the required precautions. The House of Lords did not think window cleaning was so inherently dangerous an operation that it should not be performed at all. It is clear from the opinions of both Lord Reid and Lord Oaksey, as quoted previously, that in the House of Lords the untaken precaution approach was used. A higher care was held to be required of the employer considering the known "practice" of ignoring the dangers in this profession. The employer's argument that the plaintiff himself should have used wedges to immobilize the window sash was rejected, and the employers were held liable for not providing these themselves. We note that this is in contrast with what was agued later in the House of Lords in *Qualcast (Wolverhampton) Limited v Haynes*,[41] that an employer is entitled to rely on an experienced workman being sensible enough to avoid a danger inherent in his profession. In the present case the plaintiff had 20 years of experience. Clearly two different approaches were being used; in *Qualcast* the employers were entitled to assume that the employee will take reasonable care, whereas in the present case it was held that the employers must take account of the carelessness of the workmen. We further note that in *Christmas*, a customary method of cleaning the windows was challenged and overturned. As Lord Reid argued, the plaintiff bore "a heavy onus" for having "condemned as unsafe a system of work which has been generally used for a long time in an important trade."

2.4 Cases in which the injurer is declared nonnegligent by considerations which point towards use of the due care approach

One oft-cited case which falls under this category is that of *Corporation of Glasgow v Muir and Others*.[42] The Corporation owned an old mansion house in King's Park, Glasgow, which was being used inter alia for serving tea to visitors to the park and also as a shop for the sale of sweets and ices. At some distance from the mansion house, at the top of a hill, there was a shelter at the back of which was a boiler house, from which picnic parties could buy boiling water to make their tea. The usual practice was for these parties to have their tea in the open, but on the day of the incident it was raining and two parties had arrived. One party, comprising around 250 members, had occupied the shelter; the other group of around 30–40 people from the Milton Street Free Church asked the manageress of the mansion house, Mrs Emily Alexander, if they could use the tea-room. After paying for the facility, a tea urn weighing about 100 pounds was brought to the building by the church officer, George McDonald, and a boy named Taylor. While being carried through a passage that was five feet wide but narrowed to three feet three inches, McDonald let go his side of the urn and the hot tea scalded six children, including the plaintiff, Eleanor Muir. They were among several children who were buying sweets at the counter, and Mrs Alexander had her back to the scene as she was scooping ice-cream from the freezer. The claimants alleged that Mrs Alexander was negligent as she failed in her duty to take reasonable care of the children.

After the evidence, the Lord Ordinary dismissed the action; but the majority of the First Division of the Court of Session (the Lord President dissenting) allowed the claimant's appeal. The Corporation appealed to the House of Lords, which allowed the appeal. The issue of negligence essentially hinged on the question of what any person charged with the duty should have reasonably anticipated. She was held negligent by the First Division of the Court of Session on the grounds that she ought to have anticipated that the people carrying the urn may be careless and should have therefore removed the children from the vicinity. Based on this reasoning, Lord Carmont held that the Corporation should be liable: "even if it were proved that the actual damage to the invitee happened through the tea urn being spilt in a way that could not reasonably have been anticipated."

Having taken account of the carelessness of others, the care required of her was higher than if she were allowed to assume that those carrying the urn would use reasonable care. This is clear from the opinion of Lord Macmillan in the House of Lords regarding the standard of duty:

> The degree of care for the safety of others which the law requires human beings to observe in the conduct of their affairs varies according to circumstances. There is no absolute standard, but it may be said generally that the degree of care required varies directly with the risk involved.

This view conforms with the economic model. He went on to say that: "Those who engage in operations inherently dangerous must take precautions which are not required of those persons engaged in the ordinary routine of life." He specified those acts for which liability can be imposed: "Legal liability is limited to those consequences of our acts which a reasonable man of ordinary intelligence and experience so acting would have in contemplation." In the present case, the main question was whether, when Mrs Alexander was asked to allow a tea urn to be brought into the premises under her charge, she ought to have had in mind that it would require to be carried through a narrow passage in which there were a number of children and that there would be a risk of the contents of the urn being spilt and scalding some of the children.

He emphasized:

> she was entitled to assume that the urn would be in charge of responsible persons (as it was) who would have regard for the safety of the children in the passage (as they did have regard) and that the urn would be carried with ordinary care, in which case its transit would occasion no danger to bystanders.

He argued that the immediate cause was not the carrying of the urn through the passage, but McDonald's losing grip of his handle. Stating that she was not bound to foresee the carelessness of McDonald, he argued:

> The only ground on which the view of the majority of the judges of the first division can be justified is that Mrs. Alexander ought to have foreseen that some accidental injury might happen to the children in the passage if she allowed an urn containing hot tea to be carried through the passage and ought, therefore, to have cleared out the children entirely during its transit, which Lord Moncrieff describes as 'the only effective step'. With all respect I think that this would impose upon Mrs. Alexander a degree of care higher than the law exacts.

If translated to economic terms, this means that the expected harm does not warrant such a high standard of care.

Lord Thankerton argued along similar lines:

> The ground of the majority of judges, as I understand it, is that Mrs. Alexander, while authorising the transport of the tea urn through the entrance passage, where sweets and ices were being sold to a large number of children, omitted to remove the children altogether from the passage way, so as to avoid a danger which should have been obvious to her. In my opinion, this is to turn Mrs. Alexander into something like an insurer against any risk of danger from the tea urn. On the evidence, it is established, as I have already stated, that, if carefully carried, there was no element of danger to be reasonably anticipated from the operation of carrying the urn.

He added:

> the standard of care owed by the two persons in charge of the urn to the children was at least as high as that owed by Mrs. Alexander; they were more cognisant than Mrs. Alexander of the position in the passageway when they entered it with the urn; Mrs. Alexander knew nothing that they did not know.

84 Economic analysis of select British cases

The reference to insurance shows that Lord Thankerton too thought that the standard of care was being set much higher than what the circumstances required of ordinary people who were not in the business of providing insurance.

Lord Wright argued along similar lines:

> It is left to pure conjecture how he [McDonald] came to lose hold of the handle. It may have been a momentary physical faintness or a sudden stumble; perhaps some hot tea may have screwed down. There is no evidence and no probability that children pushed against him and caused him to lose his grip. Any defect on the floor is excluded.

He, therefore, continued:

> There seem to be only two possible alternatives, either a mere accident or negligence. In my opinion, neither hypothesis could impose liability on the appellants. As to negligence, the two men were not their servants; they were not responsible for their acts; that the men should be negligent in so simple an operation was not likely to happen. It is a mere possibility, not a reasonable probability. The men, if negligent, were no doubt responsible for their own negligence, but from the standpoint of the appellants, the risk of negligence was a mere unlikely accident which no reasonable person in Mrs. Alexander's position could naturally be expected to foresee. The same is true of an accidental slip or loss of grip. To hold the appellants liable on either basis would be to make them insurers, which, under the authorities, they are not. In my opinion, no breach of duty or negligence by the appellants to the respondents has been established.

He further added: "As a reasonable person, not having any ground for anticipating harm, she was entitled to go on with her work and leave the church party to do what was proper."

Lord Romer argued that while there was a need to take precautions against unusual risk, in the present case since it is

> unknown what was the particular risk that materialised it is impossible to decide whether it was or was not one that should have been within the reasonable contemplation of Mrs. Alexander or of some other agent or employee of the appellants, and it is accordingly also impossible to fix the appellants with liability for the damage that the respondents sustained.

Lord Clauson held:

> the crucial question in this matter appears to me to be whether Mrs. Alexander ought as a reasonable woman to have had in contemplation that, unless some further precautions were taken, such an unfortunate occurrence as that which in fact took place might well be expected.

We find that the reasoning by which the majority of the judges of the First Division held the defendant negligent points towards the untaken precaution approach, and the basis of the nonnegligent verdicts of Lord Ordinary, Lord President and the House of Lords appears to be the due care approach. The former held that Mrs Alexander should have taken account of the possibility that the urn may not be carried carefully and therefore implicitly set a higher standard of care for her, and they found her actual level of care to be short of that required under the circumstances. On the other hand, the latter argued that she was entitled to assume that the urn would be carried with due care and the standard of care required of her was the lower level that would be expected of "an ordinary reasonable person" in Mrs Alexander's position, and therefore, they found her actual precaution level to be adequate and held her nonnegligent.

One may argue that the untaken precaution of "removing the children" would not have been cost-justified for the following reasons. First, the safe carriage of the tea urn did not present any reasonably foreseeable difficulty; that two men should have been able to carry it easily was attested to by many, and the accident in question was the first one that had occurred. By Lord Macmillan's description:

> When they entered the passage-way they called out to the children there congregated to keep out of the way and the children drew back to let them pass. Taylor who held the front handle had safely passed the children when, for some unexplained reason, McDonald loosened hold of the other handle.

There was no evidence about what caused McDonald to lose his grip; no witness was produced who actually saw the accident, there was no evidence that the children jostled him and there was no defect in the floor. The court was left to conjecture whether it was a "momentary physical faintness" or a "temporary muscular failure," and Lord Wright finally concluded that it "was a mere possibility, not a reasonable possibility." Second, the burden of precautions – that is, of sending the children outside – was high since it had been a wet afternoon and there was another picnic party comprising some 250 members. Finally, one has to keep in mind the *ex ante* estimate of damage and, as Lord Thankerton put it, not "give undue weight to the fact that a distressing accident has happened."

In one of the leading negligence cases of England, *Bolton v Stone*,[43] the finding of nonnegligence was based on the fact that there did not exist any cost-justified untaken precaution that could have prevented the injury. On August 9, 1947, the plaintiff, Miss Bessie Stone, was standing on the highway in front of her garden gate on Beckenham Road, Cheetham Hill, Manchester, when she was struck on the head and injured by a ball hit in the course of a match on the adjacent Cheetham Cricket Ground. She brought an action for damages against the Committee and members of the club, though not the visiting batsman who had hit the ball. The plaintiff's claim was based on the alternative grounds of nuisance and negligence, the nuisance being alleged to consist of the striking of the ball into Beckenham road and the negligence based on three untaken precautions. These were: (i) placing the cricket pitch too close to the road, (ii) failure to erect a fence of sufficient height to prevent balls being struck into the road (iii) and failure to ensure that cricket balls would not be struck into the road. Although it was unanimously held at all stages of litigation that an isolated act of causing damage by striking a person on the highway by a cricket ball hit from adjacent premises cannot be described as nuisance, regarding the negligence question there was a difference of opinion. The trial court acquitted the defendants of negligence; the plaintiffs appealed to the Court of Appeal, which reversed by a majority. The House of Lords unanimously allowed the appeal of the defendants.

The evidence regarding the first two[44] alleged untaken precautions was the following. The club had been in existence and the ground had been used for cricket since 1864, and houses on Beckenham Road were not built until 1910. During the construction the builder arranged with the club that a small strip of land at the Beckenham Road end of the ground should be exchanged for a strip at the other end. The effect of this was that in the case of a straight drive – the hit in the present case – Beckenham road was a few yards closer to the batsmen than the opposite end. However, balls were very rarely hit over the fence, which was seven feet high but 17 feet above the cricket pitch because of the upward slope of the ground towards the side in question, whereas it was about 12 feet on the other end. The particular ball had travelled 78 yards before passing over the fence and about 25 yards further before striking Miss Stone. Mr Brownson, who lived next door but substantially nearer to the ground, gave evidence that the ball had struck his house or fallen in his garden some five or six times. Two members of the club of over 30 years standing, Mr Milsom and Mr Bolton, said that the hit was "altogether exceptional and greater than anything previously seen on the ground."

On the evidence before him, the trial judge L. J. Oliver found in favour of the defendants stating: "this ground is quite large enough for all practical purposes of safety, particularly having regard to the height of the fence above the pitch. In 38 years experience no one has been ever injured before."[45] The Court of Appeal[46] was divided on the question of whether the defendants failed to exercise the care that the circumstances required. While L. J. Singleton and L. J. Jenkins thought that they had failed to do so, L. J. Somervell dissented. The majority opinion was based on the reasoning that, given the evidence that balls had been hit before, it could "reasonably be expected to happen again sooner or later," depending on the skills of the batsmen and bowlers, including visitors about whom the defendants may not know anything. Singleton argued: "An accident of this kind does not happen in the ordinary course of things if proper care is exercised." It was suggested that raising the height of the fence was one option, since it "had been shown by experience to be inadequate"; also if the wickets had been placed "at equal distances north and south a hit over the northern hoarding would have had an additional carry of twenty-one feet." Even regarding the hit in question it was stated that there was no expert evidence to show that the hit was of an exceptional nature.

Jenkins, speaking about the standard of care required in the circumstances argued:

> That the defendants, being the occupiers of the ground, and using it as they did for the purpose of playing cricket matches organised by them, were under some duty to prevent balls being hit out of the ground to the danger of persons in Beckenham Road, I have no doubt. It is less easy to define the precise extent of duty. To hold the defendants under an unqualified duty to prevent balls being hit into the road in any circumstances would, I think, be to place an unreasonably heavy burden on them.

He went on to say:

> Legitimate as the playing of cricket may be, however, a cricket ball hit out of the ground into a public highway is obviously capable of doing serious harm to anyone in the highway who may happen to be in its course, and I see no justification for holding the defendants entitled to subject people in Beckenham Road to any reasonably foreseeable risk of injury in this way.

He argued that since there was a probability of an injury, adequate precautions should have been taken. He even went to the extent of suggesting the stopping of the game on that cricket ground altogether:

> It was also, I think suggested that no possible precaution would have arrested the flight of this particular ball, so high did it pass over the fence. This seems to me an irrelevant consideration. If cricket cannot be played on a given ground without foreseeable risk of injury to persons outside it, then it is always possible in the last resort to stop using that ground for cricket. The plaintiff in this case might, I apprehend, quite possibly have been killed.

His estimate of the expected harm was so great that he thought stopping the activity was a justified precaution to take in this case.

The House of Lords unanimously held the defendants nonnegligent by asserting that one does not take steps against every foreseeable risk, one "takes precautions against risks which are reasonably likely to happen." Lord Reid argued:

> In my judgment, the test to be applied here is whether the risk of damage to a person on the road was so small that a reasonable man in the position of the appellants, considering the matter from the point of view of safety, would have thought it right to refrain from taking steps to prevent the danger. In considering that matter I think that it would be right to take into account not only how remote is the chance that a person might be struck, but also how serious the consequences are likely to be if a person is struck, but I do not think that it would be right to take into account the difficulty of remedial measures.

We note that this reasoning is inconsistent with the economic model. The cost of precautions is an important factor in the decision about the degree of care to be exercised. He went on to state: "If cricket cannot be played on a ground without creating substantial risk, then it should not be played there at all." From this it may be inferred that the burden of precautions is irrelevant in the case of substantial risk because then there is no question of comparing the costs and benefits – the activity should not be undertaken at all. This kind of reasoning clearly contradicts the economic model in which the costs and benefits for *all* kinds of risks are compared.

Lord Radcliffe allowed the appeal, stating that he was doing it "with regret" because he had "much sympathy with the decision that commended itself to the majority of the members of the Court of Appeal." This was because he thought it was fair that the appellants have to "compensate for the serious injury" as a result of the sport that they have organized on their grounds. He, however, distinguished clearly what was fair and culpable: "the law of negligence is concerned less with what is fair than with what is culpable, and I cannot persuade myself that the appellants have been guilty of any culpable act or omission in this case." Lord Radcliffe explicitly clarified the issue of breach of duty in the present case by stating:

> One may phrase it as 'reasonable care' or 'ordinary care' or 'proper care' – all three phrases are to be found in decisions of authority – but the fact remains that, unless there has been something which a reasonable man would blame as falling beneath the standard of conduct that he would set for himself and require of his neighbor, there has been no breach of legal duty, and here I think the respondent's case breaks down.

From the reasoning of the judges, we find that the trial court used the due care approach in holding that the ground was sufficiently large, and therefore there was no breach of duty. The Court of Appeal and the House of Lords both used the due care approach; the former held the defendants negligent while the latter held them nonnegligent. From the law and economics perspective, we can say that the difference in verdict arose due to differences in opinion regarding what constituted the due care level and therefore the existence or otherwise of cost-justified untaken precautions. In the search for individualized due care in the circumstances, the Court of Appeal desisted from setting a standard that was too high: "To hold the defendants under an unqualified duty to prevent balls being hit into the road in the circumstances would, I think, be to place an unreasonably heavy burden on them."[47] Nevertheless, the court identified a high standard of care based on the reasoning that the defendants knew that the risk of harm to persons on the highway existed and the magnitude of harm could have been great – "plaintiff could quite possibly have been killed." Regarding the precautions, the court's reasoning shows that while both increasing the height of the fence and repositioning the wickets were cost-justified, only the latter satisfied the cause-in-fact requirement.

L. J. Somervell and the judges of the House of Lords held that the standard of care required in the circumstances was lower than what the majority of the Court of Appeal had in mind. Somervell, in his dissenting opinion, argued: "games, notably, cricket are part of ordinary life, and that available fields will often and necessarily be adjacent to highways."[48] He went on to add:

> The steps that a reasonable occupier would take would depend on the circumstances. If the field is in the heart of the city surrounded by roads on which there is constant traffic it may well be that the reasonable occupier would have to see that in no foreseeable circumstances could a ball reach a highway. For a village playing field adjacent to a little frequented highway *the duty would be less*. (emphasis added)

Lord Reid reiterated this view in the House of Lords when he summed up saying:

> On the whole, of that part of the road a ball would fall there would often be nobody and seldom a great number of people. It follows that the chance of a person ever being struck even in a long period of years was very small.

Regarding the standard of care he added:

> What a man must do, and what I think a careful man tries not to do, is to create a risk which is substantial. Of course, there are numerous cases where special circumstances require that a higher standard shall be observed and where that is recognized by the law, but I do not think that this case comes within any such special category.

The approach of the House of Lords can be compared with an attempt to locate the due care level by asking whether there existed any cost-justified untaken precaution that would have prevented the accident. The court put a much lower estimate on the probability of harm since it was a less frequented highway, and although there was evidence that balls had crossed the fence, no one had been injured before. Even Ms. Stone said that this was the first time she had seen a ball cross the fence in the 12 years of her stay. Members of the club described the hit that had caused the injury as "the biggest hit" in nearly three decades. Therefore, the court concluded that the risk was remote, in fact, "very remote." On the other hand, the precaution of raising the height of the fence would not have been sufficient to prevent the ball in question since, as Mr Milson, a defendant and a member of the club said, "it cleared the fence at Beckenham road end by 'many' feet." Repositioning the pitch or instructing players from refraining from hitting a six would be costly; stopping the playing of cricket would obviously be prohibitively costly. Thus, concluded Lord Radcliffe:

> that a reasonable man, taking account of the chances against an accident happening, would not have felt himself called upon either to abandon the use of the ground for cricket or to increase the height of his surrounding fences.

He would have done what the appellants did. In other words, he would have done nothing.

One may argue that the difference of opinion arose using the same approach to determine negligence because this was, as both Somervell and Lord Reid put it, "a borderline case." The majority of the Court of Appeal set a higher standard of care and thus found that cost-justified untaken precautions existed at the actual level of care taken by the defendants. The House of Lords, on the other hand, took the due care level to be on the lower side and thus could not identify any cost-justified untaken precautions that could have prevented the accident. Since no cost-justified untaken precautions were found, the defendants would be nonnegligent by the untaken precaution approach as well.

Another case in which the defendants were adjudged nonnegligent because no cost-justified untaken precaution could be identified was that of *Latimer v Aec Limited*.[49] The defendants owned a factory employing around 4,000 people and spread across about 15 acres in Southall. On the floor there were channels in which an oily cooling agent known as "mystic" collected. One afternoon there was a heavy rainstorm that caused the factory floor to be flooded; the oil rose out of the channels because the iron lids that covered them were not watertight and mixed with the water on the floor. After the rain subsided, a thin oily film was left on the surface; the factory put 40 men to spread about three tonnes of sawdust on the floor to reduce the slipperiness. Twenty-four volunteers were kept to continue the work of cleaning the floors and passages. Despite this, the claimant, who was a horizontal milling machine operator at the factory, slipped on a part of the floor where sawdust was not applied, and a barrel which he was putting on to a trolley, rolled onto and injured his ankle. He claimed damages on the ground of breach of statutory duty and negligence at common law. Although the former claim was rejected at all stages of litigation, the verdict on the negligence question was not unanimous. While Judge Pilcher for the Queen's Bench Division held the defendants guilty of negligence, the Court of Appeal reversed the judgment. The plaintiff appealed to the House of Lords, which affirmed the nonnegligence verdict and dismissed the appeal.

The central issue, as Lord Asquith of Bishopstone put it, was:

> At common law the question can be whether, having regard to the nature and extent of the risk created by the slippery patches on the floor, a reasonably careful employer would have suspended all work in this fifteen acre factory and sent the night shift home or, whether, having done all he could (and did) do with the sawdust at his disposal, the forty production service men in the afternoon, and twenty-four volunteers between the end of the day shift and beginning of the night shift, he would have allowed the work to proceed.

The trial judge Pilcher concluded that a reasonable employer would have closed down. He held:

> in permitting the plaintiff to do his work in a part of the factory where the floor was slippery, and therefore, dangerous, took the risk that he might

sustain an injury and thus be liable for the injury which the plaintiff in fact sustained owing to the dangerous condition of the premises.

Judge Pilcher was of the opinion that it was not possible for the factory owner to take any further steps to make the floor less slippery, so they ought to have closed down the portion of the factory that was still slippery, if not the whole factory.

In the Court of Appeal, L. J. Singleton, refuting this argument, said:

> If the test is, as I believe, what a reasonable employer would have done in those circumstances, I fail to see that there is any breach by the employers of the duty which they owed, and I fail to see, too any evidence on which a finding that the employers were negligent in not closing the factory can be based.

L. J. Denning gave a lucid explanation of why he thought Judge Pilcher had erred in his judgment:

> "it seems to me that [Pilcher J] has fallen in error by assuming it would be sufficient to constitute negligence that there was a foreseeable risk which the defendants could have avoided by some measure or other, however extreme. That is not the law. It is always necessary to consider what measures the defendant ought to have taken, and to say whether they could reasonably be expected of him. In a converse case, for example, a brave man tries to stop a runaway horse. It is a known risk and a serious risk, but no one would suggest that he could reasonably be expected to stand idly by. It is not negligence on his part to run the risk. So here the employers knew that the floor was slippery and that there was some risk in letting the men work on it; but, still they could not reasonably be expected to shut down the whole works and send all the men home. In every case of foreseeable risk, it is a matter of balancing the risk against some measures necessary to eliminate it. It is only negligence if, on the balance, the defendant did something which he ought not to have done, or omitted to do something which he ought to have done. In this case, in the circumstances of this torrential flood, it is quite clear the defendants did everything they could reasonably be expected to do. It would be quite unreasonable; it seems to me, to expect them to send all the men home. I agree, therefore, that there was no negligence at common law.

L. J. Hodson agreed with this judgment.

The House of Lords attested the reasoning, with the exception of Lord Oaksey who simply described it as "an error of judgment in circumstances of difficulty" and held that "such an error of judgment does not amount to negligence." The reasoning of the House of Lords was that the untaken precaution in question – that of shutting the factory or at least that part where the accident occurred – would not lead to a finding of negligence because what is at issue is what steps a prudent man ought to have taken, and in the circumstances of the case, it cannot be said that he ought to have shut the factory. The evidence showed that the defendants took a number of measures to remedy the slipperiness and no one other than the plaintiff slipped or experienced any difficulty. The danger was, therefore, not of a degree to make a reasonable employer close down the 15-acre factory and send the night shift home. Lord Tucker said:

> I do not question that such a drastic step may be required on the part of a reasonably prudent employer if the peril to his employees is sufficiently grave, and to this extent it must always be a question of degree, but, in my view, there was no evidence in the present case which would justify a finding of negligence for failure on the part of the respondents to take this step.[50]

He went on to argue:

> The learned judge seems to have accepted the reasoning of the counsel for the appellant to the effect that the floor was slippery, that slipperiness is a potential danger, that the respondents must be taken to have been aware of this, that in the circumstances nothing could have been done to remedy the slipperiness, that the respondents allowed the work to proceed, that an accident due to slipperiness occurred, and that the respondents are, therefore, liable.

He argued:

> This is not the correct approach. The only question was: Has it been proved that the floor was so slippery that, remedial steps not being possible, a reasonably prudent employer would have closed down the factory rather than allow his employees to run the risk of continuing work?

Lord Tucker did not think so:

> The absence of any evidence that anyone in the factory during the afternoon or night shift, other than the appellant, slipped, or experienced any difficulty, or that any complaint was made by or on behalf of the workers, all points to the conclusion that the danger was, in fact, not such as to impose on a reasonable employer the obligation placed on the respondents by the trial judge.

The difference in conclusion arose from a difference in the estimates of expected harm; while the trial judge thought that the expected harm was large enough to warrant closing of the factory, the House of Lords thought that the expected harm was not large enough. Lord Tucker also pointed out that sufficient evidence was not there to conclude that the condition of the factory was such that no other remedial measure could be taken.

Lord Reid agreed entirely with this reasoning. Lord Asquith of Bishopstone also followed the same line of reasoning and concluded: "What evidence the learned judge had before him suggests, to my mind, that the degree of risk was too small to justify, let alone require, closing down." He said that the appellant himself testified that "you always get a certain amount of grease about"; his co-worker Ampstead concurring to this added that on "numerous occasions" (four or five times) he had seen "mystic" well up from the channels in the floor of the factory owing to flooding. The appellant admitted that, except for the accident to himself on this occasion in August 1950, he has never known any accident to happen to anyone in the factory through these causes. The respondent's safety manager, Mr Milne, did say that he would not have gone on to the floor in the condition it was in and that it would be too dangerous to do so, but this was held to be essentially an ex post statement, and he as the safety manager had not thought that there was any danger, nor did he know what further steps than those actually taken would be required for the safety of the employees.

From the reasoning of the judges at various stages, we can infer that the crux of the matter was whether the untaken precaution of closing the factory partially or fully was cost-justified. While Judge Pilcher thought that it was, considering that the risk could only be avoided by that measure, the Court of Appeal and the House of Lords did not think so. The latter emphatically argued that a reasonable employer would consider the expected harm of not taking the precaution and the burden of precautions. Here, apart from the appellant, no one had fallen during the afternoon or night shift and the closing of the 15-acre factory with 4,000 workers would entail huge costs (although even approximate estimates were not placed before the court by the defendants). On balance, it was argued, a reasonable factory owner would not have shut the factory. The difference in the opinions arose because the implicit assumption was that the individualized due care ought to have been kept at a lower level than what Judge Pilcher had set. The owners had done everything to mitigate the effects of the unprecedented storm; further measures like shutting down would involve far more costs than the expected harm it would prevent, it could be inferred that the defendants did what any reasonable person would do – not shut down. However, requiring the factory to bear the costs of injury nevertheless would reduce the negligence rule to that of strict liability. Since no cost-justified untaken precaution could be found, the defendants would be nonnegligent by the untaken precaution approach as well.

The question may be raised in this case about who had the last opportunity to avoid the accident? Surely, the claimant could have requested the cleaning "volunteers" to check the floor near the place of accident, since he was a worker in the factory and not a visitor unaware of the slipperiness of the floor. In terms of information cost, it would certainly have been cheaper for him to give the exact location of the floor that needed attention than for the cleaners to find out for themselves in a 15-acre factory with thousands of men at work.

Wells v Cooper[51] was a case where the defendant was held nonnegligent using the due care approach, but what constituted due care in the circumstances presented some difficulty. The plaintiff, Mr Albert Wells, went to the defendant's house to deliver fish and was asked to stay back for a cup of tea. After drinking the tea, he was leaving through the back door when the door handle came away in his hand and he lost his balance, fell to the ground from a raised concrete platform immediately outside the door and was injured. The door needed a fairly stiff pull to shut it properly, as a draught excluder had been fitted to the bottom of it and there was a strong wind blowing on that day. The door handle had been fitted four or five months earlier by the defendant himself, and consisted of a lever type handle fixed by a base plate that was held to the door by four three-quarter-inch screws. It was because he thought the previous door handle unsafe that he installed the present one. The defendant had some experience as an amateur carpenter, well accustomed to doing small jobs of replacement and repair about the house and believed his fixing of the new handle was secure and better than the earlier one.

It was alleged that the "insecure handle was an unusual danger of which the defendant knew or ought to have known and against which he should have taken reasonable care to guard the plaintiff." The questions that were raised by the plaintiff were: ought the defendant have foreseen that if the handle came away when a person tried to pull it that person might suffer injury and if so, would the defendant have known that the screws were inadequate to fix the handle to the door firmly enough to prevent the likelihood of such an occurrence? Instead of three-quarter-inch screws, one-inch screws should have been used. The trial judge Stable dismissed the claim on the ground that the accident was not one that was reasonably foreseeable, and the plaintiff appealed to the Court of Appeal.

L. J. Jenkins read the judgment of the Court of Appeal. Their reasoning was as follows:

> We do not think that the mere fact that he did it himself instead of employing a professional carpenter to do it constituted a breach of his duty of care. No doubt some kinds of work involve such highly specialized skill or knowledge, and create such serious dangers if not properly done, that an ordinary occupier owing a duty of care to others in regard to the safety of premises would fail in that duty if he undertook such work himself instead of employing experts to do it for him. . . . But the work in question was not of that order.

It was further held that the degree of care and skill required of him ought to be measured not by the degree of competence he actually happened to possess, but rather that which is expected of a reasonably competent carpenter.

> Otherwise, the extent of protection that an invitee could claim in relation to work done by the invitor himself would vary according to the capacity of the invitor, who would free himself from liability merely by showing that he had done the best he was capable, however good, bad or indifferent that best might be.

Regarding the actual skill of the defendant, the court went on to argue that in relation to the "trifling and perfectly simple operation such as fixing a new handle," the defendant's experience of domestic carpentry is sufficient to justify his inclusion in the category of reasonably competent carpenters. When he chose three-quarter-inch screws he believed they would be adequate; the two experts' evidence that any reasonably competent carpenter should have foreseen that three-quarter-inch screws would be inadequate was taken to be of no value, as they were in the nature of wisdom after the event. As to whether the standard differed from that required of an independent contractor, the court held that,

> the standard of care is no more than reasonable care, whether an independent contractor is employed or not. . . . Each case of this kind depends on its own particular facts, to which the broad principle of reasonable care must be applied with common sense.

The task of finding the facts and applying the principles is that of the court of first instance, and the Court of Appeal agreed with most of the findings of the trial court except that the issue of negligence depended on the unforeseeability of the injury. According to them, the defendant had used reasonable care, which is evident from the fact that the handle was securely in place for four or five months of constant use prior to the accident. The plaintiff was not able to establish that it was the untaken precaution of using one-inch screws that caused the accident.

We find that the Court specifically concluded that the standard of care is that of reasonable care on the facts of the case. The reference, therefore, is not to any common standard of care required. Counsel for the plaintiff argued that if the defendant had employed a professional carpenter as an independent contractor to fix the new handle, and the carpenter had used three-quarter-inch screws with the same results, the defendant would have been liable to the plaintiff for the carpenter's negligence. Accordingly,

> the defendant must be liable here because it cannot be that the standard of care to be required of an invitor who does the relevant work himself is lower than it would have been if he had employed an independent contractor to do it for him.

This reasoning was considered fallacious by the court, which held that:

> The invitor is to take reasonable care and the standard required of him is not raised to anything higher than that by the circumstances that he may choose to employ an independent contractor to do the work for him. As we have said before, it does not follow that because the degree of care and skill exercised by the independent contractor falls short of the standard required of him under his contract with the invitor it also falls short of the standard required of the invitor as between himself and his invitee. The two standards are by no means necessarily the same."

Another important negligence case in which there was disagreement at various stages of litigation regarding the standard of care required of an employer towards his employees was that of *Qualcast (Wolverhampton) Limited v Haynes*.[52] In this case, Mr Haynes, who was a moulder employed for some three months at the foundry at Wolverhampton, sustained injuries while casting at the moulding boxes when a ladle of molten metal slipped and the metal splashed on his ankle and foot. This was the account that the county court judge Norris took as evidence. Mr Haynes had, however, said that he was carrying a ladle of molten metal along a passage in the foundry when he stumbled over an obstruction, and this caused the metal to splash on his foot. Since the learned judge disbelieved this, the case came to centre on two alleged grounds of negligence: that the employers of Mr Haynes (i) failed to provide any or proper spats[53] or other sufficient protective clothing; and (ii) failed to provide a safe system of work and safe and proper plant and equipment. In the end, these reduced themselves into the question of the duty of the employers to provide the plaintiff with protective clothing. The judge found that the responsibility for the injury was in greater part that of the plaintiff himself and apportioned the blame as 25 percent to the defendants and 75 percent to the plaintiff. The defendants appealed against this verdict to the Court of Appeal, and the plaintiff cross-appealed that there was no contributory negligence on his part. The Court of Appeal upheld the judgment of Judge Norris. The defendants appealed to the House of Lords, which held that the plaintiff was solely responsible for the injury.

The facts regarding the items of protective clothing were that the defendants kept a stock of spats at their foundry that any workmen who asked for them could use free of cost, and in addition, pairs of protective boots were also available that could be obtained after paying only the cost price to the defendants. Although the defendants had put up a notice that the boots could be obtained at those terms, no notice was put up regarding the spats. Judge Norris found:

> He [the plaintiff] knew that there were spats and boots in the stores; that spats were to be had for the asking and the strong boots at a price which the defendants consider to be reasonable; and he decided to wear ordinary boots which he bought himself for the purpose of his work.

However, after considering a number of authorities, some of them unreported cases, regarding the issue of provision of protective clothing at the workplace and liability of the employers, he concluded:

> In the present case, the spats and boots were there, and the plaintiff knew they were there, but he was never told that they must be worn. He decided the matter himself. In view of this, I feel that my judgment must be in favour of the plaintiff.

In the Court of Appeal, Lord M. R. Evershed reviewed the primary facts of the case to ascertain whether the defendants fell short of their common law duty "of an employer in such a case to take reasonable care for the safety of his workmen." He considered the argument of the counsel for the plaintiff that "molten metal is of a temperature of something like thirteen hundred degrees centigrade. From that fact it is, of course, plain that if it gets on the skin or the body it is likely to do serious and painful injury." Lord Evershed went on to argue: "If, then, that is the nature of the hazard, I think that the obligation of the defendants extended to more than merely having the spats available in case any experienced moulder thought he would like to ask for them." Referring to Lord Morton of Henryton in *Paris v Stepney Borough Council*, he argued that "the extent of duty will depend in some degree on the gravity of the hazard which is involved and of the consequences which may ensue if damage is suffered." He, therefore, concluded that since "the defendants in the present case did nothing at all other than have the gaiters ready for those who asked, I think that they fell short of their duty."

This conclusion was affirmed by L.J. Parker, who explicitly stated that the common law duty of an employer was "to take reasonable care so as to carry on his operations as not to subject those employed by him to unnecessary risk," and there was risk of serious injury by burning in this case. He held:

> It seems to me perfectly clear, in those circumstances, that there is a duty on employers, not only to have protective clothing available, but to inform anybody coming into their employment that they have got that equipment, and to take some steps to educate the men to wear the equipment for his own safety.

The steps could range from mere advice to making the wearing of protective clothing a rule, depending on the extent of the hazard. Parker went on to say: "In the present case the employers did nothing." He considered the answer given by the defendants: "the plaintiff was an experienced moulder; he was thirty-eight years old, and he had been all his life in the trade." However, he found that explanation inadequate: "Even so, from the defendants' point of view they would not know that he knew or would have any chance of knowing that they had equipment available." L.J. Sellers was not so clear about the case to reach such a conclusion on his own. He thought the plaintiff was experienced enough to know the dangers inherent in his occupation. He, nevertheless, concurred with the others that

> the defendants might have done a little more . . . they might have put an accompanying notice about the availability of spats alongside the notice about the boots which were for sale; or they might, through the usual channels, have sought to impress on their workmen that they should wear them.

He concluded that this was "a narrow and border-line matter" and that there was "a very slight breach," and therefore, quite reluctantly, felt that he was bound to support the learned judge and dismiss the appeal.

98 Economic analysis of select British cases

In the House of Lords, Lord Keith of Avonholm referred to this reluctance of Sellers and how the Court of Appeal had felt bound to uphold the conclusion of Judge Norris. Lord Keith went on to show that the conclusion was erroneous and should therefore be reversed. He argued that when the accident happened the plaintiff was wearing ordinary boots that he had bought for the work. He was not ordered or advised by the defendants to wear protective clothing. The foreman, Kenneth Charles Bloor, testified:

> had the plaintiff been a learner he would have advised him about wearing the protective clothing, but as he was an experienced man he considered that he did not need any warning; he knew and appreciated the risks of the metal splashing attaching to his work.

In view of these facts the learned judge had said:

> Now, if I were not bound by authority I should decide that the plaintiff was so experienced that he needed no warning and that what he did was with the full knowledge of all the risks involved, and that there was no negligence on the part of the defendants.

Lord Keith argued that the cases referred to by the learned judge were different in material respects from the facts of the present case. He emphasized:

> In the sphere of negligence where circumstances are so infinite in their variety it is rarely, if ever, that one case can be a binding authority for another. A case may announce a principle which may be capable of application in other cases, but I know of no principle that, in all cases and all circumstances, an employer is liable for failing to see that a foundry man is supplied or supplies himself with spats and boots or, at the lowest, is exhorted or pressed with ardour to avail himself of such protection.

Regarding the meaning of the word "provide," he held: "In considering whether there is a common law duty on an employer to provide something, the scope of the obligation must vary with the particular circumstances of the case." In this case, the spats being available, the employers did not have "a further duty to bring pressure to bear on him to use them, a pressure which, on the evidence, he would have ignored and might have resented."[54] In terms of the economic model, we can interpret this as saying that the marginal care of bringing pressure on the plaintiff to wear spats was not cost-justified, since the spats were already available for protection from harm and the plaintiff, being an experienced worker, may have resented the pressure. Lord Keith held: "the Judge's conclusion is not a conclusion of fact but a conclusion of law reached on an erroneous assumption that he was bound by a series of inapplicable authorities." Lord Denning, holding that the conclusions of the cases cited by the learned judge were actually "nothing more than propositions of good sense," argued: "the standard of care must be fixed by the judge as if he were a jury, without being rigidly bound by authorities. It changes as the conditions of work change." He thought that the Court of Appeal ought to have corrected the judge's error and ruled as the judge would have if he had not felt bound by authority and "found that the employers had not been guilty of negligence."

One crucial aspect which was pointed out by the House of Lords was that both Judge Norris and the Court of Appeal had taken the duty of the employer as that owed to all the workmen. In fact, as Lord Keith pointed out: "The duty owed by the employers was a duty owed to the plaintiff. This is not necessarily the same as the duty owed to others of the workers. The duty may vary with the worker's knowledge and experience." Lord Radcliffe also added: "An experienced workman dealing with a familiar and obvious risk may not reasonably need the same attention or the same precautions as an inexperienced man who is likely to be more receptive of advice or admonition." The reasoning of Judge Norris and the Court of Appeal seem to point towards the untaken precaution approach, and that of the House of Lords was the due care approach. The former held that the employers ought to have done "more than merely having the spats available." This conclusion was reached even after they had accepted the reason for not doing more:

> The judge found, and I am fully prepared to accept his finding, that the defendants did not do so because they thought that the plaintiff, being an experienced moulder, should be taken as knowing as he did know what the risks were.

One may infer that the court did not think that the employers were entitled to assume that any particular workman would use reasonable care. They set a higher standard of care towards all workmen irrespective of their knowledge and experience.

The House of Lords allowed the appeal on the ground that since the workman in question was experienced, the employers were entitled to assume that he would take reasonable care. Lord Radcliffe pointed out clearly:

> "however much attention is concentrated in these cases on the adequacy of the system of working at the place of work, actions of negligence are concerned with the duty of care as between a particular employer and a particular workman.

Lord Keith argued: "It is clear on the evidence that the employers did advice inexperienced men to wear spats, and possibly others as well." Since the plaintiff had been a moulder all his life and the spats were provided, it cannot be held that "the employers had a further duty to bring pressure on him to use them."

In this important chapter, 17 British cases are included in which the reasoning regarding negligence determination is discussed in detail. Many of the cases form the basis for judgments on the negligence question in other common law countries. We note that the case of *Upson* covered in this chapter contains *the* most important judgment where the untaken precaution approach can be identified, and we find it cited in many of the judgments that are covered in later chapters. Landmark cases like *Wagon Mound*, *Bolton v Stone* and *Home Office* have been instrumental in laying down some of the core principles governing various aspects of negligence determination. This chapter, therefore, forms a very significant part of the book because through these cases many of the concepts that are vital to the economic analysis of liability rules are introduced and explained. The cases also highlight how the final verdict hinges on factoring in all the costs and benefits. For instance, in *Miller v Jackson*, Lord Denning in his now-famous reasoning brought in the "loss to society," which would result from the closing of the cricket ground. This made the cost of precautions very high, and an injunction could be averted.

Notes

1 A schematic arrangement would be provided in the Appendix to give an at-a-glance idea of the findings of the study.
2 [1970] A.C. 1004 (HL).
3 [1932] A.C. 502.
4 Lord Diplock, while quoting this statement in this case, said about it: "Used as a guide to characteristics which will be found to exist in conduct and relationships which give rise to a legal duty of care this aphorism marks a milestone in the modern development of the law of negligence."
5 1945 (70) CLR 256.
6 1898 (3) 430.
7 Overseas Tankship (U.K.) Ltd. v Morts Dock & Eng'g Co. (*The Wagon Mound (No. 1)*), 1961 A.C. 388 (P.C. Austl.).
8 Overseas Tankship (U.K.) Ltd. v The Miller SS Co. Pty. Ltd. [1967] 1 A.C. 617.
9 [1921] 3 K.B. 560. This case laid the rule that if the defendant is guilty of negligence, then he is responsible for all the "direct" consequences of the breach, whether foreseeable or not.
10 It may seem odd that the same conduct by the same defendants yielded these different findings. Lord Reid explained why this did not imply any failure on the part of the plaintiffs in *Wagon Mound (1)* because the fire happened when the manager of the plaintiffs resumed welding operations in the wharf. Therefore, if in the former case the plaintiffs had set out to prove that it was foreseeable by the engineers of the *Wagon Mound* that this oil could be set alight, they might have found it difficult to refute the counter reply that then this must also have been foreseeable by their manager. Then there would have been contributory negligence, which was at the time a complete defense in New South Wales.
11 To be discussed in section 2.3.
12 With respect to this aspect of negligence determination, Gilles (2002) states: "To be sure, a number of later English cases have relied on Lord Reid's discussion of the standard of care in Wagon Mound No. 2. But the propositions about the standard of care for which Wagon Mound No. 2 is most often cited are (1) that a reasonable person does not neglect a small foreseeable risk if there is no good reason for neglecting it, and (2) that a reasonable person balances the risk against the disadvantages of avoiding it. Remarkably, I have found no English case relying on Wagon Mound No.2 for the proposition that a reasonable person does not balance risks and precaution costs if the risk is 'substantial'."
13 [1977] Q.B. 966. The case is also known for its lyrical opening by Lord Denning, which finds pride of place on the Club's webpage.
14 This case has been discussed in section 2.4.

15 (1879) 11 Ch D 852.
16 Weinrib (2007).
17 [1981] 1 W.L.R. 349.
18 [1959] 1 W.L.R. 1168.
19 [1949] SC 9.
20 The latter case is discussed in section 2.3.
21 The full quote can be found in the case of *London Passenger Transport Board v Upson and Another* discussed in section 2.3.
22 [2011] EWCA Civ.623.
23 [2013] EWCA Civ.262.
24 [2016] EWCA Civ.544.
25 [1951] A.C. 367.
26 [1948] A.C. 155.
27 *Upson v London Passenger Transport Board* [1947].
28 788 F.2d 1260 (7th Cir., 1986). This case is discussed in Chapter 4, section 4.3.
29 [1949] 2 K.B. 291.
30 We note that regarding the duty question there was a difference of opinion. While L. J. Bucknill held that the deceased owed a duty to the omnibus driver not to stand on the step of the lorry since he "ought to have had in contemplation the drivers of other vehicles, as being affected by the very dangerous position which he took on the lorry", L. J. Denning thought "the deceased man owed no duty to him."
31 2nd edition, p. 464.
32 This was in turn a quote from the judgment of L.J. Atkin in *Ellerman Lines, Ltd. v Grayson* (1919 (2) K.B. 535).
33 The damage was apportioned as follows: one-fifth was attributed to the deceased and four-fifths to the two injurers. Between the latter, it was divided as two-thirds to the omnibus driver and one-third to the lorry driver.
34 [1938] (1) All(ER) 126.
35 [1924] A.C. 419.
36 [1952] 2 Q.B. 608.
37 [1973] Q.B. 889.
38 [1922] 1 A.C. at 144; 1921 ALLER 201.
39 [1953] A.C. 180.
40 This refers to the decision of the House of Lords in *London Graving Dock Co. Ltd. v Horton* [1951] that an occupier can allow his premises to remain defective and dangerous with impunity so long as he gives the men warning of the risk or the danger is so obvious that they must be aware of it.
41 Discussed in subsection (iv).
42 [1943] A.C. 448.
43 [1951] A.C. 850.
44 With respect to the third, Lord Porter said that it "seems to point to some unspecified method of stopping balls from reaching the road while a game is in progress on the ground."
45 *Stone v Bolton* [1948] MAA 1.
46 *Stone v Bolton* [1950] 1 K.B. 210.
47 We note that in the case of *Miller v Jackson*, it was held that every time a ball was hit out of the grounds causing injury, there would be negligence.
48 Here we find a hint of a customary norm. Even Lord Oaksey in the House of Lords argued: "There are many footpaths and highways adjacent to cricket grounds and golf courses on to which cricket and golf balls are occasionally driven, but such risks are habitually treated by both the owners and committees of such cricket and golf courses and by the pedestrians who use the adjacent footpaths and highways as negligible, and it is not, in my opinion, actionable negligence not to take precautions to avoid such risks."
49 [1953] A.C. 643.

50 We note that "peril," like "risk" in the legal sense, means what economists call "expected harm."
51 [1958] 2 Q.B. 265.
52 [1959] A.C. 74. In subsection (i), we encountered one important case on the same issue, i.e. *Paris v Stepney Borough Council*.
53 Spats are, as Lord Evershed explained, "a form of legging which would protect the instep and the lower joints of the leg against splashing of heated or molten metal."
54 The plaintiff suffered injury on September 16, 1954, and after few months of disability had completely recovered. He brought his claim on March 22, 1957. When he had returned to work he did not wear the spats. Lord Denning argued, "If the warning given by the accident made no difference, we may safely infer that no advice beforehand would have had any effect."

References

Buckley, Richard A. (2007), *Buckley: The Law of Negligence*, United Kingdom, LexisNexis Butterworths.

Demsetz, Harold (1997), 'The Primacy of Economics: An Explanation of the Comparative Success of Economics in the Social Sciences', 35 *Economic Inquiry*, 1.

Farnsworth, Ward and Mark F. Grady (2009), *Torts – Cases and Questions*, 2nd ed., New York, Aspen Publishers.

Gilles, Stephen G. (2002), 'Symposium on Negligence in Courts: The Actual Practice: The Emergence of Cost-Benefit Balancing in English Negligence Law', 77 *Chicago-Kent Law Review*, 489.

Hepple, B.A. and M.H. Matthews (1974), *Tort: Cases and Materials*, London, Butterworths.

Heuston, R.F.V. and R.A. Buckley (1992), *Salmond and Heuston on the Law of Torts*, 20th ed., London, Sweet and Maxwell.

Keeton, W. Page et al. (1984), *Prosser and Keeton on the Law of Torts*, 5th ed., St. Paul, Minnesota, West Publishing Co.

Kidner, Richard (2002), *Casebook on Torts*, 7th ed., New Delhi, Oxford University Press.

Lakshminath, A. and M. Sridhar (2007), *Ramaswamy Iyer's: The Law of Torts*, 10th ed., Nagpur, LexisNexis Butterworths Wadhwa.

Noah, Lars (2000), 'General Tort Principles: The Role of Statutes in Common Law Adjudication: Statutes and Regulations: If Noncompliance Establishes Negligence per se, Shouldn't Compliance Count for Something?' 10 *Kansas Journal of Law and Public Policy*, 162.

Rogers, W.V.H. (2010), *Winfield and Jolowicz on Tort*, 18th ed., London, Sweet and Maxwell.

Schwartz, Victor E., Katherine Kelly and David F. Partlett (2010), *Prosser, Wade and Schwartz's Torts – Cases and Materials*, 12th ed., New York, Thompson Reuters Foundation Press.

Singh, G.P. (2010), *Ratanlal and Dhirajlal: The Law of Torts*, 26th ed., Nagpur, LexisNexis Butterworths Wadhwa.

Weir, Tony (2004), *A Casebook on Tort*, 10th ed., London, Sweet and Maxwell.

APPENDIX 2.A Schematic representation of the 17 cases analyzed

Case type and No.	Approach (s) Used for Negligence Determination	Names of the cases
2.1 [four]	Defendant held negligent by reasoning pointing towards the due care approach	Home Office v Dorset Wagon Mound (2) Miller v Jackson Knightley v Johns
2.2 [three]	Defendant held negligent by reasoning pointing towards the untaken precaution approach	Lang v LTE Belka v Prosperini Parmasivan v Wicks
2.3 [five]	Defendant held negligent by reasoning pointing towards both the approaches	Paris v Stepney B C LPTB v Upson Davies v Swansea Rouse v Squires General Cleaning Contractors v Christmas
2.4 [five]	Defendant held nonnegligent using the due care approach.	Glasgow Corp v Muir Bolton v Stone Latimer v Aec Ltd Wells v Cooper Qualcast v Haynes

3
ECONOMIC ANALYSIS OF SELECT INDIAN CASES

In this chapter, we examine Indian cases along the same lines as in the earlier chapter. We will divide the cases into three[1] categories:

3.1 Cases where the injurer is declared negligent by considerations which point towards use of due care approach

One important negligence case in this category is *Rural Transport Service v Bezlum Bibi and Others*.[2] In October 1969, Taher Seikh, who was about 25 years old, was travelling on a bus run by the appellant on the route Burdwan to Nasigram via Khetia and Bhatar. When he boarded the bus at Khetia, it was very crowded and the conductor asked him and other passengers to go on to the roof. He occupied a place on the right side. However, Taher was struck by an overhanging branch of a tree when the bus swerved to the right in an attempt to overtake a cart. Taher fell down and died the following day at the hospital due to the multiple injuries sustained during the fall. His mother, Bezlum Bibi, and brother were awarded damages after deducting some amount on the grounds of contributory negligence by the Motor Vehicles Accident Claims Tribunal, Burdwan. The defendants appealed to the Calcutta High Court challenging the award and denied that there was any negligence on the part of the driver or the conductor and claimed that the accident was entirely due to the fault of the deceased who was not supposed to travel on the roof. The High Court affirmed the Tribunal's verdict that the driver and conductor were negligent but held that the deceased was nonnegligent. They, therefore, dismissed the appeal.

The Tribunal had held the driver and conductor negligent on the basis of the evidence placed on behalf of the claimants. Two co-passengers of the deceased, Abdul Mannan and Nabu Seikh, stated that it was the conductor who asked them to climb on the roof, as the bus was overcrowded and there was no accommodation inside the bus, and they did not do it to evade purchasing a ticket. They further added that the bus was running at high speed, and while overtaking a cart swerved on to the right and went on to the kutcha flank of the road and then Taher was struck by the branch and he fell. It was the shouts from his co-passengers that made the bus stop some 300–400 cubits ahead. The Tribunal held that asking the passengers to travel on the roof amounted to negligence and but for that negligence the accident would not have occurred. The High Court attested the Tribunal's finding: "that inviting passengers to travel precariously on the roof of an overcrowded bus was itself a rash and negligent act." It further held: "and that apart when passengers were being made to travel on the roof a greater amount of care and caution on the part of the driver was called for." His act of leaving the metallic track and swerving onto the kutcha path while trying to overtake a cart in excessive speed was also rash and negligent. The High Court affirmed that the accident resulted from the rash and negligent act of both the driver and the conductor of the appellant.

Regarding the negligence of the deceased, the reasoning of the High Court differed from that of the Tribunal. The Tribunal had held: "there was contributory negligence on the part of the deceased because had the deceased taken reasonable care about his own safety he would not have travelled on the roof of the bus." The High Court, however, argued:

> the Tribunal failed to appreciate that ... not only the deceased but a number of passengers were invited by the appellant's employees to travel in that manner. Being invited to do so it would be reasonable to think on the part of such passengers that they would be safely carried to their destination, the bus being driven with such care and caution so as to ensure a safe journey for them.

The High Court further held:

> Where the passengers including the deceased were made to travel in that fashion on such an assurance, contributory negligence would be no defence because the deceased was not bound to take such care as the defendant contends but had a right to assume that the defendant would do things rightly and carefully so as to ensure a safe journey for him.

We find that both the Tribunal and the High Court held the driver and conductor negligent by using the due care approach and in addition the failure to adhere to a norm – that of not travelling on the roof. The High Court used individualized calculations of due care, and in this case since the conductor had invited the passengers to travel on the roof set a high standard. It is a principle of law that the due care level varies with circumstances; in this case given the overcrowded bus, the conditions of rural roads and passengers on the roof, the due care level was much higher than otherwise. By that standard, the driver was grossly negligent.

In determining the negligence of the deceased, the Tribunal used the untaken precaution approach but applied the reasoning erroneously. It held the deceased guilty of negligence on the grounds that he ought to have refused to climb to the roof; the implicit assumption was that the deceased should have taken account of the negligence of the other parties – something to the effect that, if the bus were to be driven negligently, as often happens, the passengers on the roof would be hurt. In saying that "if the deceased had taken reasonable care for his safety the deceased would not have travelled on the roof of the bus," the implicit assumption was that there were three options open to him, namely: travelling inside the bus, travelling on the roof of the bus and not travelling. This can be inferred because given the fact that the first option did not exist, the expected cost of travelling on the roof would have to be weighed against not travelling at all. Having been invited to travel on the roof of the bus, the deceased would attribute a lower probability of harm compared to a situation where he had taken a seat on the roof on his own. Thus, the expected harm for him would be lower. The burden of precautions would have been not travelling at all. On balancing the two, the deceased did not find it cost-justified to take the precaution of "not travelling on the roof." So he ought to have been adjudged nonnegligent by the untaken precaution approach as well. Travelling on the roof would be negligent when they are doing so by themselves. The High Court held him nonnegligent by using the due care approach. It was emphasized that since the deceased had been invited to travel on the roof, and such a mode of travelling was adopted as a common method by other passengers at the instance of the conductor, the passengers had a right to expect that such travelling would be reasonably safe. The High Court, therefore, dismissed the appeal.

One case in this category which dealt with injuries to one's horse due to the negligence of the defendant was *Jung Bahadur Singh v Sundarlal Mandal and Others*.[3] The plaintiff had a horse and the members of his family used to ride on it. On the September 10, 1954, his nephew, Gulab Narain Jadhav, was proceeding on the horse towards Nathanagar when he decided to get down near a bridge called Champanala. He held the reins and was standing at the side of the road when he saw a bus coming from the opposite direction. The plaintiff alleged that although his nephew raised his hand and signaled the bus to stop, and it was broad daylight, the driver did not pay heed and dashed against the horse causing injuries which resulted in his horse becoming permanently lame. He claimed damages against the owner and driver of the bus for rash and negligent driving. The trial court dismissed the claim and the plaintiff appealed to the first appellate court, which held the defendants liable. The owner of the bus appealed to the Patna High Court questioning the principles of law followed and also raised the issue of contributory negligence of the plaintiff's nephew. The Patna High Court affirmed the negligent verdict of the appellate court and held that there was no contributory negligence.

Among the two defendants, it was only the owner of the bus who contested the suit. The driver did not appear nor did he file a written statement contesting the claim of the plaintiff and was not examined in the suit. According to the owner, the plaintiff's horse was straying unattended on the road, and when the bus neared

Champanala it blew the horn and the horse moved away from the road. When the bus had crossed the bridge, the horse suddenly came and dashed against it. The driver, despite all efforts could not avoid the accident. The trial court held that on the evidence "it could not be concluded that the accident was caused by the negligent driving of defendant No.2," and therefore, the plaintiff was not entitled to any compensation. When the plaintiff appealed, the learned Subordinate Judge of Bhagalpur held the driver negligent for driving on the wrong side of the road. The driver of the bus did not contest the joint decree and damage award. However, the owner appealed to the Patna High Court on many grounds, among them the verdict that the driver was negligent and that his negligence being the effective cause of the horse's injury was erroneous in law.

The plaintiff-respondent combated the evidence put forth that the bus had crossed the bridge when the accident occurred. The Patna High Court accepted that the plaintiff's nephew was standing on the side of the road and had given a signal for the bus to stop, which the driver ignored. and came at a high speed from the opposite direction on the wrong side. The learned Justice Raj Kishore Prasad argued: "A duty is owed by one user of a road to another or his property. A principle is that – any particular user owes a duty to another particular user not to do or omit anything he might reasonably anticipate might injure the other." It was held that a vehicle should be driven at a speed that enables the driver to stop within the limits of his vision, and failure to do this will almost always result in the driver being held, in whole or in part, responsible for the collision. Regarding the untaken precaution identified by the learned Subordinate Judge, he referred to Clerk and Lindsell[4]:

> Though being on the wrong side of the road is evidence of negligence, it is slight evidence only, for the rule of the road necessarily is not inflexible. For example, if a collision can be better avoided by going on the wrong side, it is not merely justifiable to do so but obligatory.

He went on:

> He would have easily averted the incident and its consequential injury to the horse if he had only observed the above ordinary rules of the road ... The horse was within kicking distance of the bus and it was standing not out of the range of collision. Even then defendant 2 not only was driving on the wrong side of the road but was driving it in speed as, found by the Court of appeal below.

The High Court, therefore, held that the driver was negligent and it was his negligence that was the effective cause of the accident. We can infer that the High Court thought that driving in high speed was the "but for" cause of the accident.

On the issue of contributory negligence it was held that the plaintiff was on the left side of the road and had given the signal to stop, knowing that the horse had a tendency to get frightened by noise. However, the counsel for the owner of the bus strongly urged[5] that

> mere absence of negligence on the part of the plaintiff would not be sufficient to show that he was not guilty of contributory negligence and, further that knowledge by the plaintiff of an existing danger or of the defendants' negligence is a very important element in determining whether or not he has been guilty of contributory negligence.[6]

The High Court set itself to the task of ascertaining "whether one party could have reasonably avoided consequences of the other party's negligence." The court found that at the time of the incident, the plaintiff's nephew was standing with his horse at the brink of a ditch. He could not have moved further to the left. He did raise his hands to signal the bus to stop. The High Court held:

> P.W. 2 [the plaintiff's nephew], could not possibly have knowledge of the danger to come, or, of the negligent act of defendant 2 in not heeding the signal to stop the bus, in breaking the ordinary rule of the road, and in committing breach of his duty which he owed towards P.W.2 and the horse.

The learned justice, therefore, held that he could not have avoided the consequences of the defendant's negligence and hence was not contributorily negligent.

From the reasoning given it is clear that the trial court dismissed the claim merely on the ground of the evidence not pointing to the negligence of the driver. The first appellate court examined the evidence and held the driver to be negligent by the due care approach since he had been driving on the wrong side of the road. The Patna High Court also used the due care approach to hold both the driver negligent and the plaintiff's nephew nonnegligent. It held that there were many untaken precautions; the driver should have stopped the bus or slowed down the speed and taken it to the left side of the road. These were cost-justified because it would have averted a greater harm in terms of injury to the horse or the person with the horse. Regarding the question of contributory negligence, the High Court held that the plaintiff's nephew was entitled to assume that the driver would take reasonable care. This was made clear by the following statement:

> P.W.2 could not possibly have anticipated that defendant 2 would not, in spite of his signal to stop, slow down the speed of the bus, or, stop it, or pass by the left side of the road which would have clearly avoided the collision, because in that case the bus would have been beyond the kicking distance of the horse.

The implicit assumption is that the plaintiff's nephew set a lower probability of collision since he had given a signal to the bus and expected the driver to pay heed to it. Thus, he attached a lower expected harm from the collision than from falling into the ditch, and he was held to be justified in doing that. The untaken precaution of "moving further to the left" was, therefore, not cost-justified; thus, no contributory negligence could be ascribed.

Krishna Goods Carriers Private Limited, Delhi v Union of India[7] involved an accident at a railway level-crossing. On September 23, 1961, at about 1.30 a.m. in the night a driver of Krishna Goods Carriers [the plaintiffs] was returning to Delhi from a circus in Meerut in a Mercedes truck belonging to the company. A friend who had accompanied him to the circus was also driving a truck, and they were proceeding in their respective trucks along the Meerat-Delhi road when they reached the public level-crossing between Meerat city and Kharkhoda Railway Station. Finding the gates open and no warning of the danger of any approaching train, they proceeded to cross. His friend had safely crossed ahead but the plaintiff's driver suddenly saw a goods train travelling at full speed from the Hapur side towards Meerat city in front of his truck. It was claimed that despite his efforts, the truck dashed against the wagon next to the engine of the train, as a result of which the truck was damaged. On November 22, 1963, the company brought a suit alleging that the front portion of the truck including the engine was completely smashed and claimed the amount that they had to spend in repairs. The trial court dismissed the suit on the grounds that the plaintiff's driver was guilty of contributory negligence and hence could not recover. The plaintiff appealed to the Delhi High Court, which allowed the appeal holding that the accident occurred due to the negligence of the railway employees and the plaintiff cannot be held guilty of contributory negligence.

The level crossing in question had iron gates on both sides and there was a cabin and lodging for the gateman. The practice of the railways was not only to close the gates but also to signal with a red light the approach of a train. At the time of the accident, the gates were open and the gateman was absent from duty. The defendant, Northern Railway, denied their liability on the grounds that "the accident was not due to the negligence of the Northern Railway Administration or its servants but it was due to the carelessness and negligence of the driver of the plaintiff." They argued that it was a moonlit night and the driver could easily see the railway track and hear the whistle of the engine. The defendant's argument was: "True we invited the driver to cross the line by reason of the gate being unlocked, but we did not invite him to leave his common sense behind. He could have averted the danger." The trial court judge, after inspecting the site and examining the evidence, gave the verdict that although the railway was negligent, it was the plaintiff's driver who was "the author of his own wrong." The learned judge stated:

> The Railway was no doubt negligent in not closing the gate to warn the public of the approaching train but the plaintiff's driver was all the more negligent in not having a proper lookout from both sides of the road at the level crossing in question.

In the Delhi High Court, Justice Rohtagi examined the report of the Railway Accident Enquiry Committee, which said that at the time of the accident the gates were open, the gateman was absent from duty and "the accident was the direct result of this failure" of the gateman to close the level crossing. The Committee had held the plaintiff's driver also responsible for the accident because although he saw the train approaching, he attempted in a hurry to pass the railway line hoping to pass over before the train arrived on the level crossing. The learned justice found that the train was running at a speed of 27 miles per hour, and the engine driver admitted that he did not stop the train, although he knew that it was his duty to do so if he found the gates open. It was a goods train with no scheduled timing. Given that the evidence regarding visibility at night was conflicting with the plaintiff's side alleging that it was a cloudy night, the learned justice held that no conclusive evidence could be taken regarding this or whether a whistle would be audible in the rumbling of the train. It was held that the alleged untaken precautions, namely, "(i) omission to close the gate; (ii) the absence of the gatekeeper; (iii) the lack of a warning system at the crossing; (iv) excessive speed of the train; (v) failure to stop after seeing that the gate is open" all represented breaches of the duty to take care.

Regarding the issue of whether the plaintiff's driver was also negligent, Justice Rohtagi argued:

> It being the duty of the railways, where its line crosses a public highway on the level, to keep the gates closed when a train is approaching, a passenger along the highway who finds the gates open is reasonably entitled to assume that no train is approaching and that he may cross with safety, for the act of the railway in leaving the gates open 'amounts to statement, and a notice to the public, that the line at that time is safe for crossing.'
>
> *(North Eastern Railway v. Wanless (1894) 7 HL 12)*

The Court further added that a passerby is

> *not bound to look so carefully to see as he would be if there had been no such invitation.* The passerby, whether he is a highway pedestrian, a motorist, or a truck driver, is entitled to assume in the absence of warning that conditions are usual. The open gates amount to an invitation that the plaintiff can safely pass and if he is injured he is entitled to recover. (emphasis added)

Numerous authorities were cited in support of this contention. Based on this, it was held that the trial judge had erred in holding the plaintiff's driver negligent for the reckless way in which he crossed the line. The learned justice concluded:

> The driver thought, as anybody would think, that as the gates are not closed no train was coming, and therefore he might go over the crossing in safety without taking the precaution of looking up and down the line, or any other such precaution as might otherwise be necessary. If that be so, there was no want of reasonable care on his part.

We find in this case the negligence of the Northern Railway Administration and its employees was determined by the due care approach at both stages of litigation.

The five alleged untaken precautions were held to be cost-justified. The Court even clarified it by stating:

> It is, I think, now clearly established that the railway must take reasonable care to prevent danger at these crossings, and this is an obligation which keeps pace with the times. As the danger increases so must their precautions increase. The railway cannot stand by while accidents happen and say: 'the people using our crossing must look out before entering.' Safety is their concern. It is their trains which help to cause the accidents, and it is often the increased number of trains which increases the danger as well as the increased traffic on the road. The greater the risk of injury the greater the duty of care. . . . They must do all that is reasonably required of them, in the shape of warnings, whistles, and so forth so as to reduce the danger to people using the crossing.

It is clear that the court was referring to the duty of care being commensurate with the extent of harm. In this case, with the increase in the number of trains the expected harm was also larger.

The main issue before the courts was whether the plaintiff's driver was negligent. While the trial court held the plaintiff's driver negligent using the untaken precaution approach, the Delhi High Court reversed the verdict using the due care approach. Here the question posed was, given that the defendants' servants were negligent, what level of care was reasonable on the part of the plaintiff's driver. The trial court thought that the care required was higher than the level required if the railway had not been negligent. However, the High Court firmly rejected this view, holding that the plaintiff was not bound to take a higher care level just because the railway was negligent. This difference in conclusions arose because while the trial court held that he should have kept a look-out for negligent behavior, the High Court explicitly stated that the plaintiff was entitled to assume that the railways would take reasonable care for the safety of the public and therefore, he could interpret open gates as an indication that it was safe to cross. This case is interesting because here, like in the American case of *Haeg v Sprague*,[8] the plaintiff's driver actually saw the train approaching despite the open gates and proceeded to cross ahead of it.

One important negligence case was *Klaus Mittelbachert v The East India Hotels Ltd*.[9] in which the plaintiff, Klaus Mittelbachert, a German national, was seriously injured as a result of which he became paralyzed and after suffering from numerous ailments died of acute cardiac arrest about a decade after the accident. The plaintiff, at the time of the incident, was about 30 years of age and was a co-pilot with Lufthansa airlines. He had checked into Hotel Oberoi Intercontinental located in Zakir Hussain Marg, New Delhi, during a lay-over period between flights from Bangkok to New Delhi on August 11, 1972, and then on to Frankfurt on August 14, 1972. In the afternoon of August 13, the plaintiff had been swimming in the pool for some hours when he decided to take a dive from the diving board. He hit his head on the floor of the pool and fractured his skull, and he was left a cripple until his death on September 27, 1985. He had filed the suit on August 11, 1975,[10] for recovery of damages alleging that "the accident was caused by what in the circumstances amounted to a trap." The diving board suggested a proper depth of water into which a swimmer could dive. The hotel owed the plaintiff a duty to take care and ensure his safety. Having failed to do so, they were guilty of negligence. The defendants denied the allegations, saying that the accident was caused solely due to the negligence of the plaintiff himself. The Delhi High Court held the defendants guilty of negligence and ruled out any contributory negligence on the part of the plaintiff.

From the evidence, the following facts emerged. On the day of the accident, the plaintiff had been in the swimming pool since 2.30 p.m. and swam twice or thrice, every time taking an hour's rest in between. Around 6.00 p.m. he wanted to take a final swim with a dive from the three-metre high diving board. On the diving board, he started by taking two to three steps and made a dive with his head forward and arms stretched and closed over his head. He sustained injury on the first dive. He was taken out bleeding from the right ear and appearing to have paralyzed his arms and legs. He was rushed to Holy Family Hospital and after eight days, he was flown to Germany under medical escort. The defendants had argued that the plaintiff had been performing dangerous acrobatics under the influence of alcohol and had been warned by the hotel staff. There was a caution board near the diving board. Also, since he had been in the pool since 2.30 he was exhausted. The defendants further alleged that since the plaintiff had been suffering from meningitis it was possible that he got an attack of epilepsy while diving, which prevented him from diving with accuracy. The plaintiff agreed that he had ordered a bottle of beer but said that he did not take it but had intended to take it after the swim and before going for dinner. This was corroborated by Mrs Rose Marie Gausmann, who gave mouth-to-mouth resuscitation to the plaintiff immediately after the accident, and had he taken the beer she would have smelt it. She also said that the caution board was not there at the time of the accident and she saw it only when she stayed in the hotel around eight weeks later.

After examining the evidence, Justice Lahoti reached the conclusion that the plaintiff was not drunk. He reasoned:

> Assuming that he either alone or by sharing with others had consumed beer, it cannot be said that he had consumed alcohol in such quantity as would have caused enough intoxication to impair his alertness or lessen his normal senses so as to have deprived him of capacity to take care of himself.

Further, while examining the allegation that the plaintiff's hands were not above his head as should have been and it was that posture that caused the injury, Justice Lahoti argued:

> the swimming pool is expected to be so designed with so much depth of water and such placement of the diving board as to exclude danger even to

amateurs and learners. The posture of the plaintiff at the time of diving loses all its significance looked at from this angle.

He also argued that it was the duty of the employees of the hotel to prevent the plaintiff from swimming when they noticed that he was drunk or exhausted or was swimming or diving in the pool in an unusual manner. We note that Justice Lahoti thought that the defendants were subject to a high level of care if they actually "saw" the plaintiff being careless and that warning him would have been effective in preventing the accident. The testimony regarding the negligence of the plaintiff was deemed inconsistent and the plaintiff was held to be nonnegligent.

The next question concerned the standard of duty which the hotel owed to its guests. In general, Justice Lahoti held: "A person, who enters or walks into any premises, if the premises be open to accept entry, and there be nothing warning against his entry, has a right to assume that he is walking into a safe premises." Besides, he argued: "In the commercialized world degree of care would also be determined by reference to the price which is being charged. . . . Higher the charges, higher the degree to take care." He went on to state:

> there is no difference between a five-star hotel owner and insurer so far as the safety of the guest is concerned. In the hotel culture the stars assigned to a hotel are suggestive of the professional expertise, achievement and quality of the services available at the hotel and professed and projected by it to the public at large holding out invitation to the prospective guests to stay at the hotel – an assurance to quality, safety and hazardlessness of the services offered and available at the hotel.

He held that this high standard of care cannot be diluted by a general notice – "at your own risk." He argued that the presence of the diving board was an invitation to guests to use it and "it implied a warranty as to safety – that the swimming pool was structurally and from architectural point of view so designed as to be safe." After examining the evidence regarding the design and conformity with the prevalent standards, Justice Lahoti concluded that the defendant's swimming pool "was structurally so designed as to achieve just the bare minimum of depth at the plummet point." It was held that although a three-metre diving board required a minimum depth of 12 feet at the plummet point, the hotel failed to meet that standard. He concluded: "A five star hotel cannot be said to have discharged its duty to care towards its guests by observing bare minimum standards of safety. It should have gone by preferred standards."

Having established that the design of the swimming pool was defective, the Court held that the swimming pool represented a trap and could be considered hazardous. Justice Lahoti argued:

> A five star hotel charging a high or fancy price from its guests owes, a high degree of care to its guests as regards quality and safety of its structure and

services it offers and makes available. Any latent defect in its structure or service, which is hazardous to guests, would attract strict liability to compensate for consequences, flowing from its breach of duty to take care.

We note that although here there is a reference to strict liability, the rule of simple negligence with the defense of contributory negligence is being applied. He went on to argue:

A five star hotel cannot be heard to say that its structure and services satisfied the standards of safety of the time when it was built or introduced. It has to update itself with the latest and advanced standard of safety.

We find that the defendants were held negligent by the due care approach – they had not met the preferred standards of safety considering their five-star status. The plaintiff was held nonnegligent also by the due care approach – given that he was paying for high quality services, he was entitled to assume that he would be free from danger. The defendants should have "redesigned and renovated" when the standards changed in 1970 (the defendants had been adhering to the 1956 standard). The court held: "The least which could have been done by the defendants in the year 1970 was to have removed the three metres spring board from above the swimming pool leaving it available only for swimming and not for diving." The court, thus, identified a cost-justified precaution which, if taken, could have prevented the accident.

One oft-cited negligence case is *Municipal Corporation of Delhi v Subhagwanti and Others*,[11] which concerned appeals arising out of three suits filed by the heirs of three persons who died when the Clock Tower situated opposite the Town Hall in the main Bazaar of Chadni Chowk belonging to the Municipal Corporation of Delhi (MCD) collapsed. The three suits, one filed in 1952 by Subhagwanti and others who were the heirs of deceased Ram Prakash, the other filed in 1952 by Munshi Lal and others who were the heirs of deceased Panni Devi and by Kuldip Raj, whose father Gopi Chand was also among those who died as a result of the collapse of the Clock Tower. These were tried by the Subordinate Judge, First Class, Delhi, and disposed by a common judgment granting damages to all three parties. The trial court held that it was the duty of the Municipal Committee (the MCD was formerly called the Municipal Committee) to take proper care of the buildings, so that they should not prove a source of danger to persons using the highway as a matter of right. The Municipal Committee filed appeals in the High Court on all three suits. On November 17, 1959, the High Court disposed of all the suits by a common judgment in which the damages awarded to Subhagwanti was maintained and those awarded to the other two parties was reduced. The MCD brought these appeals to the Supreme Court of India against the decree of the High Court.

The High Court had held that it was the duty of the Municipal Committee to carry out periodical examination for the purpose of determining whether deterioration had taken place in the structure and whether any precautions were necessary to strengthen the building. The verdict was based on the statements of Shri. B. S. Puri, Retired Chief Engineer, P. W. D., Government of India, and Mr Chakravarty, Municipal Engineer, that the building was 80 years old and the life of the structure of the top storey, having regard to the type of mortar used, could only be 40 to 45 years, and the middle storey could be saved for another decade. The High Court also considered the testimony of Mr Puri that the Clock Tower had collapsed due to the thrust of the arches on the top portion. He was of the opinion that if an expert had examined the building specifically for the purpose he might have found that it was likely to fall. He further said that when he inspected the building after the collapse and took the mortar in his hands he found that it had deteriorated to such an extent that it was reduced to powder without any cementing properties. Given the evidence, the High Court applied the doctrine of *res ipsa loquitur*.

In the Supreme Court, the main question presented in the appeals was whether the appellant was negligent in looking after and maintaining the Clock Tower and was liable to pay damages for the death of the persons resulting from its fall. The appellants also contended that the doctrine of *res ipsa loquitur* should not have been applied. It was argued that the fall of the Clock Tower was due to an inevitable accident that could not have been prevented by the exercise of reasonable care or caution. It was also suggested that there was nothing in the appearance of the Clock Tower that should have put the appellant on notice with regard to the possibility of danger. Justice Ramaswami accepted the evidence placed in the High Court regarding the age and normal life of the building and held that in the absence of any earthquake or any other unforeseen natural event, the fall of the Tower "tells its own story" in raising an inference of negligence. The doctrine of *res ipsa* therefore applied to the case.

The Supreme Court then went on to consider what it described as "the main question" in this case, namely, whether the appellant as the owner of the Clock Tower abutting on the highway, is bound to maintain it in proper state of repairs so as to not cause any injury to any member of the public using the highway and whether the appellant is liable if the defect is patent or latent. That is, it considered the duty question. The appellant had urged that there were no superficial signs on the structure that might have given the warning to the appellant that the Clock Tower was likely to fall, and since the defects were latent, the MCD could not be held guilty of negligence. The Supreme Court held that:

> In view of the fact that the building had passed its normal age at which the mortar could be expected to deteriorate it was the duty of the appellant to carry out careful and periodical inspection for the purpose of determining whether, in fact, deterioration had taken place and whether any precautions were necessary to strengthen the building. The apex Court accepted the finding of the High Court that there was no evidence to show that any such inspections were carried out on behalf of the appellant. Even if any inspection was carried out, they were "casual and perfunctory in nature.

It held:

> The legal position is that there is a special obligation on the owner of the adjoining premises for the safety of the structures which he keeps besides the highway. If these structures fall into disrepair so as to be of potential danger to the passers-by or to be a nuisance, the owner is liable to anyone using the highway who is injured by reason of the disrepair. In such a case, it is no defence for the owner to prove that he neither knew nor ought to have known of the danger. In other words, the owner is legally responsible irrespective of whether the damage is caused by a patent or a latent defect.

It referred to the English case of *Wringe v Cohen*[12] in which J. Atkinson had stated:

> By common law it is an indictable offence for an occupier of premises on a highway to permit them to get into a dangerous condition owing to non-repair. It was not and is not necessary in an indictment to aver knowledge or means of knowledge."

The Supreme Court held that:

> Applying the principle to the present case it is manifest that the appellant is guilty of negligence because of the potential danger of the Clock Tower maintained by it having not been subjected to a careful and systematic inspection which it was the duty of the appellant to carry out.

We note that here the Supreme Court is adopting the due care approach to arrive at a finding of negligence. It also identified the untaken precaution, namely, "careful and systematic inspection," which could have averted the accident. The building was way past its normal life and that warranted not just "casual and perfunctory" inspection but something more than that.

One case in which the determination of contributory negligence of the victim came up for scrutiny was the case of *Smt. Sarla Dixit and Another v Balwant Yadav and Others*.[13] It concerned an accident which occurred on March 16, 1975, at 11.00 a.m. when Capt. Rama Kant Dixit was riding a scooter on his way from Chandra Prasth Colony towards Mall Road, Morar, within the city of Gwalior. A truck was coming from the side of Gola-ka-Mandir on a road measuring 25 feet and running west to east and there was an intersection with Indraprastha Road that ran from north to south, and Rama Kant was on this road proceeding southwards. When he had entered the intersection, the truck came from the western side at high speed and dashed against the scooter, killing Rama Kant instantaneously and injuring Ramji Sharma, who was riding pillion on the scooter. The wife of the deceased, Smt. Sarla Dixit, filed a suit claiming compensation before the Gwalior Tribunal. The Tribunal ruled in favour of the claimants but reduced the compensation by three-quarters on the grounds of contributory negligence of the deceased.

Aggrieved by the award, the claimants appealed to the High Court of Madhya Pradesh, Jabalpur Bench, Gwalior. The defendants preferred cross appeal against the award. The High Court held that the deceased was not guilty of contributory negligence and hence the entire negligence rested on the driver of the truck. The award was seen to be too low and the claimants appealed to the Supreme Court of India. The defendants challenged the finding of the High Court that Rama Kant was not guilty of contributory negligence.

In the Supreme Court the negligence question concerned whether the accident occurred solely due to the negligence of the truck driver or whether the deceased had contributed to the accident. It was reiterated that the accident occurred on the intersection of two roads, the deceased travelling from the southward direction on the north-south road and the truck coming eastwards on the east-west road. From the evidence given by the pillion rider Ramji Sharma, and the photographs of the place of accident, it was clear that the scooter was already mid-way on the intersection when the collision took place because the right side of the scooter dashed against the left front wheel of the truck. Ramji Sharma further testified that Rama Kant had sounded the horn when he entered the intersection and had given a hand signal to indicate that he intended to go across. The postmortem of the deceased also revealed that the injuries were on the right side of his body and face. The fact that he was thrown off his scooter indicated that the driver of the truck was driving very fast and he did not care for the safety of the scooterist, who was almost halfway along the intersection and visible to him in broad-daylight. He had continued to drive recklessly even after the accident and could stop only after traversing a distance of 70 feet. The truck driver was a novice, aged about 20 years without a driving licence to drive such a heavy vehicle, and it was his rash and negligent driving that caused the accident.

The Supreme Court referred to Regulation (7) of the Tenth Schedule of the Motor Vehicles Act, 1939, which reads: "7. The driver of a motor vehicle shall, on entering a road intersection, if the road enacted is a main road designated as such, give way to all traffic approaching the intersection on his right hand." The Supreme Court argued that:

> Regulation (7) could have been pressed in service against the deceased Rama Kant if it was shown that while entering the intersection, having seen the on-coming truck from his right-hand side he had not taken due precaution. Such a situation, from the facts of the present case, is found to be absent.

On the other hand it was pointed out that the truck driver had committed a breach of Regulation (6) of the very same Schedule, which reads: "6. The driver of a motor vehicle shall slow down when approaching a road intersection or junction until he has become aware that he may do so without endangering the safety of persons thereon." The truck driver was required to slow down while approaching the road intersection, and he had not done so and went on driving at full speed and threw the scooterist, who was already in the middle of the intersection. The

Supreme Court, therefore, affirmed the verdict of the High Court and held that the truck driver was solely responsible for the accident and the deceased did not contribute to the accident.

We find that the both the High Court and the Supreme Court used the due care approach to decide the negligence question of both the truck driver and the deceased. The truck driver had been driving very fast, did not have a licence to drive such a heavy vehicle and failed to comply with Regulation (6) of the Tenth Schedule of the Motor Vehicles Act, 1939, by not slowing down while approaching the intersection and endangering the safety of persons on the intersection. The deceased had sounded the horn, given a hand signal about his intention to cross and was already on the intersection when he was struck. The Supreme Court ruled that:

> There was no occasion for him to halt and give way to the truck coming from the western side and proceeding to the eastern side of road no. 7 for the simple reason that Rama Kant had already entered the intersection and had travelled almost half way across the breath of road no. 7.

From this one can infer that the Court did not think that the untaken precaution of "halting and allowing the truck to pass" was cost-justified. Implicit in this reasoning is the assumption that Rama Kant was justified in thinking that no vehicle would come speeding onto the intersection – that is, he was entitled to assume reasonable behavior on the part of road users.

One similar case of car–truck collision was that of *Pramodkumar Rasikbhai Jhaveri v Karmasey Kunvargi Tak and Others*,[14] in which the issue of taking extraordinary precautions was explicitly discussed. The case concerned an accident that occurred when the Fiat car in which the claimants were travelling to Surat from Ahmedabad collided with a truck coming from the opposite side at high speed. The truck, which was loaded with goods, toppled over to its right side and came to a halt at a distance of 20 feet. The driver of the car and the other occupants filed a suit in the Motor Accident Claims Tribunal for compensation for the injuries suffered. The Tribunal allowed the entire amount claimed, but the insurance company filed an appeal in the High Court of Gujarat, and the court reduced the total compensation and also held that the driver of the car contributed to the accident to the extent of 30 percent. The claimants appealed to the Supreme Court of India.

The finding of contributory negligence by the High Court was based on two reasons: first, the appellant who was driving the car did not slow down when he saw a speeding truck trying to overtake a car ahead of it, and second, although there was a three-foot distance on the left of the car, it did not swerve to the left on seeing the oncoming truck. These two untaken precautions were scrutinized by the Supreme Court: "We do not think that these two reasons given by the High Court fully justify the accepted principles of contributory negligence." Justice Balakrishnan went on to define what constituted contributory negligence:

> Negligence ordinarily means breach of a legal duty to care, but when used in the expression 'contributory negligence' it does not mean breach of any duty.

It only means the failure by a person to use reasonable care for the safety of either himself or his property, so that he becomes blameworthy in part as an "author of his own wrong."

Further, Justice Balakrishnan stated:

> Subject to non-requirement of the existence of duty, the question of contributory negligence is to be decided on the same principle on which the question of the defendant's negligence is decided. The standard of a reasonable man is as relevant in the case of a plaintiff's contributory negligence as in the case of a defendant's negligence. But the degree of want of care which will constitute contributory negligence, varies with the circumstances and the factual situation of the case.

While investigating the precautions that ought to have been taken, the apex Court stated:

> It has been accepted as a valid principle by various judicial authorities that where, by his negligence, if one party places another in a situation of danger, which compels that other party to act quickly in order to extricate himself, it does not amount to contributory negligence if that other acts in a way, which, with the benefit of hindsight, is shown not to have been the best way out of the difficulty.

Lord Hailsham's observation in *Swadling v Cooper*[15] was quoted:

> Mere failure to avoid the collision by taking some extraordinary precaution does not in itself constitute negligence. The plaintiff has no right to complain if in the agony of the collision the defendant fails to take some step which might have prevented a collision unless that step is one which a reasonably careful man would fairly be expected to take in the circumstances.

In the present case, the evidence showed that the total width of the road was 22 feet and there were mud shoulders on either side having a width of three feet. The truck in question had come to the central portion of the road and there was only a three-foot width of the road on the left side of the car driven by the appellant. Justice Balakrishnan held that in these circumstances it was not justified for the High Court to have found that the appellant contributed to the accident. The apex Court stated:

> It would, if at all, only prove that the appellant had not shown extraordinary precaution. The truck driven by the second respondent almost came to the centre of the road and the appellant must have been put in a dilemma and in the agony of that moment, the appellant's failure to swerve to the extreme left of the road did not amount to negligence.

We find that the High Court was using the untaken precaution approach in holding the appellant negligent. Given that the other party was negligent, extraordinary precautions – that of swerving to the left – was appropriate. The Supreme Court did not controvert the finding of the existence of an untaken precaution but was of the view that negligence (as well as contributory negligence) should be defined in terms of the due care approach.

One oft-cited case of negligence in the employment context was that of *Madhya Pradesh State Road Transport Corporation and another v Ms. Basantibai and Others*.[16] The case concerned a driver, Chunnilal, who was employed by the Central Provinces Transport Services (C.P.T.S). In September 1956, curfew was imposed because of communal riots restricting movement without a valid pass issued by the District authorities. Chunnilal was given a pass and asked to report to work. On September 16, 1956, he was proceeding towards Jabalpur depot at about 6.00 a.m. when he was stabbed in the abdomen. He succumbed to his injuries. His widow, Basantibai and three sons alleged in their suit that the management of C.P.T.S was negligent in not providing adequate arrangement for the safety of Chunnilal while he was going for his duty. They alleged that the accident arose out of and in the course of employment. During the pendency of the suit, the Madhya Pradesh State Road Transport Corporation was formed and was substituted as a defendant in place of C.P.T.S. The trial court held that the management of the C.P.T.S was negligent in not providing safety arrangement for the deceased while going to join his duty and that the accident arose out of and in the course of his employment. The defendants appealed to the Madhya Pradesh High Court.

The evidence given by Gulab Singh, who was also an employee of the C.P.T.S, Jabalpur, was that curfew was imposed from four or five days before the day of the incident and the drivers including Chunnilal were given passes and were required to reach the C.P.T.S depot at 6.00 a.m. or 6.30 a.m. where they were assigned different duties. Another witness, Gurudayal Singh, stated that on the day of the incident, at about 6.00 a.m. he saw Chunnilal in a rickshaw at the C.P.T.S depot and the rickshaw-wala told him that someone had stabbed him in the abdomen. This was corroborated by Gulab Singh. From the evidence, Justice G. P. Singh inferred that Chunnilal was stabbed on his way to duty and he died due to those injuries. The appellants agreed that no arrangement for the safety of Chunnilal was provided and it was their contention that it was not their duty to do so.

Since there was no direct precedent to provide guidance regarding the duty question, Justice Singh referred to Lord Atkin's speech in *Donoghue v Stevenson* that one must take reasonable care not to injure one's neighbours – that is, persons who are so closely and directly affected by one's act that they ought to be kept in contemplation. Lord Macmillan had also said that new duty situations could also arise: "The conception of legal responsibility may develop in adaptation to altering social conditions and standards. The criterion of judgment must adjust and adapt itself to the changing circumstances of life. The categories of negligence are never closed." After citing various authorities like Lord Pearce in *Hedley Bryne*[17] and Lord Reid in *Home Office*, Justice Singh concluded by referring to Clerk and Lindsell:

"The obligation is three-fold – 'the provision of a competent staff of men, adequate material and a proper system and effective supervision.' To these should be added: a safe place of work."

Justice Singh argued that normally an employer owes no duty of care for the safety of his employee while the employee is on his way to work. He went on to argue:

> The point, however, is whether the same rule prevails when the situation is abnormal and when as a result of outbreak of violence in the city, the law enforcement authorities promulgate curfew order requiring citizens to be within doors as the only means which can reasonably ensure their safety. In such a situation, when every citizen is expected to be within doors as a matter of safety, if an employer requires his employee to come to the place of employment in early hours of the morning, it is reasonably foreseeable that the employee is likely to suffer injury at the hands of some ruffian while on his way to join work unless adequate arrangements are made by the employer for the safety of the employee.

He concluded:

> On the principles enunciated by Lord Atkin in Donoghue v Stevenson (quoted earlier) the employer must, in the circumstances prevailing in the instant case, be held to owe a duty of care to the employee while he was on his way to the place of work.

Interpreted in economic terms, it means when the expected harm is very high, a duty exists to protect the employee.

Justice Singh even specified the precautions that could have been taken: "providing safe transport or some persons to accompany and guard him." He further added: "In case it was not possible for the employer to make any arrangement for the safety of the employee, the employer should have temporarily closed down the business as the only alternative of avoiding harm to the employee." Translated to economic terms this means that the expected harm was so great that it even warranted the precaution of closing down the business temporarily. Justice Singh further held:

> It has to be kept in view that the employee, in the instant case, unlike a police constable or a foreman, was not in such an employment where it was expected of him from the nature of employment to face the hazard of a riot.

He concluded that from the facts and circumstances of the case it can be held that a duty-situation existed and the management of the C.P.T.S was liable in negligence. We note that in this case the due care approach was used and an attempt was made to find cost-justified precautions. It was held that even closing the business was cost-justified given the risk encountered during communal riots in case other cheaper measures were not available. The employers were held to be negligent for

> not taking adequate precautions for the safety of the deceased, either by making arrangement for his protection while he was on his way to join his work, or by closing the business temporarily, if no such arrangement for the protection of the deceased was possible.

In this case, we note that although the negligence notion that is used is that of due care, negligence in the Grady sense is also established.

One extensively cited case of motor accident is that of *Pushpabai Purshottam Udeshi and Others v Ranjit Ginning and Pressing Company Private Limited and Another*,[18] which concerned an accident that occurred on December 18, 1960, near a village called Chicholli-Vad, 16 miles from Saoner, which is on the way from Nagpur to Pandhura. The car in which the plaintiff's husband, Purshottam Udeshi, was travelling was driven by Madhavjibhai Mathuradas Ved, the manager of the first opponent company, M/s Ranjit Ginning and Pressing Co. Private Ltd. The plaintiff alleged that it was because the car was driven in a rash and negligent manner that the accident occurred, as a result of which her husband died. The first opponent as well as the second opponent, the Union Fire Accident and General Insurance Company, Ltd., denied the allegation and claimed that the vehicle was in a perfect condition and that the accident was an inevitable one. They also said that the deceased was travelling on his own responsibility and for his own purpose. The Motor Accident Claims Tribunal, Jabalpur, found that the accident occurred due to the negligent driving of the manager and put the liability on the first opponent. The latter appealed to the High Court of Madhya Pradesh, which did not decide the question of negligence but only focussed on the liability issue, saying that the accident did not occur during the course of employment. On an application by the claimants the High Court granted a certificate, and an appeal was filed before the Supreme Court of India.

The Supreme Court took up the two issues of negligence determination and vicarious liability sequentially. The testimony of the younger brother of Purshottam Udeshi, who went to the spot soon after the accident, revealed that the car had dashed against a tree four feet from the right side of the main metalled road. On either side of the 15-foot wide straight road there were fields that were at a lower level. The tree against which the car dashed was uprooted about nine or ten inches from the ground, and the car was broken on the front side; the machine of the car had shifted from its original position by about a foot, which caused the steering wheel and the engine of the car to recede back causing the death of the occupants. From this evidence the Tribunal had concluded that it was the negligence of the driver that caused the accident. Since the opponents had pleaded that it was a case of inevitable accident, it was for them to prove it. The opposite party failed to prove this.

The Supreme Court held that if the driver had used proper care in the ordinary course of things the car could not have gone to the right extreme of the road, dashed against a tree and moved it a few inches away. The respondents put forth the argument that cattle may have strayed into the road, suddenly causing the accident. The Supreme Court rejected this argument stating:

> We are unable to accept the plea for in a country road with a width of about 15 feet with fields on either side ordinary care requires that the car should be driven at a speed in which it can be controlled if some stray cattle happened to come into the road.

From the evidence, it stood unchallenged that the car had proceeded to the right extremity of the road, which is the wrong side, and dashed against a tree, uprooting it about nine inches from the ground. The fact that the front side of the car was broken and the engine was shifted back was enough to show that the accident occurred due to the rash and negligent driving of the manager. The Supreme Court held the driver negligent and the owner vicariously liable since it thought that the deceased was acting in the course of his employment.

We find that in this case individualized due care was used. It was clear that the court was referring to some given speed level but that speed level was what that required in the circumstances. It was a metalled road with fields on either side that were at a lower level. The driver should have used the care that the circumstances demanded. Since he had not done so, he went on the wrong side of the road and dashed against the tree so violently that it was uprooted and the car was damaged badly by the impact. No specific untaken precaution was identified in this case.

One important case concerning the question whether the state was guilty of negligence was that of *Jay Laxmi Salt Works Pvt. Ltd. v State of Gujarat*.[19] In 1954, the state of Saurashtra, which is now part of the state of Gujarat, made a plan for reclamation of vast areas of land from the salty sea water by erecting a "reclamation bundh" so as to prevent sea water from flowing in several creeks in the area on the sea side of the bundh further to the claimed site and to stop the area from becoming salty. The bundh was completed in the year 1955, but in the first monsoon after its completion in 1956, due to the change in the natural course of different streams in the reclaimed area and its diversion towards the appellant's already existing factory, there occurred an increased flow and discharge of water on appellant's land and factory. On the night of July 4, 1956, the flood level rose to such an extent that water filtered into the factory breaking even the protective bundh made by the appellant on the border of its factory. The plaintiff approached the authorities and the government for redress and an amount of damages was determined by an Official Committee. When the Government refused to pay the amount, the plaintiff filed a suit against the State. The State Government gave the defense that there was no negligence either in the construction of the bundh or in the action of the officers and that the quantum of damages was unacceptable. The State also argued that the suit was barred in time, by applying Article 36 of the Limitation Act, 1908.[20] The trial court dismissed the suit as it did not find any negligence ascribing the incident to an act of God and also held that the suit was barred in time. The plaintiff appealed to the High Court, which held that the planning and construction of the bundh was done in a negligent manner but dismissed the suit saying it was barred in time. The plaintiff then appealed to the Supreme Court of India.

In the High Court, Justice Desai, who wrote the leading judgment, held that the construction of the bundh by the State could not be termed as non-natural use, as:

> the dam was erected over the land and streams of water. The purpose was to save the lands on the reclamation site from becoming useless. Therefore, the dam in question, was just like, which, an owner of a field would erect, where the boundary of his land is eroded by constant flow and rush of water.

After examining the evidence (oral and documentary) the learned Judge held that the act of planning and construction of the bundh was done in a negligent manner, as a result of which flood water entered the factory of the appellant causing extensive damage. He dismissed the suit stating that it was barred in time. The other judge who constituted the Bench, Justice Sheth, agreed with Justice Desai on the questions of fact but differed on the point that the suit was barred in time. The case was referred to a third judge, Justice Divan, who agreed with Justice Sheth.

In the Supreme Court, Justice Sahai held that:

> In a welfare society construction of dam or bundh for the sake of community is essential function and use of land or accumulation of water for the benefit of society cannot be non-natural user. But that cannot absolve the State from its duty of being responsible to its citizens for such violations as are actionable and result in damage, loss or injury.... Since the appellant suffered loss on facts found due to action of respondent's officers at the stage of construction and failure to take steps even at the last moment it was liable to be compensated.

Justice Sahai further stated: "Since construction of bundh was a common law duty any injury suffered by a common man was public tort liable to be compensated." It was argued that: "the expressions 'malfeasance', 'misfeasance' and 'nonfeasance' would apply to those limited cases where the State or its officers are liable not only for breach of care and duty but must be activated with malice and bad faith." It held: "The defective planning in construction of a bundh, therefore, may be negligence, mistake, omission but to say that it can only be either malfeasance, misfeasance and nonfeasance is not correct." It added: "The basic ingredients of torts, namely, injury and damage due to failure to observe duty has been found to have been established. In the conservative sense it was negligence." It was also held that Article 36 was not exhaustive to cover all torts. The suit was not barred in time as the case should be governed by Article 120 of the Limitation Act. The court concluded: "the damage was caused to the appellant not only because of negligence of officers but also because it was due to failure to discharge public duty and mistake at various stages." Justice Singh, in Ratanlal and Dhirajlal's *Law of Torts*, argues that the court, however, did not refer to any provision of the Constitution or elaborate on the concept of public law duty.[21]

We find that here both the High Court and the Supreme Court of India found that the State could be held liable not only for the negligence of its officers but also failure to perform a public duty properly. Thus, the due care level was higher since the interests of the community at large were involved. One can interpret this as saying the higher the expected harm, the higher the level of care required to be exercised. The due care approach seems to have been followed but the level of care was an individualized one. The Supreme Court endorsing the textbooks stated:

> the axis around which the law of negligence revolves is duty, duty to take care, duty to take reasonable care. But the concept of duty, its reasonableness, the standard of care required cannot be put in a strait-jacket. It cannot be rigidly fixed.

Another case in which the negligence of a government organization came under scrutiny was *Municipal Corporation of Delhi v Sushila Devi Smt. And Others*.[22] On the evening of August 18, 1964, two brothers, Suresh Chander and Ramesh Chander, were returning home on a scooter from their office. When they were passing Sant Parmanand Blind Relief Mission Building situated at 20, Alipur Road, Delhi, a branch of a neem tree suddenly broke and fell on the head of Suresh Chander. He was rushed to Irwin Hospital, but he succumbed to his injuries the next morning. A piece of wood was found embedded in his brain that required surgery. The deceased was survived by his widow, three minor sons and a minor daughter and his mother. They brought a suit for damages against the corporation. The learned judge sitting on the original side of the High Court held the Municipal Corporation of Delhi negligent and therefore, liable for the damages. On the one hand, the Municipal Corporation sought for the suit to be dismissed; on the other hand, the claimants sought enhancement in the amount of damages. The division Bench dismissed the appeal filed by the corporation but partly allowed the appeal preferred by the claimants and enhanced the compensation. Both parties preferred further appeals to the Supreme Court of India.

The Supreme Court held that the bundle of facts constituting the cause of action that had accrued to the claimants were – the ownership and possession of the tree resting in the corporation, its maintenance by the corporation, the fall of a branch of the tree over the deceased and the death consequent to the injury sustained. The court considered the evidence given by the Division Bench that "the tree in question was a dead tree. It had no bark, no foliage or butt." A botany professor who was examined as an expert witness testified that a tree with no bark was dried up and dying. The testimony of the garden superintendent examined on behalf of the corporation also showed that the tree was "dead, dried and dangerous." The Supreme Court noted that the Division Bench had upheld the finding recorded by the learned trial judge, that the horticulture department of the corporation should have carried out periodical inspections of the trees and should have taken safety precautions to see that the road was safe for its users and such adjoining trees as were dried and dead and/or had projecting branches that could prove to be dangerous to the passers-by were removed. Since the Municipal Corporation had not done that, they were negligent in discharging their duty. We note here that when trees are dead and dried, the probability of them falling is high and the resultant harm would be high. From the facts, it appears that it was a case of no care rather than inadequate care; it was held that the Corporation would have to take the precaution of "removing" trees.

The Supreme Court affirming this finding of the trial Court and the High Court, quoted from Clerk and Lindsell on torts[23]:

> The fall of trees, branches and other forms of natural growth is governed by the rules of negligence. When trees on land adjoining a public highway fall upon it, the owner is liable if he knew or ought to have known that the falling tree was dangerous. He is not bound to call an expert to examine the trees, but he is bound to keep a lookout and to take notice of such signs as would indicate to a prudent landowner that there was a danger of a tree falling . . . the landowner was held liable when the tree which fell had been dying for some years before and had become a danger which should have been apparent to an ordinary landowner.

The Supreme Court finally concluded:

> the law is well settled that if there is a tree standing on the defendant's land which is dried or dead and for that reason may fall and the defect is one which is either known or should have been known to the defendant, then the defendant is liable for any injury caused by the fall of the tree. The duty of the owner/occupier of the premises by the side of the road whereon persons lawfully pass by, extends to guarding against what may happen just by the side of the premises on account of anything dangerous on the premises. The premises must be maintained in a safe state of repair. The owner/occupier cannot escape the liability for injury caused by any dangerous thing existing on the premises by pleading that he had employed a competent person to keep the premises in safe repair.

The Supreme Court affirmed the verdict of the High Court that the Municipal Corporation of Delhi was negligent at common law. It stated:

> If the tree is dangerous in the sense that on account of any disease or being dead the tree or branch is likely to fall and thereby injure any passer-by then such a tree or branch must be removed so as to avert the danger to life.

We conclude that the due care approach was used to hold the corporation negligent and the untaken precaution identified by the court was removing the dead tree or branch to avert the danger.

3.2 Cases where the injurer is declared negligent by considerations which point towards use of untaken precaution approach

One case concerning the kidnapping of a newborn from the maternity ward of a hospital was that of *Government of NCT of Delhi and Others v Sudha Devi and Another*.[24] Sudha Devi had delivered a baby boy by a caesarean section on the July 7, 2003, at 2.30 p.m. in G.T.B. Hospital, Shahdara. At 4.30 a.m. the next day, the baby was found missing. Sudha Devi had been administered pain killers, sedatives and antibiotics as is the usual practice after a caesarean and that had affected her mental alertness. Since she was kept in a female ward, male members were not allowed and she had no female relatives. One lady from her neighbourhood, Indu, had volunteered to accompany her to the hospital. When the infant could not be found, Sudha Devi filed a suit against the hospital authorities and also the Government of NCT Delhi and the Union of India. The trial court passed a decree in her favour. The defendants appealed to the Delhi High Court.

From the testimony of Indu, it was established that she had taken her young son with her to the hospital and about 4.30 a.m. had to take him to the toilet. On her return, she found the newborn baby missing. Dr N. K. Sinha, who was posted at the hospital, confirmed the timing of the birth and the disappearance of the infant and stated that the female ward was taken care of by a professor of the Gynaecology Department; the department had security to check the entry and exit of patients and their attendants and only authorized persons were allowed. The learned trial judge held that it was the duty of the hospital to ensure that the patients who were admitted did not suffer any harm. He argued that extra care was required at the maternity ward because young mothers were there, particularly those who had undergone caesarean sections and were not in their full senses. The hospital, the Government of NCT of Delhi and the Union of India were held jointly liable to satisfy the decree. The reasoning suggests that because the probability of harm was high in this ward, and since young mothers were not fully alert and capable of taking care of their infants, extra care was required.

In the High Court, Mr Avnish Ahlawat, learned counsel for the appellants, urged that merely because security is deployed at the hospital does not mean that the patients and their attendants are absolved of the duty to take care of themselves and their children and wards. Further, since the Government of NCT, Delhi, does not charge any money, it is not responsible for the safety of the patients admitted at the hospital. He urged that it was the duty of Indu, the attendant of Sudha Devi, to take care of the infant. Justice Pradeep Nandrajog went on to deal with the concept of negligence before turning to the present case. He stated:

> The jurisprudential concept of negligence defies any precise definition. We do not intend to catalogue the various definitions of negligence but would note that each definition recognizes two essential components of negligence, that is to say: (i) The existence of a duty to take reasonable care which is owed by the alleged tortfeasor to the person aggrieved; (ii) The failure to attend

the duty of reasonable care. On the proof of the twin, the resultant damages which are the direct and inevitable (i.e. reasonably foreseeable) consequences of negligence have to be borne by the tortfeasor qua the injured person.

We note that in this definition, the resultant damages are said to be those which are "the direct and inevitable (i.e., reasonably foreseeable) consequences of negligence." There is no mention of the indirect but reasonably foreseeable consequences of negligence. We noted earlier that in *Wagon Mound (1) Re Polemis* was overruled and it was held that not only the direct but also the indirect consequences of negligence should be included in damages provided they are foreseeable, and *Wagon Mound (2)* added the criteria of reasonable foreseeability. The way in which Justice Nandrajog defined damages would, in terms of the economic model, mean a lower estimate of "harm" and hence a lower standard of care. The Learned Justice Nandrajog added: "The degree of care required to be taken depends on the surrounding circumstances of each case and varies proportionately with the risk to be encountered and the magnitude of the prospective injury." Here we find that "risk" is used to denote the probability of harm. We also note that this way of arriving at the standard of care conforms with the economic model.

The learned justice elaborated on the concept of negligence: "Further, a person may reasonably be expected to take extra care on account of better knowledge of the facts." He added:

> No doubt, a person is in general, entitled to assume that others will comply with statutory regulations but not that they will take reasonable care to look out for themselves or will take reasonable steps to avoid common risks when experience shows negligence to be common.

This position of the High Court becomes clearer in its reference to the case of *Upson* when it said that that decision

> applied the principle in relation to drivers of vehicles being aware of the fact that at controlled crossings pedestrians had a tendency to cross over even when the signal for the pedestrians is red in colour. It was held that in view of this fact of pedestrians being negligent being known to drivers an extra duty to be vigilant at controlled crossings was required to be maintained by the drivers keeping in knowledge negligent pedestrians.

He explicitly stated:

> A higher degree of care is required of those who know of or ought to foresee the presence of the disabled; the immature; the feeble minded or persons with a feeble body. Similarly, the duty of care owed to a child will be more strict so as to take into account the likelihood of the child being endangered by the act of the tortfeasor.

Regarding the assertion of the counsel for the appellants that since the hospital did not charge any fee it had no duty, the High Court held that: "Merely because the defendant is exercising a common calling akin to a charitable cause does not exclude the duty of reasonable care to be observed." In the present case, the High Court reasoned that the fact that the hospital authorities had accepted that they owed a duty of care to the patients can be inferred from the following:

> Referring to the facts of the instant case, the fact that an untoward incident may happen at the maternity ward and it being anticipated stands proved by testimony of D2/W1, Dr. N.K. Sinha, the Additional Medical Superintendent of the hospital who stated that security persons are deployed in each ward to regulate and check the entry and exit of the patients and their attendants. The denial in cross examination to the suggestion that people had unrestricted entry in the ward, evidences that those in charge of the hospital were aware that entry of unauthorized persons has to be prevented inside the hospital. The hospital authorities have thus accepted that they owed a duty of care to the patients and the newly born at the Maternity Ward, to protect their person and their belongings, having regard to the condition which were reasonably anticipated i.e. entry of unauthorized persons in the wards. Thus it was necessary, indeed it was the duty of the hospital authorities, to take effective measures to secure that the ward was watched and protected from unauthorized persons, prohibiting their entry within the precincts of the Maternity Ward.

The court held that the hospital authorities and the Government of NCT, Delhi, which had established the hospital, were jointly liable and absolved the Union of India of any liability on the ground that it neither established nor maintained the hospital.

We note that this case can be interpreted both ways – along the due care approach as well as the untaken precaution approach. It was clearly argued that what constitutes due care depends on the circumstances and that common negligence has to be factored in. The untaken precaution in this case was preventing the entry of unauthorized persons in the wards. Since it could be anticipated that they would enter despite the presence of guards, extra caution was required. Also, the hospital had not met the due standards of care.

3.3 Cases where the injurer is declared negligent by considerations which point towards use of both the approaches

Of the Indian cases, one case that predominantly uses the untaken precaution approach to determine the negligence of the injurer is *Vidya Devi and Another v Madhya Pradesh State Road Transport Corporation and Another*.[25] The accident occurred on July 24, 1968, in Jabalpur at the crossing of two roads, the Katni Road, which goes from the bus-stand to Katni, and Stadium Road, which is a side road going from Shahid Smarak to the stadium. A bus owned by the Madhya Pradesh State Road Transport Corporation and driven by Abdul Bashir came from the bus stand and was proceeding towards Katni when it collided with a motorcycle that came from the Shahid Smarak side, driven by Inderjeet Singh, who sustained a fractured skull that led to his death soon after. His widow, Vidya Devi, and infant son, Amarjeet Singh, claimed damages in negligence against the bus driver. The Motor Accident Claims Tribunal, Jabalpur, dismissed the claim on the ground that the plaintiffs failed to prove the negligence of the bus driver, and the facts and circumstances of the case indicate that the victim was solely responsible. The claimants appealed to the Madhya Pradesh High Court, which held that both the victim and the bus driver were negligent and apportioned the liability.

The bus driver claimed to have been travelling at a speed of 10 miles per hour when the motorcycle came from the Shahid Smarak side at an excessive speed and collided with the bus on its right hand side over the right front wheel. One of the witnesses, Nathulal, gave evidence that the bus was running at moderate speed and the motorcycle collided with the front head-light of the bus on the right hand side. Another witness, Suraj, stated that the motorcycle, after it came upon the intersection, turned towards the right and at that stage the impact occurred. The High Court did not accept this as correct, for it held that had it been as this witness described the bus would have hit the motorcycle from behind. The witnesses testified that the motorcycle collided with the bus on its right hand side over the right front wheel, and as a result of the impact the motorcycle was dragged on the road up to a distance of about 30 cubits; the deceased was found lying under it. None of the witnesses said that the motorcycle came under the wheels of the bus or that the bus hit it from behind. Both the witnesses said that the bus and the motorcycle had blown the horn while approaching the crossing. Although not designated as such, the Tribunal took Katni Road as a main road. Based on these facts, the Tribunal held the deceased to be solely responsible.

In the Madhya Pradesh High court, Justice G. P. Singh noted that the bus driver did not say in his evidence that he had kept a look-out for traffic coming from the side road, could not say at what point of time he first saw the motorcycle before the collision nor that it was not possible to see the motorcycle approaching the intersection even if he had kept a good look-out. The learned justice argued:

> Experience shows that sometimes vehicles suddenly come from a side road although it is not reasonable for their drivers to do so. Had the driver of the bus kept a proper look-out, it is quite possible that he would have seen the motorcycle coming from the side road and possibility of collision occurring would have been reasonably apparent to him and he could have stopped his bus in time to allow the motor-cycle to pass in front of him and the accident may have been averted.

He further noted that every driver of a motor vehicle is required by Section 78 of the Motor Vehicles Act to drive in conformity with the driving regulations contained in the Tenth Schedule to the Act. According to regulation 6:

The driver of a motor vehicle shall slow down when approaching a road intersection, a road junction or a road corner, and shall not enter any such intersection or junction until he has become aware that he may do so without endangering the safety of persons thereon.

On the basis of the evidence, the High Court found the bus driver negligent.

Regarding the negligence of the deceased, the High Court concluded that it was clear from the evidence "that the motor-cycle was coming not at a moderate speed and the deceased wanted to cross the intersection before the bus could cross it." It added: "the very fact that the motorcycle after the impact dragged on the road with the deceased for about 30 cubits shows that its speed was not moderate and the deceased was not able to control it." Moreover, the deceased was "coming from a side road and ought to have allowed the bus to pass which was proceeding on the main road." He, therefore, violated regulation 7 of the Motor Vehicles Act:

The driver of a motor vehicle shall on entering a road intersection, if the road is a main road designated as such, give way to the vehicles proceeding along that road, and in any case give way to all traffic approaching the intersection on his right hand.

Justice Singh concluded: "In our opinion, the deceased was negligent for his own safety and his negligence substantially contributed to the accident."

The Tribunal used the due care approach to hold the deceased solely responsible for the accident. From the reasoning of the High Court we can infer that it also used the due care approach in holding the deceased negligent – he was driving at excessive speed and did not adhere to regulations. In the determination of negligence of the bus driver, the High Court relied heavily on the untaken precaution approach. Reference was made to various British judgments, in particular the principle emphasized by the House of Lords in *London Passenger Transport Board v Upson*,[26] that a reasonably careful driver does not always assume that other users of the road, whether drivers or others, will behave with reasonable care, and the driver guards against the negligence of others when experience shows such negligence to be common. The reasoning points to the reliance on the due care approach as well because he violated traffic regulations in not looking out for traffic from the side road while approaching a crossing. Justice Singh also cites Charlesworth's *Negligence* [5th Edition, p. 495] to note that to keep a good look-out for other traffic, especially at a road crossing, is a duty of the driver of a vehicle.[27]

One important case in this category is *The Municipal Corporation of Greater Bombay v Shri Laxman Iyer and Another.*[28] It concerned a collision that occurred on August 15, 1989, between a bus belonging to the Corporation and a bicycle that Kumar, an 18-year old boy, was riding. His parents, the claimants, alleged that the severity with which the bus dashed against the bicycle was so great that he was thrown some distance and he sustained various injuries that resulted in his death. The Motor Accident Claims Tribunal for Greater Bombay held the driver negligent and solely responsible and awarded damages. The corporation appealed to the Bombay High Court, which affirmed the verdict of the Tribunal. It then appealed to the Supreme Court which held that although the driver was substantially to blame, the deceased was negligent too.

Regarding the evidence, the corporation initially claimed that the deceased had suddenly come from the left side of the bus from Chembur Railway Station at a very high speed and instead of taking the left turn, took a right turn in contravention of traffic regulations. When the bus driver saw the cyclist coming from the wrong side he immediately applied the brakes and halted the bus. Despite this the cyclist was unable to control the cycle and dashed against the bus from the right corner of the bus, and as a result he fell down. However, as the case progressed the Tribunal noted a significant change in the stand taken by the corporation. On being examined, the driver stated that he was driving the vehicle at a very slow speed and stopped the vehicle when he saw the bicycle at a distance of 30 feet. The cyclist dashed against the front of the bus. After examining the evidence, the High Court noted that "there was ample scope for avoiding the collision between the cycle and the bus." Both the Tribunal and the High Court rejected the stand of the Corporation that the bus had come to a halt prior to the incident because had that been the case, the bicycle would not have been thrown to a distance of four to five feet. Both the Tribunal and the High Court, therefore, held the driver solely responsible for the accident.

The corporation appealed to the Supreme Court on the grounds that the High Court verdict regarding negligence was erroneous because the accident occurred more on account of the negligence of the victim. Justice Arijit Pasayat questioned the evidence:

> Even according to the stand of the Corporation, the victim was seen by the driver from a distance of about 30 ft and the vehicle was moving at a snail's pace. If that be so, it is not understood as to how it became totally impossible for the driver to avoid the accident has not been substantiated by proper evidence.

The learned justice noted that the horn was not blown by the driver. Also, the application of the brakes and the collision was almost simultaneous. The Supreme Court, therefore, held that the bus driver was substantially responsible for the accident. Regarding the negligence of the victim, it noted that the victim did act in contravention of traffic regulations. The apex Court noted:

> Where an accident is due to negligence of both parties, substantially there would be contributory negligence and both would be blamed. In a case of contributory negligence, *the crucial question on which liability depends would be whether either party could, by exercise of reasonable care, have avoided the consequence of other's negligence. Whichever party could have avoided the consequence of other's negligence would be liable for the accident.* (emphasis added)

The Court argued that in the circumstances of the present case, the liability must be apportioned, and they fixed the share of the corporation as three-quarters and that of the deceased as one-quarter.

We find that the Tribunal and the High Court used the due care approach to arrive at the negligent verdict for the defendant. Since the stand of the corporation changed, the inference about the speed and application of brakes was made on the basis of the facts that the impact of the collision was so great that the deceased was thrown to a distance of four to five feet. That could not have happened had the bus driver been driving slowly as claimed and had stopped *prior* to the collision. The reasoning of the Supreme Court points towards use of the untaken precaution approach for the determination of the driver's negligence, as he should have taken greater care in view of the victim's negligence. He may or may not have been negligent by the due care approach. The victim was negligent by the due care approach. We can say that he was negligent by the untaken precaution approach by inference because in this case the cares of the two parties are substitutes.

Another case in which the reasoning clearly points towards the untaken precaution approach is *Sundara Shetty v K. Sanjeeva Rao (Deceased by L. Rs.) and Others*.[29] On January 27, 1967, an accident occurred in which Gunapala Shetty, a boy aged nine years was going to school after the mid-day recess with his brother, Dhanapala Shetty, when he was hit by a car from behind. As a result of the injuries sustained during the accident, the boy lost strength in his left hand and left leg, lost his memory, was unable to speak and became a cripple for life. The claimant, the victim's father Sundara Shetty, alleged that the accident occurred because the car was driven in a rash and negligent manner and filed a petition before the Motor Accidents Claims Tribunal, South Kanara, Mangalore, for compensation. The defendants K. Sanjeeva Rao (who subsequently died) and the driver, K. Santharama, denied that the accident was due to the rash and negligent driving but was entirely due to the negligent conduct of the boy himself. The Tribunal held that the claimants failed to prove that the driver was negligent and dismissed the claim. The claimants then appealed to the Karnataka High Court, which allowed the appeal.

At the time of the accident, K. Santharama Rao was going from his cloth shop situated in the heart of the town to his house, which was at a distance of two furlongs[30] from the shop, for his mid-day meal. The car in which he was travelling belonged to the partnership firm M/s K. Sanjeeva Rao, and the regular driver of the car was also present in the car at the time of the accident. The road on which the car was being driven was ascending for half a furlong or so. The accident happened on the ascent near the house of K. Santharama Rao. According to the defendants, a black cow charged at the boys who were walking on the right side of the road. A frightened Gunapala Shetty ran towards the left side of the road and dashed against the car, which was going on the correct side, slowly and carefully. The then member of the Tribunal, Shri K. Channabasappa, held that the claimants failed to prove that the driver was rash and negligent and dismissed the petition. The claimants then appealed to the Karnataka High Court in Miscellaneous First Appeal, and the court ordered a fresh trial with a direction that both parties should be given the opportunity to furnish additional evidence. When the earlier judgment was reiterated and the petition for compensation dismissed even after the remand, the claimants appealed to the Karnataka High Court under the Motor Vehicles Act, 1939.

The High Court considered the crucial question: "Whether it is the car that dashed against the boy or it is the boy that dashed against the car?" In that context, the testimony of the driver was examined. He had stated that at the time of the accident he was driving slowly at about five km/hr on the left side of the road. When the car was about ten to 15 feet from the house, he saw two children proceeding towards the school on his right hand side. A cow was about five to six feet away and was charging at them. He further elicited that "the children were moving hither and thither on the road." Then suddenly one of the boys ran towards his left towards the car. Although he applied the brakes about one to two feet from the place of the impact, the boy dashed against the front grill of the car and fell down. He denied that on the spur of the moment he had pressed the accelerator instead of pressing the brakes as one of the witnesses, Bhaskara Bhandary, gave evidence that the regular driver of the car had told him that. The court argued that had the regular driver been examined as a witness, he would have refuted the denial of K. Santharama. Moreover, the mahzar, marked Exhibit P-2, clearly indicated that the car went about ten feet before it halted. The driver had denied this too. From these the court concluded that although the car was being driven at a slow speed before, when he pushed the accelerator the car spurted forward and hit the boy.

The High Court held that the reasoning of the Tribunal, that because the speed was low the driver could not be held negligent, was incorrect. It was argued that speed was a relative term. The observation of Justice Venkatarama Iyer who delivered the judgment of the Madras High Court in the case of *Gobald Motor Service Ltd. v Veeraswami Chettiar*[31]:

> A speed that would be reasonable on the fine concrete road would not be expected on a road which is full of ruts and under a state of repair. What might be regarded as a safe speed in an uninhabited area might become dangerous in a congested area. The speed which might be harmless during restful hours of the night might be reckless during business hours of the day. Whether in a given case the speed was excessive or not must be determined on a consideration of all the circumstances.

Further, Lord Du Parcq's observation in *London Passenger Transport Board v Upson* was quoted: "no speed is reasonable which is not adjusted to the circumstances of the moment, including the fact that the driver is approaching a pedestrian crossing and may pull up quickly and within a very short distance." In the present case, since the driver was approaching a school zone he should have been prepared to pull up within a second's notice. Moreover, when he actually saw the boys moving hither and thither, it was "his duty to so adjust his speed as to be able to stop his vehicle within a moment's time in case of exigency." The court stated: "He has further admitted that he saw a cow coming to charge them and further expected that the cow was about to butt them. In the circumstances, the prudent course for the driver of the car was to pull up the car at once." The High Court, therefore, concluded:

> That being so, without more, it becomes clear the accident is the result of the rash and negligent driving of the car in question by its driver, especially so having regard to the great responsibility cast on the driver of the car while passing through the school zone in the circumstances in which Santharama Rao was driving the car.

The Court further held: "It is well established that it is not enough for the driver to try to be careful in driving. He should further anticipate common folly of others which he knows, by experience, would generally occur." Lord Uthwatt's observation from *London Passenger Transport Board v Upson* was quoted: "A driver is not, of course, bound to anticipate folly in all its forms, but he is not, in my opinion, entitled to put out of consideration the teachings of experience as to the form those follies commonly take." They also quoted from Clerk and Lindsell on torts[32]:

> There has also been a tendency in recent years to stress the fact that a reasonable man will not assume that other people will always act carefully and will therefore be prepared for lapses and unreasonable acts on the part of others.

Based on this reasoning the Court concluded: "The facts of the present case demanded greater care on the part of the driver of the car because children of tender years cannot even be imputed with contributory negligence."

From the reasoning of the High Court, it is clear that they adopted both the approaches to reach this negligence verdict. The case that had been dismissed by the Tribunal for lack of evidence and failure to prove negligence on the part of the claimants took a different turn in the High Court. The testimony of the driver, K. Santharama, formed the basis of a finding of negligence. The court used the standard of individualized care, on the argument that what is rash varies with circumstances. In this case, since he was driving through a school zone, had seen the cow charging at the boys and the frightened boys moving around here and there, he should have stopped the car immediately. In the given situation, driving at even five km/hr, was rash and negligent. That the Court was using the untaken precaution approach as well to arrive at the higher standard is clear because it explicitly stated that it is not enough to drive carefully; one must also anticipate the folly of others, in this case the children. The untaken precaution identified by the Court was "to pull up the car at once."

Another case in this category that involved multiple tortfeasors is *Sushma Mitra v Madhya Pradesh State Road Transport Corporation*.[33] The plaintiff was travelling from Jabalpur to Chhindwara on a bus owned by the Madhya Pradesh State Road Transport Corporation, when around seven km from Jabalpur on the Jabalpur-Nagpur highway, a truck coming from the opposite direction crossed the bus in such a way that her right elbow was severely injured. The plaintiff alleged that as a result of the injuries she has suffered a permanent disability of the right hand and claimed damages on the grounds that it was the negligence of the two drivers of the vehicles involved that caused her injuries. The trial court held that it was the plaintiff herself who was at fault and dismissed her claim. She appealed to the Madhya Pradesh High Court, which held the two drivers as negligent and exonerated her of any fault.

The trial court's argument was that since there was no evidence of a head-on collision as alleged by the plaintiff or any physical contact between the two vehicles, it was because the plaintiff's elbow was protruding from the bus the accident occurred. She alone was responsible for her injuries and therefore, not entitled to any damages. The Madhya Pradesh High Court reexamined the evidence and found that the plaintiff was unable to give the exact course of events because she fell unconscious because of the injury. Relying on whatever little evidence was given by the bus driver, Moolchand, the High Court found that the truck was visible from a distance of a furlong and at the time of the accident both vehicles were running at a speed of 25 to 30 miles/hr. From the testimony of the conductor, Tahil Ali and the plaintiff, the High Court found that she was sitting in the fourth row near the window with her right elbow protruding out. She suffered injuries when the truck brushed against her hand but did not come into contact with any part of the bus. The High Court held that despite the fact that the plaintiff's elbow was protruding from the window, "the drivers of the bus and the truck must be held to be guilty of negligence."

The reasoning of the High Court was as follows. Both Justice G. P. Singh and Justice Raina argued that the common habit of passengers to rest their elbows on the windows of vehicles in which they are travelling must be taken into account by drivers. Justice Singh held:

> It is a matter of common experience that passengers who sit adjoining a window very often rest their arm on the window sill by which act the elbow projects outside the window. The driver of the bus must have these passengers also in contemplation and, therefore, while overtaking or crossing another vehicle on the road he must not come too close to the vehicle that is overtaken or crossed and he must leave sufficient gap between the vehicles to avoid injury to these passengers.

He went on:

> The driver of a vehicle coming from the opposite direction owes a similar duty while crossing a passenger bus. He too must have in contemplation passengers sitting near the windows of the oncoming bus who may have their hands resting on the windows. And in crossing the bus he must not only avoid contact with the body of the bus but he must also avoid coming in contact with the elbow of any passenger that may be resting on the window and

projecting outside the body of the bus. He must therefore, take precautions to move to his near side and leave sufficient gap for preventing any mishap.

He argued that even if resting one's elbow on the bus window was a foolish or negligent thing to do, "it must enter into the contemplation of a reasonable driver for the foresight of a reasonable man on the basis of which cases of negligence have to be solved, takes into account also common negligence of human behavior." He quoted the oft-cited judgment of *Upson* in this regard.

Justice Raina further elaborated this aspect by emphasizing the need to take greater care given that this was a common practice among passengers travelling on the highway. Even in crowded places, this is a common feature. He argued:

> In streets of big towns it is a common experience to find rickshaws tongas loaded with children whose various limbs protrude outside the vehicle. The driver of a vehicle cannot therefore be absolved from negligence merely on the ground that he passed his vehicle in such a manner that its body did not come into contact with the body of another vehicle carrying passengers on the road.

Regarding the duty question, he specifically held:

> While driving or passing a vehicle carrying passengers it is the duty of the drivers to pass on the road at reasonable distance from other vehicle so as to avoid any injury to the passengers whose limbs might be protruding beyond the body of the vehicle in the ordinary course.

He conceded that in extremely crowded places vehicles may have to cross or overtake each other at close quarters, but if this is done slowly and after adequate warning by blowing the horn then there would be no negligence if someone is hurt despite all the efforts. Justice Raina further added that it is a well-known rule of the road that when two vehicles are approaching each other from opposite directions, each must keep to left for the purpose of allowing the other to pass. He stated: "Failure to observe this is prima facie evidence of negligence."

Regarding the question of the victim's negligence, the defendants' case was that in resting her arm on the window sill the plaintiff failed to take reasonable care of her safety, and this was a contributory factor to the accident. Justice Singh argued that this was a common practice and since the vehicles were on roads outside a town, traffic was not heavy and there was enough space to pass without coming too close to cause these kinds of injuries. There was no evidence of a horn being blown and the plaintiff disregarding the warning. In fact, the vehicles were moving at such high speeds that they must have crossed each other in a split second, leaving no time for the plaintiff to withdraw her hand. He concluded:

> In these circumstances, I do not think that the plaintiff can be said to have failed to take reasonable care of her safety in resting her arm on the window

of the bus. After all 'a reasonable man does not mean a paragon of circumspection' and if most of the passengers behave in the manner the plaintiff did it would not be right to hold that a reasonable man would have behaved in a different manner.

Justice Raina while examining the issue quoted from Halsbury's Laws of England[34]:

> A person is guilty of contributory negligence if he ought reasonably to have foreseen, if he did not act as a reasonably prudent man, he might hurt himself. The plaintiff is not usually bound to foresee that another person may be negligent unless experience shows a particular form of negligence to be common in the circumstances. If negligence on the part of the defendant is proved and contributory negligence by the plaintiff is at best a matter of doubt, the defendant alone is liable.

He concluded:

> Passengers travelling in motor vehicles in crowded areas no doubt owe a responsibility to keep their limbs within the motor vehicles but on long journeys it would be too much to expect a passenger not to allow any part of his body to protrude at all beyond the body of the vehicle. Resting of elbow on the window sill, as stated previously, is extremely common even for passengers of reasonable prudence and therefore, the plaintiff cannot be held guilty of contributory negligence.

The reasoning seems to be that expected harm would be higher in crowded places and care required would also be higher compared to the roads taken during long journeys.

We note that in this case the exact circumstances of the accident could not be ascertained because the drivers did not give evidence to that effect. The conductor was busy issuing tickets and the plaintiff fell unconscious at the time of the accident. In view of this, the High Court, relying on various authorities on the issue, held that adverse inference may be drawn. One point of contention could be whether the road was narrow or broad enough at the point where the two vehicles crossed each other. While the conductor of the bus stated that the metalled portion of the road was only 12 feet, which meant that the two vehicles could not cross each other without leaving the road sufficiently by moving onto the Kutcha portion, Justice Singh argued that "the road was wide enough for the two vehicles to cross leaving a reasonable gap to avoid any accident even though the vehicles were moving at a speed of twenty-five or thirty miles." Regarding the determination of negligence, we find that the trial court used the due care approach to hold the victim guilty of negligence and took this as a complete defense so that the victim could not recover anything. The due care was also set very high. However, the High Court can be said to have used the due care approach to hold the drivers negligent and the victim nonnegligent. This is because the individualized standard was set lower for the victim, and for drivers it would be higher because the bus was proceeding on a highway. From the reasoning given in the course of the litigation, we can also arrive at the following interpretation: that the victim could be held negligent by the due care approach for having failed to take care of her own safety and the drivers could be held negligent by the untaken precaution approach based on the common knowledge that passengers usually keep their arms protruding from windows on long journeys.

Since both the parties are negligent, the situation is symmetric. We can say that the victim could be held negligent by the untaken precaution approach on the grounds that roads in India are not always of the same width at all places, and vehicles often move at very high speed on highways even if they are not supposed to do so according to regulations. The victim ought to have kept the common negligence of motor drivers in mind and kept her hand inside the bus. This certainly would not be expecting too much of her.

Another similar action for personal injuries in which the untaken precaution approach was clearly used was the oft-cited case of *Ishwardas Paulsrao Ingle v General Manager, Maharashtra State Road Transport Corporation, Bombay and Others*.[35] The accident occurred on May 21, 1979, when Ishwardas, then a student of standard XII, was travelling with his two sisters on a bus belonging to Maharashtra State Road Transport Corporation plying on the route from Buldana to Solapur. There were three stops en route – Mera, Deulgaon-Raja and Bhivgaon – and the trio had boarded the bus at the Mera stop. When it reached the Bhivgaon stop, the bus brushed against a stationary bus, as a result of which Ishwardas's right hand got crushed and it was left hanging by the skin only. He filed a petition with the Motor Accident Claims Tribunal, Buldana, for damages alleging that the accident occurred due to the negligence of the bus driver, Shaikh Matin. The corporation denied that the driver was driving in a grossly negligent manner and argued that it was the negligence of the plaintiff that caused his injuries. The Tribunal, after evaluating the oral and documentary evidence, dismissed the petition. The plaintiff then appealed to the Bombay High Court, and its Aurangabad Bench pronounced the verdict that the driver of the bus was negligent and no contributory negligence could be attributed to the victim.

The evidence given by the two rival parties was conflicting. Both parties said that the accident occurred at the Bhivgaon stop when the bus dashed against a bus plying on the route from Jalna to Jafrabad, which was at the time stationary. However, while the plaintiff's side alleged that the bus was driven at a high speed and the horn was not blown, the driver stated that on seeing the stationary bus in the opposite direction he had changed the gear to third gear, his speed was about 25 to 30 km/hr and he was blowing the horn. Further, the conductor, Ashok Tambat, said that in the previous stop he had warned the victim to keep his arm inside the bus when he saw that he was sleeping by resting his head on his hand. Refuting this, his sister Sushila said when their bus dashed against the stationary bus the passengers got a jerk and were thrown up from their seats and the right hand of Ishwardas was thrown out of the window. The bus driver said that there were some people, including children, sitting under a banyan tree to the left of the bus. When the bus had crossed part of the stationary bus, he saw a boy of about eight to ten years of age crossing from left to right. In order to save the boy, the bus swerved to the right side, applied the brakes and stopped. A co-passenger testified that the victim had kept his hand outside the window, that the bus was not being driven at a high speed and that the driver had blown the horn. The Tribunal found that the account of the accident given to the police by the victim and that given before the Tribunal were contradictory and could not be considered trustworthy. Therefore, based on the defendant's evidence that the plaintiff was travelling with his elbow outside the window, the Tribunal held him negligent and absolved the defendants of liability.

The Bombay High Court held that this verdict was erroneous and the trial court had made "a mountain out of a mole hill" in relying on the contradictions in the two statements as the basis of its judgment. Justice W. U. Wahane argued that a young boy who has had to have his right hand amputated would be under mental stress and deserves immunity. In fact, after scrutinizing the evidence he held that the driver did not leave sufficient space while crossing the stationary bus. Since he had already crossed three-quarters of the bus, there would have been no dash if enough space had been left. The High Court held:

> Because of the abrupt turn to the right side, the bus dashed with the stationary bus. Even then the driver did not stop the bus and swerved the same to his right side and thus crossed completely the stationary bus. In fact, such course could have definitely been avoided if the bus would not have been in speed and within the reach of the driver's control. We are aware that man may lie but not the circumstances. Thus, the circumstances clearly demonstrate that the evidence of the driver, conductor and alleged co-passenger is not trustworthy as they want to save Sk. Matin.

Further, the High Court held that the trial court's verdict, which was based on the defendants' allegation that the victim was resting his elbow on the window sill, is incorrect because it is "a usual phenomenon" and "there is no prohibition against this." It is seen at crowded places and on highways. It was the driver's duty to take all steps that a person of ordinary prudence would take to ensure the safety of the passengers. The learned justice held: "The driver of the bus in question cannot be said to be unaware of the fact that the passengers were in the habit of putting their hands outside the bus." Therefore, the fact that he did not leave sufficient space in between the two vehicles is enough to prove that he was negligent. Moreover, based on this reasoning the learned justice concluded that the plaintiff cannot be said to be negligent at all merely because he rested his elbow on the window. The learned justice cited various cases in which the facts were similar and where the same conclusion was reached using similar reasoning. One of these, the case of *Sushma Mitra*, has been discussed earlier.

We find that the Tribunal had used the due care approach to hold the victim negligent and placed the entire responsibility of the accident on him. The High

Court held the driver negligent by both approaches. From the evidence placed and the circumstances of the accident the High Court argued that the plaintiff was able to prove that the "bus was in speed, the driver had not blown the horn, not stopped the bus or reduced the speed after sighting the stationary bus at the bus stand." Also, the driver should have left sufficient space because it was likely that passengers' arms may be injured. The defendants' claim that the driver had swerved to the right to save the boy who had come in the way was an attempt to show that the precaution of swerving was cost-justified given that the expected harm to the boy was greater than the harm to the passengers that could occur if there was a sudden jerk. The Tribunal had accepted it. The High Court factored in the expected harm to the passengers who were likely to keep their arms outside the bus. It reasoned that the precaution that should have been taken in the circumstances, even if one were to believe that the boy came in front of the bus (which, on cross-examination, the driver denied to have told anybody), was applying the brakes and stopping the bus. Since the speed was high, the driver could not control the bus and swerved to the right and caused the accident. It can be argued that since it was a bus stand, the driver should have anticipated that there would be people walking around, and he should have driven slowly. As far as the plaintiff was concerned, the High Court argued that he was doing something that was not barred by law. So he was nonnegligent by the due care approach.

The case of *Union of India v United India Insurance Company Limited and Others*[36] dealt with a batch of cases arising out of an accident at a railway crossing in Kerala, and in these the negligence determination was undertaken using mainly the due care approach. The accident occurred on May 5, 1979, at an unmanned level – crossing at Akaparamba (near Kalady) in Kerala when a hired passenger bus was hit by the Jayanthi Janatha Express at about 3.00 p.m. and 41 passengers and the driver were killed, while some other passengers sustained injuries. The dependents of the deceased and injured persons filed petitions with the Motor Accident Claims Tribunal, Ernakulam. In one batch of cases, the Tribunal by a judgment dated February 2, 1986, held the driver of the bus negligent and passed awards against the owner of the bus and the insurance company but dismissed the claim against the railways on the grounds that there was no negligence on the part of the driver of the railway engine concerned or the railway administration. The insurance company appealed against the award and objections were preferred by the claimants. The appeals and cross-objections were partly allowed by the High Court, making the railway administration also liable on account of its negligence in regard to the accident. In both of these, it was held that an award could be passed against the railways, which was accepted by the High Court. The Union of India appealed to the Supreme Court of India against all these judgments.

The motor vehicle in question was owned by K. Arunamugham of Arni, Tamil Nadu, who was hired by employees of the Survey and Land Records Department of Tamil Nadu for a trip to Trivandrum, Cochin, Kalady, Guruvayoor, etc. in Kerala. On May 7, 1979, the bus started at Trivandrum for Cochin. Since there was some delay on the way, the passengers were finding fault with the driver and this angered him so that he threatened to abandon the bus and leave the passengers in a forest. By noon, the bus reached Cochin and proceeded to Kalady via Angamally. The bus was to cross an unmanned level-crossing at Akaparamba at about 3.00 p.m. The railway-crossing had no gates or stiles and even the "caution board" was moth-eaten and the writings thereon could not be deciphered by anyone, even if one was inclined to read. The train was visible to the driver and the passengers at a distance of one km. The driver drove the vehicle and was crossing the railway line when the vehicle stopped on the track and did not move. Despite the cries of panic by the passengers, the bus did not move and the train struck it, and in the impact the bus was moved 500 metres. The train was running at a speed of 75 km per hour, which would mean that it would have taken about 40–50 seconds to reach the level crossing.

Regarding the negligence of the engine driver it was argued by the Supreme Court that there was no evidence of his negligence. The argument was:

> In fact, if he had applied the brakes when he saw the bus about 100 ft. away while the train was running at a speed of 75 km. per hour, there would have been a derailment of several compartments of the train itself.

We can infer that the untaken precaution of "stopping the train" was not cost-justified because had the train stopped it would have been at a greater cost – that of derailment of several of its compartments.

As far as the obligations of a driver and conductor of a motor vehicle are concerned, Clause (f) of Rule 100 of the rules made by the Government under the Motor Vehicles Act, 1939, was referred to, where it was stated that the conductor of a stage carriage while on duty shall:

> while crossing an unmanned railway level-crossing with his vehicle, require the driver to stop the vehicle on the road at the place notified for such stoppage by appropriate signboard as set out in the Third Schedule to these Rules and on stopping, shall get down and after making sure that no train is approaching the level crossing from either side, walk ahead of the vehicle until it has safely crossed the level-crossing.

From this, the Supreme Court inferred that the rule postulates the existence of a signboard, requiring the conductor to "get down." However, since the signboard was moth-eaten and no writing was visible, it was held by the Supreme Court: "Hence in our view no special obligations created by the rule, which were in addition to the common law requirements can be said to apply." We can say that the Court did not think that the due care level would be higher, requiring the conductor to "get down" from the bus. Thus, there was only a common law duty as applicable to a prudent person – to "stop," "see and hear" and find out if any train was coming.[37] The Court distinguished the care requirement on the part of a driver of a motor vehicle in case of an unmanned level crossing and one which had a gateman.

In the former, the driver was required to "stop the vehicle, look both ways to see if a train is approaching and thereafter only drive his vehicle after satisfying himself that there was no danger in crossing the railway track." However, where a level crossing is protected by a gateman, "it will be too much to expect of any reasonable and prudent driver to stop his vehicle and look out for any approaching train." The standard of care required of a driver of a motor vehicle would be lower at level crossings that are manned. In the present case, the Supreme Court held the driver negligent for failing to stop the vehicle at the unmanned crossing. The Supreme Court, thus, affirmed the finding of negligence of the Tribunal and the High Court.

Regarding the negligence of the railways, the Supreme Court referred to Section 13 of the Railways Act, 1890,[38] and argued that the provision does not cast a direct obligation on the railway administration unless a requisition is made by the Central Government. The courts, have, therefore, often relied on the common law duties contending that

> the Railways, as an occupier of the level-crossing for the purpose of running railway trains which are inherently dangerous to those who use the public road at that point, has special responsibilities as a responsible body to see that accidents are kept at a minimum.

The Court further argued:

> The test of breach at common law is again the test of a reasonable or prudent person in the particular fact situation – of course the amount of care, skill, diligence or the like, varying according to the circumstances of the particular case. The standard of foresight is again that of a reasonable person. Such a person is also expected to take into account common negligence in human behaviour.

In the present case, the Supreme Court affirmed the High Court's finding that "applying common law principles, the railways must also be deemed to be negligent in not converting the unmanned level-crossing into a manned one with gates – having regard to the volume of rail and road traffic at this point." The High Court had noted that

> 300 vehicles pass through this point and six express trains cut across this public road everyday (obviously there must be other non-express or passenger and goods trains every day). The population is dense in Kerala and more so near Kalady, the pilgrimage centre connected with Shri Jagadguru Adi Shankaracharya.

In economic terms, this is translatable as saying that the burden of precautions should be commensurate with the expected harm. The larger the expected harm, given the actual circumstances, the greater the precautions that are required. To determine what precautions would have been appropriate it referred to the English case of *Llyods Bank Limited and Another v Railway Executive*,[39] in which the Court of Appeal held that even when the road traffic reached a level of 75 to 100 vehicles, the Railways ought to have, if it was a public road, put up gates and a watchman, as required by statute.

The Supreme Court endorsed the view of the High Court that "absence of gates and caution board" constituted the untaken precaution that was cost-justified in the circumstances and would have averted such a "severe accident." It was observed that

> the bus driver was from Tamil Nadu, he was not familiar with this place in Kerala state where the accident occurred, there was no caution board or other indication to show that the road was cutting across a railway line, and there were no gates or handrails to alert the passer-by.

The next question that arose was whether the omission on the part of the Central Government to take a decision whether or not to exercise powers under Section 13 of the Railways Act, 1890 – in particular under clauses (c) and (d) of Section 13 – amounted to a breach of a statutory duty, giving rise to a cause of action for damages based on negligence. The Supreme Court put it as whether one could derive a common law "ought" from a statutory "may." It went on to add:

> it does not always follow that the law should superimpose a common law duty of care upon a discretionary statutory power. Apart from exceptions relating to individual or societal reliance an exercise of statutory power – it is not reasonable to expect a service to be provided at public expense and also a duty to compensate for loss occasioned by failure to provide the service. An absolute rule to provide compensation would increase the burden on public funds.

The apex Court quoted Halsbury's Laws of England[40] regarding the general expectation of the community so far as the railways are concerned: that a plaintiff

> is entitled to rely on reasonable care and proper precautions being taken and, in places to which the public has access, he is entitled to assume the existence of such protection as the public has, through custom, become justified in expecting.

It referred to the English case of *Stovin v Wise*[41] and the Australian case of *Sutherland Shire Council v Heyman*[42] to draw the conclusion that not only did the "general expectation of the community" condition hold in the present case but also one could conclude that

> a policy to pay compensation could be inferred if the power was intended to protect members of the public, from risks against which they could not guard themselves i.e. having regard to the expense involved or the highly technical

nature of safeguards needed to be taken or because the safeguards have to be taken in the premises of the public authority.

We find that the condition of "general reliance" that was being employed can be interpreted as follows: There are situations where the expected harm is great but the precautions required to prevent such harm, although cost-justified, are such that the public cannot afford to take them. Since these "inherently perilous" situations are created by public authority, cause of action in negligence arises. The Supreme Court quoted from *Stovin v Wise* a crucial aspect of law:

> Reliance or dependence in this case is in general the product of the grant (and exercise) of power designed to prevent or minimize a risk of personal injury or disability recognized by the legislature as being of such magnitude or complexity that individuals cannot, or may not, take adequate steps for their protection. This situation generates on one side (the individual) a general expectation that the power will be exercised and on the other side (the authority) a realization that there is a general reliance or dependence on its power to act.... The control of air traffic, the safety inspection of aircraft and the fighting of a fire in a building by a fire authority may well be examples of this type of function.

In the case of railways, it was emphasized by the Supreme Court that the running of trains has been recognized as inherently dangerous and "certainly creates in the minds of the public a general expectation that safety measures – which the public cannot otherwise afford, have been taken by the railway administration." On the basis of this reasoning, the Supreme Court concluded that

> the non-exercise of public law or statutory powers under section 13 (c) and (d) did create a private law cause of action for damages for breach of statutory duty. The case falls within the exception where a statutory 'may' gives rise to a common law 'ought.'

Thus, we find that the Supreme Court adopted both the approaches in the determination of the negligence of the railways because it identified the untaken precaution of "absence of caution board and gates" to be cost-justified in the circumstances and also after "taking account the common negligence of others." As far as the engine driver was concerned, the due care approach was used to determine the negligence question. He could not have averted the accident, except by stopping the train, but it was found that stopping the train was not cost-justified. As far as the Central Government was concerned, the court relied on custom to hold them negligent under common law.

Another case in which both the approaches to negligence determination were used was that of *State v Bhalchandra Waman Pethe*.[43] In that case two sisters were knocked down by a motor car when they were on the pedestrian crossing on the road near Churchgate in Bombay. One of the sisters, Kunda, aged about 20 years, died as a result of the injuries suffered in the accident, and the other one, Vidya, aged about ten, was injured. The incident occurred on February 15, 1964, when the accused was driving his car on the Marine drive, later known as Netaji Subhash Road, from north to south. The trial court held the driver negligent and sentenced him to six months and two months imprisonment in each of the counts and imposed a fine of Rs.2000 and Rs.200, respectively. It was felt that the sentence was inadequate and the case was directed to be placed before the Bombay High Court. The High Court held that the accused was guilty of negligent and rash behavior and imposed six months of simple imprisonment in addition to the punishment deemed fit by the learned trial magistrate.

The evidence placed before the Court was as follows: There was a pedestrian crossing situated at the junction of "B" Road and Netaji Subhash Road. There was a bus stop at the northern side of "B" Road corner, and Natraj Hotel was at the southern corner of that road. The pedestrian crossing was indicated by two broken transverse lines opposite the bus stop and two transverse broken lines opposite the Natraj Hotel on the southern side, and boards were placed on both sides with "Pedestrian Crossing" written on it. Vidya testified that they had gone to the University Club House, situated at "B" Road to attend some function. Since they were a bit early, they decided to take a stroll along the sea wall. They were crossing the road between the northern side of the transverse lines, indicating the pedestrian crossing when the accused, driving at a very high speed, knocked them down. She did not recall the sound of a horn. On cross examination, she said that before stepping on to the crossing, they looked and saw that there were no vehicles in the vicinity but only one car at a long distance away from them approaching them from the right side, but she could not tell its position on the road. She denied that on seeing the car they ran and dashed against the car. Kunda had given a statement on the day after the accident in which she said that they were crossing the road from east to west in front of Natraj Hotel, and she did not remember whether she was crossing through the pedestrian crossing.

One eye-witness, Rupsingh (considered by the court as an independent witness), was examined 17 days after the incident, and he said that just before the incident he had come out of the "C" Road on the Netaji Subhash Road and was on the left side of the third row. According to him the accused was driving at about 40 miles per hour, he had heard the sound of brakes being applied and saw the accused knocking down the two girls and then halting about five to seven feet from the hedge. Rupsingh did not stop his car because he had to go to the Congress House. The accused had said that he was driving at 20 to 25 miles per hour and that the girls were running in front of the car. The learned trial court magistrate estimated that the speed at which the accused was driving was 48 miles per hour and held him negligent, but he added that the sisters also contributed to the accident.

In the Bombay High Court, Justice Patel dealt with all the arguments placed by Mr Jethmalani challenging the conviction. First, the objection to considering Rupsingh as an independent witness was dismissed on the grounds that the delay in examining him was due to the general apathy of people to get involved in criminal cases. Second, the contention that an attempt has been made to shift the point of impact because Kunda had said that she did not remember whether she was crossing through the pedestrian crossing was held to be misplaced because the marks of the brakes, broken glass of lamps and the testimony of a police officer who went to the scene all went to show that the "two girls were knocked down only within the northern set of lines" on the pedestrian crossing. Third, the Supreme Court rejected the contention that Rupsingh may not have been able to give a proper estimate of the speed at which the accused was driving his car. It took account of Mr Jethmalani's view that the speed of 48 miles per hour as put by the learned trial magistrate was too high and conceded that it could be less – around 35 miles per hour.

Regarding the question of rash and negligent driving, the apex Court distinguished between rashness and negligence as follows:

> When one does an act with utter indifference to the consequences of which the doer may be conscious and which he hopes may not take place, one is said to be rash, while criminal negligence is neglect to take that precaution which a reasonable and prudent person is expected to take under the circumstances obtaining in a given case.

Justice Patel referred to the regulations framed by the Commissioner of Police under the Bombay Police Act, which define respective duties of the pedestrian and the driver of a car at these crossings.[44] It explicitly states:

> 4. (B) (i) No driver of a vehicle shall have precedence over a pedestrian who is actually on the carriageway at such crossing ... (v) No pedestrian shall cross any street except at the demarcated pedestrian crossings where there exist.

Justice Patel held that in law,

> a clear duty is imposed on the driver of a motor vehicle to allow the pedestrian to cross the road. Having regard to clause (v) of the Regulations which imposes a restriction on the pedestrian, the least that one can say is that the driver of a vehicle approaching a pedestrian crossing must keep a look-out to see if any pedestrian is trying to cross the road at that point. Even if one assumes that these rules may not be known to all motor drivers, which they are bound to know, even so an ordinarily prudent man would approach a pedestrian crossing in such a way that he should be able to stop the car when it reached it if necessary. In other words he would not continue the normally high speed when he is nearing a crossing.

The Supreme Court referred to the case of *Upson*, and although the case did not appear to be relevant in deciding the present issue, it was held that some of the general observations made were held to be useful. For instance, Lord Porter's observation:

> If the driver could and ought to have seen the plaintiff hurrying towards the crossing before she reached the taxi-cab and to have anticipated that she was about to or might hasten across the crossing and did not do so, undoubtedly he would be guilty of negligence at common law.

Further, the oft-cited reference of Lord du Parcq to the observations of Lord Dunedin in Fardon v Harcourt-Rivington:

> If the possibility of the danger emerging is reasonably apparent, then to take no precautions is negligence; but if the possibility of danger emerging is only a mere possibility which would never occur to the mind of a reasonable man, then there is no negligence in not having taken extraordinary precautions.

Applying these principles in the present case, Justice Patel argued:

> These observations suggest that a person who is driving a motor car owes a duty to the members of the public to keep a look-out on the road and more so when approaching a pedestrian crossing where he would normally expect a pedestrian to cross the road. *The reasoning in this case also illustrates that regard must be paid to the habits of the public.* (emphasis added)

The Supreme Court rejected Mr Jethmalani's contention that the vision of the accused was obstructed, as there were two other cars to his left. From the evidence it was clear that the cars were in a line, side by side, and the accused had said that he was not overtaking any of the cars. The court reasoned:

> Now, if that is so, when the width of the road which the girls had to cross was about 12.8 meters, i.e., at least about forty feet if not more, it cannot be pretended that he did not notice them. If the girls were walking at ordinary pace of four miles per hour then if the accused were travelling even at thirty miles per hour he would be at a distance of about eighty meters when the girls entered the crossing from the kerb. If he had been watchful he would have seen the girls entering the road from a distance of about eighty meters.

The fact that it was Saturday, around 5.30 p.m. and the accused was nearing a pedestrian crossing with the boards visible from a distance, the accused was bound to have his vehicle under such control that he could stop if necessary at the crossing. We may interpret this in economic terms by saying that the expected harm was higher in the circumstances and therefore warranted a higher degree of care. The court stated:

> If he had been on the look-out he could, even from a distance of about eighty meters of the crossing, have seen the girls entering the road between

the two lines. It was too late when he applied the brakes. If he had seen them and still continued at the same speed at which he was going, he was too rash.

The court concluded that, having regard to the circumstances, it could be stated without doubt that "the accident was the result of the negligence and rashness on the part of the accused." Regarding the issue of contributory negligence of the victims, the Supreme Court rejected the trial court's verdict saying: "It is not the law and it cannot be the law, that unless there was no car on the road no pedestrian is to cross the road, even at a pedestrian crossing since the condition can rarely be satisfied."

We find that the question of negligence was decided in the trial court by the due care approach. In the Bombay High Court, both approaches were used. He was held negligent for not adhering to regulations, driving too fast and in addition for not keeping in mind "the common habits of the public." The principles followed in *Upson* were found to be applicable here and were used to reach a verdict of negligence. Rashness was attributed to the accused: "If he had seen them and still continued at the same speed as he was going, he was too rash."

Another case, *Minor Veeran and another v Krishnamoorthy and Another*,[45] involved a minor boy, Veeran, who had been knocked down by a lorry at Always when he was trying to cross the road along with many others. On the day of the accident, April 29, 1956, around 11.30 a.m., 20–25 boys from the nearby Arabic School had gathered on the roadside to cross it. They waited for a bus approaching from the south to pass and then ran across the road. A lorry was about 75 to 100 yards behind the bus and when some of the boys had crossed, the accident occurred. The plaintiff, aged six years old, filed a suit through his father and next friend for damages for personal injuries sustained due to the accident. Munsif Mr G. Kurien held that since the road was straight and the second defendant, the lorry driver, could see that a group of boys were ready to cross the road, if he had exercised reasonable care he could have avoided the danger. He held that the driver was solely responsible for the accident. On appeal by the first defendant – the owner of the lorry – District Judge Mr Balakrishna Menon argued that it was for the plaintiffs to prove that the driver was driving the lorry in a rash and negligent manner and the evidence placed before it did not show that. He set the decree of the lower court aside and dismissed the suit. The plaintiffs appealed to the Kerala High Court, which restored the Munsif's award.

The reasoning which the Munsif had stated was as follows: when the driver saw that 20–25 boys were ready to cross the road, he should have reduced his speed and "driven the lorry in such a manner as to have it under control if any mishap is going to happen by the crossing of the boys across the road." Regarding the contributory negligence of the plaintiff, he argued:

> As a general proposition, children are incapable of negligence and therefore equally of contributory negligence. The reason is that children could not be expected to take that care which the law expects of adults and act which in the case of adults might amount to negligence cannot be set down against the

children so as to deny them redress. The law has necessarily to make allowance for their inexperience and infirmity of judgment.

The District Judge looked at the evidence and argued that the alleged speed of 25 to 30 miles could not be seen to be dangerous because what is considered as dangerous speed depends on circumstances. The learned judge elaborated:

> In a narrow congested road even a speed of 10 miles per hour will be dangerous. In a straight open road with no obstruction, or traffic, even a speed of 40 miles per hour will not be dangerous. Here the road is proved to have a width of 30 ft. as seen from the evidence of PW 5. It was straight road except for a slight bend. So the driver had good visibility he could not have been going at a high speed, because within 8 ft. of the impact, he had stopped the lorry as proved by PW 5. That means the lorry was going at slow speed at not even 20 miles per hour. And the brakes of the lorry were exceedingly effective. In such circumstances I am unable to conclude on the evidence available that the plaintiffs have proved that the 2nd defendant was driving the lorry in a rash or negligent manner.

We can say that he meant that the standard should be calculated with respect to the risk involved, when the road is congested greater expected harm warrants greater care. However, when the road is straight and wide with good visibility, a higher speed was justified.

In the Kerala High Court, Justice M. Madhavan Nair went into the question of what constitutes negligence and stated:

> A reasonable man would so regulate his conduct as to avoid producing any undesirable consequences which he foresees as probable. That is the normal standard of careful conduct. If the conduct in question falls short of that standard it is negligent. Here, the question is not of whether the defendant did actually foresee the consequences that happened as probable. The question is only whether he, as a reasonable man ought to have foreseen them.

He went on to the question of what each party is entitled to assume:

> Of course every workman constantly, and justifiably, takes risks relying on others to do their duty and trusting that they have done it. But that is far from saying that everyone is entitled to assume, in all circumstances, that other persons will be careful. In the case of an adult person, an amount of care on his part attributable to a reasonable man in the circumstances may be expected and correspondingly the duty of care owed to him may be reduced. In case of a child, having regard to its age, its mental development and other attendant circumstances, not much of care can be expected and accordingly the duty of care owed to it must then be of a higher standard."

Justice Nair relied heavily on the observations in *Upson* in support of his reasoning. He stated that it is settled that men must use care driving vehicles on highways, especially so when there are pedestrians waiting to cross and particularly if they are schoolchildren. He argued:

> The evidence is clear that the 2nd defendant, when he was about 75 to 100 yards away from the spot could well see the boys about to cross the road. The evidence further shows that as soon as the bus passed, when there was a space of 75 to 100 yards in front of the lorry, the boys began to cross the road. There were 20 to 25 boys of tender age to cross the road. The boy in question was only less than six years and the road was 30 ft. wide. The accident that happened, in the circumstances, must have been foreseen or ought to have been foreseen by the 2nd defendant.

Regarding whether the speed was reasonable, he quoted Lord du Parcq in *Upson*: "no speed is reasonable which is not adjusted to the circumstances of the moment, including the fact that the driver is approaching pedestrian crossing and may have to pull up quickly and within a very short distance." Applying this to the present case, Justice Nair held that:

> having seen the school-boys about to cross the road, it was the second defendant's duty to have proceeded at such speed as to be able, if necessary, to stop before he reached the crossing place. Proof here is that the lorry could be stopped only after 8 feet beyond the place of accident. There is no merit in saying that the boys were at fault in crossing the road after seeing the lorry coming down at a distance of 75 to 100 yards. It is common experience that boys, in crossing a road, do not often behave with 'reasonable care.'

Regarding the untaken precaution of "slowing down when he saw the boys," although the District Judge had said that "even if he had slowed down the vehicle and the boy suddenly jumped on to the road when it reached near him, it will not be possible to avert an accident," Justice Nair was of the view that but-for that precaution the accident would not have occurred. He argued that the driver was driving the lorry at a much higher speed or else a "lorry proceeding at 30 miles per hour could well be stopped within 15 yards. The evidence, accepted by the Courts below, is that when the assemblage of boys began to cross the road, the lorry was at a distance of 76 to 100 yards." He held that the driver was, therefore, solely responsible for the accident.

It is clear that the Munsif was applying both the approaches to hold the driver negligent, but the District Judge used the due care approach in reaching a verdict of non-negligence. In the Kerala High Court, Justice Nair again used both the approaches – the driver was driving at great speed and, having noticed the children from a distance, had not slowed down the vehicle. The High Court used non-individualized due care in this case. We note that in this case, again, the defendant actually saw the plaintiff crossing in front of him and did not slow down. He could be considered rash – as was done in *State v Bhalchandra Waman Pethe* discussed earlier.

In this chapter, the 20 Indian cases considered were classified into three categories. We find that most of the cases were either where the injurer was held negligent by the due care approach or the use of both the approaches. The cases have been classified by the approach used in the final verdict. We note that the use of the untaken precaution approach is more pervasive than this categorization shows because even when the due care approach was used to reach the final verdict, in some cases like that of *Rural Transport Corporation v Bezlum Biwi*, the untaken precaution approach is used at the stage of the Tribunal. Since the cases were taken from varied accident contexts, the different kinds of untaken precautions that can be cost-justified have come to the fore. We note that in a highly populated country like India, with vehicles carrying more passengers than their capacity permits, with some having to travel on the roof or with body parts protruding out of vehicles, the untaken precaution approach assumes great significance.

Notes

1 There are six categories, but the 20 cases that were selected could be classified in one of three categories only. Notably, no case involving a nonnegligent verdict in the case of the defendant at the final stage of litigation could be found.
2 AIR 1980 Cal 165.
3 AIR 1962 Pat 258.
4 Clerk and Lindsell on Torts, 11th edition, 1954, pp. 368–370.
5 Referring to the Calcutta High Court judgment in *Smt Jeet Kumari v Chittagong Engineering and Electric Supply Co. Ltd.* [1947 AIR (Cal) 195: 1946 (2) ILR (Cal) 433].
6 Barnes and Stout in their book, *Cases and Materials* (p. 111), have raised this very point in relation to the American case of *Haeg v Sprague Warner and Co., Inc.* 202 Minn 425, 281 N.W. 261: "The facts in *Haeg* are a bit unusual, in that the plaintiff actually observed the defendant acting carelessly. The rule in the Restatement (Second) of Torts § 466 is that plaintiffs have a duty to protect themselves from the negligence of others about which they know or *have reason to know*." The case is discussed in Chapter 4, section 4.1.
7 AIR 1980 Del 92.
8 As mentioned earlier, this case will be discussed in detail in Chapter 4, section 4.1.
9 AIR 1997 Del 201.
10 After his death, his legal representatives applied for liberty to prosecute the suit in his place, alleging survival of the cause of action to them. The defendants had opposed it, saying that the cause of action would not survive and the claim arising out of the injuries sustained by the deceased plaintiff would die with the death of the plaintiff.
11 AIR 1966 SC 1750.
12 (1940) 1 KB 229: 161 LT 366: 56 TLR 201: (1939) 4 All ER 241.
13 AIR 1996 SC 1274: (1996) 3 SCC 179.
14 AIR 2002 SC 2864: (2002) 6 SCC 455.
15 1931 AC 1: 1930 ALLER 257: 100 LJKB 97 (HL) AC.
16 1971 ACJ 328: 1971 MPLJ 706.
17 (1964) AC 465: (1963) 3 WLR 101: (1963) 2 All ER 575: 107 SJ 454 (HL).
18 AIR 1977 SC 1735: (1977) 2 SCC 745.
19 (1994) 3 JT 492: (1994) 1 SCC 1: (1994) 4 SCC 1.
20 According to Article 36 of the Limitation Act, 1908, if the suit is filed after two years from the date the cause of action arose, then the suit could be dismissed.
21 Singh (2010), p. 58.

22 AIR 1999 SC 1929: (1999) 4 SCC 317: 1999 ACJ 801.
23 16th edition, 1989, pp. 546–547.
24 2008 (153) DLT 70.
25 1974 ACJ 374: 1974 MPLJ 573: AIR 1975 MP 89.
26 This case has been discussed in section 2.3.
27 We note the dissent of Greene MR in the case of *London Passenger Transport Board v Upson and Another*, where he had specifically pointed out this duty issue. This case was discussed in Chapter 2, section 2.3.
28 (2003) 8 SCC 731: AIR 2003 SC 4182.
29 1981 AIR (Kar) 84.
30 A furlong is an old English word to denote an eighth of a mile.
31 1953 AIR (Mad) 981.
32 12th edition, at para 711.
33 1974 ACJ 87 (M.P.).
34 [1959] 3rd edition, p. 90.
35 AIR 1992 Bombay 396.
36 JT 1997 (8) SC 653 655: (1997) 8 SCC 683: AIR 1998 SC 640.
37 In the United States, it has been held that there is no absolute duty at common law to get down from the vehicle invariably. See the cases of *Goodman* and *Pokora* discussed in Chapter 4.
38 In particular, clauses (c) and (d) are relevant here: "The Central Government may require that, within a time to be specified in the requisition or within such further time as it may appoint in this behalf, . . . (c) suitable gates, chains, bars, stiles or handrails be erected or renewed by a railway administration at places where a railway crosses a public road on the level; (d) persons be employed by a railway administration to open and shut such gates, chains or bars."
39 [1952] (1) All E.R. 1248.
40 Volume 34 *Negligence* [1984], 4th ed.
41 (1996) 3 All ER 801 (HL): (1996) AC 923: (1996) 3 WLR 388.
42 1985 (157) CLR 424. The doctrine now stands rejected in Australia by the decision in *Pyrenees Shire Council v Day* (1998) 72 ALJR 152 (Aust) in which C. J. Brennan observed: "If community expectation that a statutory power will be exercised were to be adopted as a criterion of a duty to exercise the power it would displace the criterion of legislative intention – the appropriate criterion is legislative intention" (p. 158).
43 1966 AIR (Bom) 122.
44 Published in 'Maharashtra Government Gazette', Part 1, dated September 12, 1968.
45 AIR 1966 Ker 1972.

References

Gandhi, B.M. (2006), *Law of Torts*, 3rd ed., Lucknow, Eastern Book Company.
Heuston, R.F.V and R.A. Buckley (1992), *Salmond and Heuston on the Law of Torts*, 20th ed., London, Sweet and Maxwell.
Lakshminath, A. and M. Sridhar (2007), *Ramaswamy Iyer's: The Law of Torts*, 10th ed., Nagpur, LexisNexis Butterworths Wadhwa.
Rogers, W.V.H. (2010), *Winfield and Jolowicz on Tort*, 18th ed., London, Sweet and Maxwell.
Singh, Ram (2004), 'Economics of Judicial Decision-Making in Indian Tort Law. Motor Accident Cases', *Economic and Political Weekly*, June 19, 2613–2616.
Singh, G.P. (2010), *Ratanlal and Dhirajlal: The Law of Torts*, 26th ed., Nagpur, LexisNexis Butterworths Wadhwa.
Weir, Tony (2004), *A Casebook on Tort*, 10th ed., London, Sweet and Maxwell.

APPENDIX 3.A Schematic representation of the 20 Indian cases analyzed

Case type and No.	Approach (s) Used for Negligence Determination	Names of the Cases
3.1 [eleven]	Defendant held negligent by reasoning pointing towards the due care approach	*Rural Transport v Bezlum Biwi* *Jung Bahadur v Sundarlal Mandal* *Krishna Goods Carriers v Union of India* *Klaus Mittelbachert* *MCD v Subhagwanti* *Sarla Dixit v Balwant Yadav* *Jhaveri* *Basanti bai* *Purshottam Udeshi* *Jay Laxmi Salt Works Private Ltd. v State of Gujarat* *Sushila Devi*
3.2 [one]	Defendant held negligent by reasoning pointing towards the untaken precaution approach	*Govt. of NCT v Sudha Devi*
3.3 [eight]	Defendant held negligent by reasoning pointing towards both the approaches	*Vidya Devi* *Laxman Iyer* *Sundara Shetty* *Shushma Mitra v MPSTC* *Ishwardas Paulsrao Ingle v General Manager, MSRTC* *Unioin of India v United India Insurance Company* *State v Bhalchandra* *Veeran v Krishnamoorty*

4

ECONOMIC ANALYSIS OF SELECT AMERICAN CASES

In this chapter, we analyze American cases along the same lines as the British and Indian case analyses done in earlier chapters.

4.1 Cases where the reasoning points towards the adoption of the due care approach in holding the injurer negligent

One important automobile collision case in this subsection that is important more for the determination of negligence of the plaintiff is *Haeg v Sprague, Warner and Co. Inc.*[1] The collision occurred in broad daylight at the right-angle intersection, three miles south of the southern limits of the city of Minneapolis, of county highway 52 also known as Nicollet Avenue and rural Hennepin County road, known as 86th street south. The plaintiff, Edward Haeg, was approaching in his truck from the west along the latter road that ran from east to west. Harry Thompson, a salesman for the defendant Sprague, Warner and Co. Inc. approached in his car from the south on Highway 52, which lies north and south. The country was flat with a clear view and there were no disturbing circumstances on either road at the time of collision. The plaintiff brought an action in the District Court for Hennepin County to recover damages sustained in the collision. The case was tried before Judge Frank E. Reed and a jury which gave a verdict in favour of the plaintiff. The defendant appealed to the Supreme Court of Minnesota alleging contributory negligence on the part of the plaintiff. The majority opinion was that the plaintiff was guilty of contributory negligence and therefore, the trial court decision was reversed and a verdict was entered for the defendant.

From the evidence it was found that Thompson's car was coming from the plaintiff's right and had a right of way. However, he would have forfeited that right if he were driving at an excessive speed. While the plaintiff alleged that he was travelling at 50 to 60 miles per hour until the collision, Thompson admitted to a speed of 45 miles per hour until the moment that he saw that the plaintiff was not going to give him the right of way. The district court held him negligent for the high speed, not believing his story that he had reduced it to "half speed" at the time and place of the collision. The plaintiff had testified that he had seen Thompson's car several times, and when he entered the intersection, it was still about 100 to 125 feet away and was not slackening his speed. He stated: "I entered the intersection first, and I expected him to slack up and let me through." The plaintiff's case all along was based on his right to assume that Thompson would exercise ordinary care to avoid the collision. The trial court held that he was nonnegligent.

In the Supreme Court of Minnesota, Justice Holt overruled this saying:

> Plaintiff's supposed reliance upon Mr. Thompson's exercise of due care is of no moment for the simple reason that it is a case, if ever there can be one, where such reliance was itself negligence. We stress again the obvious truth of fact and law that it is not due care to depend upon the exercise of care by another when such dependence is itself accompanied by obvious danger. (emphasis added)

He argued that from the evidence it can be concluded:

> Either Thompson's car had the right of way or it was in excess of 45 miles an hour. So when plaintiff entered Nicollet Avenue, Thompson's car was so close and going at such rate of speed that it was the clearest kind of negligence for plaintiff not to stop.

Justice Holt stated that in this case, the plaintiff actually saw the defendant. He stated: "Plaintiff had a clear view of the approach of Thompson's car over a long distance, knew all the time that it was coming with great speed and did not observe any checking of its momentum." He held that the fact that the collision occurred as it did shows that when he entered Nicollet Avenue Thompson's car was much closer than the plaintiff admits. Moreover, it was not that the plaintiff entered the intersection first under such circumstances as to give him the right of way. It was held that in the present case the plaintiff "had no reason to assume that the other driver would exercise reasonable care, because it was perfectly obvious either that the other was not doing so, or, if he did, that the danger of collision was still great."

Justice Peterson in his dissenting opinion argued that he did not agree with the basis of Justice Holt's decision that when the plaintiff entered the intersection the circumstances were such as to make a collision inescapable if he persisted in his attempt to cross Nicollet Avenue ahead of Thompson. He stated:

> The respective speeds and positions of the cars at that time indicated that the plaintiff would cross safely if each individual continued at his then speed.

Certainly, if Thompson slackened his speed, or if he slackened his speed and turned to the left, or if he came to a stop, plaintiff would encounter no danger.

He argued that the possibility of danger depended on whether Thompson would increase or decrease his speed during the 125 feet that separated him from the intersection. He held: "The plaintiff, present at the intersection, had a right to assume that Thompson would exercise ordinary care, which in this case meant that Thompson would slacken his speed and allow for the plaintiff's presence at the intersection." He argued that the majority opinion was that it was physically impossible for Thompson to stop his car within 125 feet but just slowing down would be enough to let the car pass through. Since Thompson *could* have done it, it was only reasonable on the part of the plaintiff to think that he *would* do it. Justice Hilton concurred with this dissenting opinion of Justice Peterson.

We find that the trial court used the due care approach to hold the defendant negligent and the plaintiff nonnegligent. The Supreme Court of Minnesota clearly used the untaken precaution approach to hold the plaintiff guilty. The main point of contention was what the plaintiff was entitled to assume when he was entering the intersection after having seen the defendant speeding towards the intersection at least four times at various distances before the collision. While at the trial it was held that he had a right to assume that Thompson will take reasonable care, the Supreme Court held that by law one should take account of the negligence of others and react accordingly. The latter held him to a higher level of care – the untaken precaution of stopping the car was seen to be cost-justified because he ought to have considered that Thompson may not stop; thus, the probability of collision and hence expected harm was larger. Barnes and Stout (1992) argue that Justice Holt's view that there is no absolute right to assume that other people will be careful is indeed the dominant rule in tort cases.[2]

Another important case famous for the categorical statement of Justice Stone that it is not due care to depend on the exercise of due care by others is *Demetrius Dragotis v Vincent Kennedy and Another*.[3] On the evening of March 13, 1931, Demetrius Dragotis was travelling as a guest along with three others in a car driven by Vincent Kennedy. It was drizzling, and when they were going eastward on trunk highway No. 10, a mile or so west of Decano, Minnesota, the left rear tire went flat. Kennedy stopped the car on the traffic lane and made no effort to go on to the shoulder, which was of adequate width to serve the purpose. Since the taillight was out, Dragotis assisted the others by holding the flashlight while they were changing the tire. An east bound car, driven by Anderson, ran into the Kennedy car and in the impact, Dragotis was injured. He sued both Kennedy and Anderson for personal injuries. The case was tried in the District Court of Hennepin County (Minnesota) before Judge Edmond A. Montgomery and a jury. At the close of the evidence, the court directed a verdict against the plaintiff by charging him with contributory negligence. Since at the time it was a complete bar to recovery, the plaintiff appealed to the Supreme Court of Minnesota, which held that although the two defendants were negligent, the plaintiff was guilty of contributory negligence and hence barred from recovery.

The two defendants were held to be negligent by the Supreme Court of Minnesota as well. In particular, Justice Stone argued that "defendant Kennedy was grossly so" on the ground that:

> With opportunity to get off the road for a tire change, it is bad enough, the conduct utterly inexcusable both as discourtesy and negligence, to obstruct a highway in the daytime as Kennedy obstructed the road on this occasion. Where darkness, wet pavement, and the absence of tail-light or other signal to warn approaching traffic are also factors, it so clearly amounts to gross negligence.

According to the testimony, visibility was reduced to a radius of not more than 30 feet. In the circumstances defendant Kennedy was grossly negligent. This argument can be interpreted as saying that since in the present case expected harm was greater, the standard of care was higher than if the same action had been undertaken in daylight. So the defendant's care level fell far below the standard.

The discussion about the plaintiff's negligence was more elaborate. It was argued that the plaintiff

> not lacking in discernment or other mental capabilities, without protest, actively participated in Kennedy's conduct. Moreover, he put himself within a foot or so of the center line of the pavement, standing or 'squatting', with the rays of the flashlight turned downward, ignoring or deliberately risking the danger of his situation and that to other cars coming from the west.

Regarding the standard of care required of him, Justice Stone reasoned: "True, plaintiff was charged with the duty to exercise only due care. But that means a degree of care commensurate with the danger." This way of defining due care is consistent with the economic model. Justice Stone went on to give the oft-cited statement:

> There is no help for the plaintiff in the rule that ordinarily one may rely upon the exercise of due care by others. That rule has no application where it is plain, as it should have been to the plaintiff, that even the exercise of great care by others may not prevent injury. *It is not due care to depend upon the exercise of care by another when such reliance is accompanied with obvious danger.* (emphasis added)

In the present case, Justice Stone argued that circumstances were such that there was obvious danger, and it "would be difficult for fancy to suppose circumstances making it more clearly unreasonable dependence upon careful conduct of others than those of this case, which plaintiff helped to create."

From the reasoning we find that the defendant Kennedy was held negligent using the due care approach. Since expected harm was higher in this case, the standard required was also higher. A cost-justified untaken precaution was identified "getting off the road for a tyre change," it was noted that the shoulder "had adequate width for the purpose" and the defendant had "opportunity" to exercise this option but did not do so. The plaintiff's negligence was determined using the untaken precaution approach as it was clearly stated that it is not due care not to take account of the negligence of others. Implicit in the reasoning is that the untaken precaution that could have prevented the incident was standing in a position while showing the flashlight so that he could keep a look-out for traffic coming from the west.

One famous negligence case concerning a railroad grade crossing which has been often scrutinized in the literature because of the opinion by Justice Holmes is *Baltimore and Ohio Railroad Company v Goodman*.[4] The accident occurred when Nathan Goodman was driving his truck at a grade crossing in an unincorporated village in Montgomery County, Ohio, when it collided with a train which was coming at approximately 60 miles per hour. He could not see the train coming because a section house blocked his view. He slowed the vehicle but did not stop and by the time he could see the train he could not stop and the train struck his truck and he was killed in the accident. His widow filed a negligence action against the railroad in the District Court of the United States for the Western Division of the Southern District of Ohio to recover damages for her husband's death. The railroad's defense was contributory negligence because it was daylight and the deceased was familiar with the crossing. The verdict was rendered for the widow. The railroad appealed to the Circuit Court of Appeals, Sixth Circuit, which affirmed. The railroad further appealed to the Supreme Court of the United States, which reversed the appellate Court's judgment.

The evidence was that Nathan Goodman was driving an automobile truck in an easterly direction and the train was running in a southwesterly direction at not less than 60 miles per hour. The plaintiff's evidence tended to show that the deceased reduced his speed, when about 40 feet from the crossing, from 10 to 12 miles per hour to 5 or 6 miles per hour, at which rate he was moving at the time of collision. The line was straight but it was stated that the track north of the crossing was obscured by buildings and other obstructions; a tool shed was 243 feet north of the crossing, and 24 feet from the west track there was a store which obstructed the line of vision to the north; the deceased could not have seen the approaching train until he was about 20 feet from the first rail, or, as the plaintiff argued, 12 feet from danger with the engine still obscured by the tool shed. The evidence was uncontradicted that the seat in which the driver was sitting was six feet from the front of the machine, and that the overhang of the railroad engine was 2.5 feet. Therefore, the front of his truck was within 11.5 feet from danger point, before he could first see past the tool shed, behind which was the approaching train. Travelling at 5–6 miles per hour, he was covering seven to eight feet per second. Therefore, he had only a 1.5 seconds interval to guide his conduct. It was not shown that Goodman looked or listened for the train, but the Circuit Court of Appeals held that "there is a rebuttable presumption that he did both."

The trial court submitted to the jury the issues of negligence and contributory negligence and the jury returned a verdict for the plaintiff. In the Court of Appeals it was argued that:

> Plaintiff accounts for the engineer's failure to see the truck when it emerged from behind the store on the theory that the tool house obstructed his line of vision, which shows, as she contends, that the train was running faster than 60 miles an hour. That may or may not be true, or it may be that there was a momentary diversion of attention, and perhaps discovery, in the brief time that elapsed before the two vehicles came in contact at the crossing – as to Goodman, for example, the looking to the south before looking north.

Regarding his duty of care, it was held:

> It is, of course, true that Goodman was required to exercise, for his own safety, the degree of care that a reasonably prudent person ordinarily would exercise in the same or like circumstances, which included 'the use of his faculties of sight and hearing.' This imposed on him the duty of looking and listening when he could do so effectively. . . . Hence it is said that, as the evidence shows he could have seen the train when within 16 or 18 feet of the track – whether he did or did not is immaterial – he was guilty of negligence as a matter of law, for, if he did not, he failed to look, or, if he looked, failed to stop before going on the crossing, and in either circumstance it was the duty of the court to direct the jury to return a verdict for defendant.

The court argued that the cases cited by the defendant in support of this contention were decided on the particular facts under consideration. These do not conflict with the later cases which "allow – if not in terms, in the adaptation of the general rule – for modifying circumstances, or for accidental diversion of the attention, to which the most prudent and careful are sometimes subject." The Court concluded: "Under these decisions we cannot hold that Goodman was guilty of negligence as a matter of law."

As for the question of the railroad's negligence, it affirmed the verdict of the jury. Regarding the contention that the operation of the train did not require, in approaching the crossing, to take into consideration obstructions not in the right of way of defendant, it argued:

> It would be too lax a rule to permit a railway company to ignore the dangers of a crossing caused by obstructions not on the property of the company, and to operate its trains as if the crossing were free of the extraordinary dangers incident to its location. The duty of those operating a train to exercise ordinary care to avoid injuring persons about to use a railroad crossing clearly requires the taking into consideration of obstructions off the right of way that render the crossing more dangerous than otherwise it would be.

In the Supreme Court, Justice Holmes noted two things related to Goodman's situation – that it was daylight and he was familiar with the crossing. Regarding the negligence question he argued:

> When a man goes upon a railroad track he knows that he goes to a place where he will be killed if a train comes upon him before he is clear of the track. He knows that he must stop for the train, not the train stop for him. In such circumstances, it seems to us that if a driver cannot be sure otherwise whether a train is dangerously near he must stop and get out of his vehicle, although obviously he will not often be required to do more than to stop and look.

It was clear that Justice Holmes thought the driver needed to take the "extra precaution" of getting down and looking because he had no way of determining whether a train was approaching.

He further argued: "it seems to us that if he relies upon not hearing the train or any signal and takes no further precautions he does so at his own risk." It is clear from here that Goodman was not supposed to assume that the other party would use due care. Justice Holmes held: "if at the last moment Goodman found himself in an emergency it was his own fault that he did not reduce his speed earlier or come to a stop." Here the untaken precautions are "reducing his speed earlier" or "coming to a stop," and further "getting out of his vehicle" to check if a train was approaching the crossing. This high standard was applicable given that the defendant had not taken due care and so Goodman could not ascertain whether a train was "dangerously near" because of obstructions blocking his line of vision. Justice Holmes famously concluded:

> it is true as said in Flanelly v Delaware and Hudson Co. 225 U.S. 597, 603, that the question of due care very generally is left to the jury. But we are dealing with a standard of conduct, and when the standard is clear it should be laid down once and for all by the Courts.

There are two aspects in this conclusion. First, the finding that in this particular case, Goodman was required to get out of his vehicle, in addition to the requirement that he should stop and look. The statement that: "if a driver cannot be sure otherwise whether a train is dangerously near he must stop and get out of his vehicle, although obviously he will not often be required to do more than to stop and look" shows that in the circumstances, Justice Holmes thought that a reasonable man ought to take the extra precaution of getting out of his vehicle. Second, setting a "fixed standard" in law to enable the courts to determine the negligence issue in general in cases of daylight automobile crossing where there is a view of the track by specifying what conduct shall be considered reasonable and prudent on the part of the automobile driver. Here the implication is to follow the rule whenever there is an obstruction in the line of vision without any reference to cost-justification.

We find that the approach adopted by the trial court and the Court of Appeals was the due care approach by which they held the railroad negligent for running the train at high speed at the railroad grade crossing and the plaintiff's husband nonnegligent because he had slowed down and listened and was entitled to assume that an approaching train would give the usual warning. The Supreme Court of the United States adopted the untaken precaution approach in holding Goodman negligent as he specified an extra precaution that was required, and the implicit assumption was that he was not entitled to think that the railroad would take due care.

The absolute standard laid down by Justice Holmes in *Baltimore and Ohio Railroad Co. v Goodman* was categorically rejected in *Pokora v Wabash Railway Co.*[5] by Justice Cardozo, and his opinion regarding the standard of care has come to be considered a landmark in negligence determination. The plaintiff, John Pokora, an ice dealer, had come to the railway grade crossing in the city of Springfield, Illinois, to load his truck with ice. The tracks of the Wabash Railway were laid along Tenth Street which ran north and south. There was a crossing at Edwards Street running east and west. Two ice depots were on the opposite corners of Tenth and Edward Streets, one at the northeast corner and the other at the southwest. Pokora driving west along Edwards street, stopped at the first of these corners to get his load of ice but found many trucks ahead of him and decided to try the depot on the other side of the way. The accident occurred while he was crossing to the other side. He filed a suit for damages and the District Court found him guilty of contributory negligence and directed a verdict for the defendants. The Circuit Court of Appeals (one judge dissenting) affirmed. A writ of certiorari took the case to the Supreme Court of the United States.

In the Supreme Court, after examining the evidence, Justice Cardozo found that Wabash Railway had four tracks on Tenth Street, a switch track on the east, then the main track and then two switches. Pokora, as he left the northeast corner had stopped, looked for approaching trains, from a point which was about 15 feet east of the switch ahead of him. A string of box cars standing on the switch five to ten feet from the north line of Edwards Street, cut off his view of the tracks beyond him to the north. He listened but when he did not hear a bell or whistle, he crossed the switch reaching the main track still listening, and then he was struck by a passenger train coming from the north at a speed of 25 to 30 miles an hour. From the evidence, Justice Cardozo concluded that "he had no view of the main track northward, or none for a substantial distance, till the train was so near that escape had been cut off."

The essential question before the jury, argued Justice Cardozo, was "whether reasonable caution forbade his going forward on reliance on the sense of hearing unaided by that of sight." The learned justice was of the opinion that:

> No doubt it was his duty to look along the track from his seat, if looking would avail to warn him of danger. This does not mean, however, that if vision is cut off by obstacles, there was negligence in going on, any more than

there would have been in trusting his ears if vision had been cut off by the darkness of the night.

He went on to say: "Pokora made his crossing in the day time, but like the traveler by night used the faculties available to one in his position." To the argument made that the plaintiff should have found other means of assuring himself of safety before venturing to cross, he reasoned:

> The crossing was a frequented highway in a populous city. Behind him was a line of other cars, making ready to follow him. To some extent, at least, there was assurance in the thought that the defendant would not run its train at such a time and place without sounding bell and whistle.[6]

Justice Cardozo went on to say:

> Indeed the statutory signals did not exhaust the defendant's duty when to its knowledge there was special danger to the traveler through obstructions on the roadbed narrowing the field of vision. . . . All this the plaintiff, like any other reasonable traveler, might fairly take into account. All this must be taken into account by us in comparing what he did with the conduct reasonably to be expected of reasonable men.

This can be interpreted to mean that the plaintiff could rely on the defendant taking due care. In case of the defendant, given that the "crossing was a highly frequented highway in a populous city," the expected harm warranted that taking due care included the sounding of bell and whistle. This reasoning is consistent with the due care approach.

The Court of Appeals had relied on the case of *Baltimore v Goodman* discussed earlier in which the Supreme Court of the United States had held:

> In such circumstances it seems to us that if a driver cannot be sure otherwise whether a train is dangerously near he must stop and get out of his vehicle, although obviously he will not often be required to do more than to stop and look.

Justice Cardozo did not go into the controversy of "the existence of a duty to stop, disconnected from a duty to get out and reconnoitre" because he felt that would lead into "the thickets of conflicting judgments" but nevertheless, concluded:

> The subject has been less considered in this court, but in none of its opinions is there a suggestion that at any and every crossing the duty to stop is absolute, irrespective of the danger. Not even in B. & O. R. Co. v. Goodman, supra, which goes farther than the earlier cases, is there support for such a rule. To the contrary, the opinion makes it clear that the duty is conditioned upon the

presence of impediments whereby sight and hearing become inadequate for the traveler's protection.

We can infer from his statement that the higher level of care would arise only when the expected harm is greater.

In the present case, however, the plaintiff had stopped before he started to cross the tracks. Justice Cardozo argued:

> If we assume that by reason of the box cars, there was a duty to stop again when the obstructions had been cleared, that duty did not arise unless a stop could be made safely after the point of clearance had been reached. . . . For reasons already stated, the testimony permits the inference that the truck was in the zone of danger by the time the field of vision was enlarged. No stop would have helped the plaintiff if he remained seated on his truck, or so the triers of the facts might find.

He continued:

> standards of prudent conduct are declared at times by courts, but they are taken over from the facts of life. To get out of a vehicle and reconnoitre is an uncommon precaution, as everyday experience informs us. Besides being uncommon, it is very likely to be futile, and sometimes even dangerous. If the driver leaves his vehicle when he nears a cut or curve, he will learn nothing by getting out about the perils that lurk beyond. By the time he regains his seat and sets his car in motion, the hidden train may be upon him. . . . Often the added safeguard will be dubious though the track happens to be straight, as it seems that this one was, at all events as far as the station, about five blocks to the north. A train traveling at a speed of thirty miles an hour will cover a quarter of a mile in the space of thirty seconds. It may thus emerge out of obscurity as the driver turns his back to regain the waiting car, and may then descend upon him suddenly when his car is on the track. Instead of helping himself by getting out, he might do better to press forward with all his faculties alert. So a train at a neighboring station, apparently at rest and harmless, may be transformed in a few seconds into an instrument of destruction.

We can say that Justice Cardozo was in effect evaluating whether the untaken precaution of "getting out of the vehicle, once the obstruction was cleared, checking and then returning" would have been effective.

The learned justice weighing the costs and benefits of the precaution concluded:

> At times the course of safety may be different. One can figure to oneself a roadbed so level and unbroken that getting out will be a gain. Even then the balance of advantage depends on many circumstances and can be easily disturbed.

He had said that this precaution was not common and not even laid down by precedent to be an absolute duty. The circumstances would determine whether the precaution should have been taken. In the present case, the options before Pokora were such that he could not have left his vehicle to get out and check if a train was coming. Justice Cardozo reasoned:

> Where was Pokora to leave his truck after getting out to reconnoitre? If he was to leave it on the switch, there was the possibility that the box cars would be shunted down upon him before he could regain his seat. The defendant did not show whether there was a locomotive at the forward end, or whether the cars were so few that a locomotive could be seen. If he was to leave his vehicle near the curb, there was even stronger reason to believe that the space to be covered in going back and forth would make his observations worthless.

We can infer that Pokora had three options before him – to leave his vehicle on the switch and go and check; to leave his vehicle in the curb and go to check; just stay in the vehicle and listen and look-out for an oncoming train. Taking the first option involved the expected harm from the box cars being shunted upon him, the second had the expected harm due to train coming upon him anyway despite the checking. Justice Cardozo held that the option of staying in the vehicle and pushing ahead with all senses alert involved the least expected harm because given the Illinois rule that bell and whistle have to be sounded, the probability of a train approaching without having sounded the warning was low. Thus, the Supreme Court found for the plaintiff and reversed the verdict of the Court of Appeals.

We find that the due care approach was used to hold the defendant negligent and the plaintiff nonnegligent. The defendant clearly violated a statutory rule. The plaintiff took the caution of looking and listening before crossing. The precaution of getting down from the vehicle was not cost-justified given that he was entitled to assume that the defendant would take due care and blow the whistle. What was appropriate in *Goodman*, need not be appropriate in other cases. The same standard need not be applicable in all cases. In this case, getting down was not cost-justified and therefore the untaken precaution of not getting down did not indicate breach of duty. Justice Cardozo gave his categorical statement in this regard: "Illustrations such as these bear witness to the need for caution in framing standards of behavior that amount to rules of law."[7]

One oft-cited negligence case which has been subject to detailed analysis[8] is *Eckert v Long Island Railroad*[9] in which the plaintiff's husband, Henry Eckert, was killed while attempting to rescue a child who had come in front of an advancing train. The incident occurred on the afternoon of November 26, 1867, when Henry was standing about 50 feet from the defendant's tracks in East New York and was in conversation with another person when he saw a train coming in from Jamaica at a speed of 12 to 20 miles per hour. The plaintiff's witnesses did not hear any warning from the train's whistle or bell. He saw a child of three or four years sitting or standing on the defendant's tracks and rushed to rescue it. Although he managed to throw the child clear of danger he was himself struck by the train and died of the injuries the same night. The plaintiff's wife, Anna Eckert, filed a suit for damages in the City Court of Brooklyn (New York) alleging that the death of her husband was caused by the negligence of the defendant, its servants and agents in the conduct and running of the train. The jury found a verdict for the plaintiff. The defendants appealed to the Supreme Court (New York) on the ground that the deceased's negligence contributed to the injury and therefore the plaintiff's case should be dismissed. The Supreme Court affirmed the judgment of the jury. The defendants appealed to the Court of Appeals of New York, which affirmed the Supreme Court's verdict by a majority, with two judges dissenting.

The defendants were held negligent by the jury because the train was being driven at a speed which was not appropriate given that the place "was a thickly populated neighborhood and one of the stations of the road." There was no warning given of the approach by means of bell or whistle. Also, the engine of the train was constructed to run either way without turning, and it was then running in reverse with the cow-catcher next to the train it was drawing and nothing in front to remove obstacles from the track. The jury verdict was affirmed by the Supreme Court and the Court of Appeals. We note that this was in conformity with the economic model – the expected harm was high enough to warrant a lower speed and greater vigilance.

The main question in the appeal was, however, whether Henry was guilty of contributory negligence. Judge Grover argued:

> The evidence showed that the train was approaching in plain view of the deceased, and had he for his own purposes attempted to cross the track, or with a view to save property placed himself voluntarily in a position where he might have received an injury from a collision with the train, his conduct would have been grossly negligent, and no recovery could have been had for such injury. But the evidence further showed that there was a small child upon the track, who, if not rescued, must have been inevitably crushed by the rapidly approaching train. This the deceased saw, and he owed a duty of important obligation to this child to rescue it from its extreme peril, if he could do so without incurring great danger to himself.

We find that the expected benefit of his action was an important consideration in the determination of the issue of contributory negligence.

We note that there was a balancing issue here when Judge Grover says "without incurring great danger to himself." The person in the position of Henry has to evaluate the expected cost of his action as well; in this case it was the risk of death. In order to determine whether there ought to be a finding of negligence, Judge Grover elaborated:

> Negligence implies some act of commission or omission wrongful in itself. Under the circumstances in which the deceased was placed, it was not

wrongful in him to make every effort in his power to rescue the child, compatible with reasonable regard for his own safety. It was his duty to exercise his judgment as to whether he could probably save the child without serious injury to himself. If, from the appearances, he believed that he could, it was not negligence to make an attempt to do so, although believing that possibly he might fail and receive an injury himself. He had no time for deliberation. He must act instantly, if at all, as a moment's delay would have been fatal to the child.

He was to weigh the chances of saving the child against the chances of being killed. If, in the instant, he thought there was a reasonable probability of saving the child, he was not negligent in attempting to do so.[10]

Judge Grover cautioned that if the probability of saving the life in question is too low, then the act of rescue may be even considered rash:

> The law has so high regard for human life that it will not impute negligence to an effort to preserve it, unless made under such circumstances as to constitute rashness in the judgment of prudent persons. For a person engaged in his ordinary affairs, or in the mere protection of property, knowingly and voluntarily to place himself in a position where he is liable to receive a serious injury, is negligence, which will preclude a recovery for an injury so received; but when the exposure is for the purpose of saving life, it is not wrongful, and therefore not negligent unless such as to be regarded either rash or reckless.

Judge Grover was emphasizing two things: first, that the object to be saved has to be valuable enough and since the law accords very high value to human life, it is worth taking a risk; second, there must be a reasonable probability of the rescue or else taking the risk will not be cost-justified.[11]

We note that in deciding whether it was reasonable on the part of Henry to have taken such a risk, the court took into account the fact that the train was advancing in excessive speed and without signal and the child would have been surely killed had Henry not rescued him. Given the danger, the act of rescue was seen to be cost-justified. We find that the untaken precaution approach is being adopted to hold the plaintiff nonnegligent.[12] In this case the plaintiff's husband actually *saw* the negligence of the defendants and acted in response to it.

Judge Allen gave the dissenting opinion in which he argued that Henry was negligent because: "He went upon the track of the defendant's road in front of an approaching train, voluntarily, in the exercise of his free will and while in full possession of all his faculties, and with capacity to judge of the danger." If in the exercise of his free will, "he chose for the purpose to attempt the crossing of the track, he must take the consequences of his act." He argued that:

> The act of the intestate in attempting to save the child was lawful as well as meritorious, and he was not a trespasser upon the property of the defendant,

but it was not the performance of any duty imposed by law, or growing out of this relation to the child, or the result of any necessity."

We find that his analysis can be interpreted as saying that since he had no duty, he cannot recover. It is of no import whether the act was cost-justified or not. The object to be saved or purpose of crossing is of no importance. Neither is it significant whether the railroad was negligent or not: "Whether the defendant was or was not guilty of negligence, or whatever the character and degree of culpability of the defendant or its servants is not material."

United States v Carroll Towing[13] is, by far, the most famous case in the economic analysis of law for laying down explicitly what has now come to be termed the "Hand Formula"[14] for negligence determination. This case concerned the sinking of a barge, *Anna C*, on January 4, 1944, off pier 51, North River. The barge was owned by Conners Marine Company and had been chartered to the Pennsylvania Railroad Co., which had loaded it with a cargo of flour that belonged to the United States. The charter required that the Conners Co. provide a bargee between the hours of 8.00 a.m. and 4.00 p.m. On that day, Grace Line Co. sent the tug *Carroll* that it had chartered from the Carroll Towing Company to "drill out" another barge. The process involved adjusting the lines of the *Anna C* in order to get to the other barge; after the other barge had been drilled out, the servants of Grace Line – a harbormaster and a deckhand improperly retied the *Anna C* lines. The *Anna C* was among six barges tied together and the tide and wind carried all of them together, until the *Anna C* hit a tanker whose propeller broke a hole in the *Anna C* below the waterline. Shortly afterwards, she careened, dumped her cargo of flour and sank. The United States sought compensation for the flour and the Conners Co. for the barge. Carroll Towing Company argued that the barge could have been kept afloat and the cargo saved if a bargee were present and had detected that she had been struck by a propeller. The District Court held the tug owner, Carroll Towing, liable to the United States, Pennsylvania Railroad and Conners Co. Railroad was held secondarily liable to the Conners Co. The Carroll Company and the Pennsylvania Railroad Co. sought review of the judgment and among other things, charged *Anna C* with a share of the damages, or at least with as much as that resulted from her sinking.

In the evidence it appeared that both *Carroll* and *Grace*, another tug owned by Grace Line, came to the help of the flotilla after it broke loose; and as both had siphon pumps on board, they could have kept the *Anna C* afloat, had they learned of her condition; but since the bargee was absent on *Anna C* it could not be reported that she was leaking. The captain of the *Carroll* had told the harbormaster and the deckhand to secure the pier since there was a strong northerly wind blowing.

Regarding the negligence of Grace Line's harbormaster aboard the *Carroll*, it was stated that the answer depended on how far his authority extended. It was established that: it was his job to tie up barges; that when he came "to tie up a barge" he had to go in and look at the barges that were inside the barges he was "handling"; that in such cases "most of the time" he went in "to see that the lines to the inside barges are strong enough to hold these barges," and that "if they are not" he "put out sufficient other lines as are necessary." Judge Hand argued that from the District Court's finding one can conclude that

> the master of 'Carroll' deputed the deckhand and the 'harbormaster' jointly to pass upon the sufficiency of the Anna C's fasts to the pier.... The harbormaster was not instructed what he should do about the fast, but was allowed to use his own judgment.

Since they were negligent in the task, they were held liable.

The next question was whether Conners Co. was negligent for the bargee's failure to care for the barge. Here Judge Hand distinguished between the damages arising out of the flotilla breaking adrift and the propeller punching a hole in the barge which he called "collision damage" and the damage due to the sinking of cargo which he called the "sinking damages." In the case of the former, the argument was that even if a bargee was present on *Anna C* there was no guarantee that the collision would have been prevented. He reasoned:

> even though we assume that the bargee was responsible for his fasts after the other barges were added outside, there is not the slightest ground for saying that the deckhand and the 'harbormaster' would have paid any attention to any protest which he might have made, had he been there. We do not attribute it as any degree of fault of the Anna C that the flotilla broke adrift.

He was in effect saying that the absence of the bargee did not satisfy the "but-for" test of causation as far as the collision damage was concerned. We note that here the question is of liability determination, which has to satisfy both the breach-of-duty test and the cause-in-fact requirement. The former was taken up in the discussion with respect to the other component of damages.

He argued that the bargee could have prevented the "sinking damages":

> if the bargee had been on board, and had done his duty to his employer, he would have gone below at once, examined the injury and called for help from the 'Carroll' and the Grace Line tug. Moreover, it is clear that these tugs could have kept the barge afloat, until they had safely beached her and saved her cargo.

Thus, the crucial question in this decision was: "whether a barge owner is slack in the care of his barge if the bargee is absent." In order to answer this question he went on to give the now – famous negligence formula:

> since there are occasions when every vessel will break from her moorings, and since, if she does, she becomes a menace to those about her; the owner's duty, as in other similar situations, to provide against resulting injuries is a

function of three variables: (1) The probability that she will break away; (2) the gravity of the resulting injury, if she does; (3) the burden of adequate precautions. Possibly it serves to bring this notion into relief to state it in algebraic terms: if the probability be called P; the injury, L; and the burden, B; liability depends upon whether B is less than L multiplied by P: i.e., whether B less than PL.

He continued:

> Applied to the situation at bar, the likelihood that a barge will break from her fasts and the damage she will do, vary with the place and time; for example, if a storm threatens, the danger is greater; so it is, if she is in a crowded harbor where moored barges are constantly being shifted about.

We note that Judge Hand was saying that the duty to take the precaution of having a bargee on board depended on the expected harm, which varied according to circumstances. At night, even in a busy harbour if the custom is not to have a bargee on board then "the situation is one where the custom should control." One can infer that, if the level of activity was low, then the balancing approach will have to give way to custom. However, he added: "We leave that question open."

Returning to the issue of the precaution of having a bargee on board, it was held:

> it is not in all cases a sufficient answer to a bargee's absence without excuse, during working hours, that he has properly made fast his barge to a pier, when he leaves her. In the case at bar the bargee left at five o' clock in the afternoon of January 3rd, and the flotilla broke away at about two o' clock in the afternoon of the following day, twenty-one hours afterwards. The bargee had been away all the time, and we hold that his fabricated story was affirmative evidence that he had no excuse for his absence.

The fact that the bargee had no excuse has been emphasized by Judge Hand. He had also stated: "the barge must not be the bargee's prison, even though he lives aboard; he must go ashore at times." One can infer that had the bargee been able to give a convincing excuse, the balance could have tilted in his favour. Essentially, it is an aspect of the cost of the untaken precaution – having a bargee on board.

In the present case, Judge Hand reasoned:

> At the locus in quo – especially during the short January days and in the full tide of war activity – barges were being constantly 'drilled' in and out. Certainly it was not beyond reasonable expectation that, with the inevitable haste and bustle, the work might not be done with adequate care. In such circumstances we hold – and it is all we do hold – that it is a fair requirement that the Conners Company should have a bargee aboard (unless he had some excuse for his absence), during the working hours of daylight.

We note that Judge Hand was in effect stating that the Conners Co. should have taken account of the negligence that is usual in the circumstances and taken adequate care to protect their own barge. The untaken precaution of having a bargee on board was cost-justified in the circumstances. Although it was negligent not to have the bargee on board, the Conners Co. was not held liable for the "collision damages" because the cause-in-fact requirement was not satisfied.

From the reasoning, we infer that Judge Hand was using the due care approach in holding the defendants guilty – the "harbormaster" did not perform that which he was authorized to do as part of his duty and failed to secure the barges after "drilling" out the one he had been asked to. As regards the contributory negligence of the plaintiff, the untaken precaution approach was being used. Knowing that "drilling" in and out of barges was often done without adequate care, the Conners Co. should have been cautious in requiring his bargee to be on board during the working hours of the day. They were not entitled to rest on the assumption that the harbormasters would perform their tasks with due care, and hence they had to ensure that the bargee in question was present during the day – the period when expected harm was greatest due to enhanced activity in the harbour.

In *Putt v Daussat*,[15] both parties in a motor vehicle collision case filed suits against each other. In the first suit, Mrs Christina M. Putt, claimed damages from the defendant, Mr Damon A Daussat and his liability insurer, St Paul Fire and Marine Insurance Company. A counter-suit was filed by Mr Daussat against Mrs Putt and his own liability insurer since Mrs Putt had no liability insurance, alleging that the insurance company was liable under the uninsured motorist coverage provided by the policy. The two suits were consolidated for trial and appeal. In the first suit, the trial court held that Putt was negligent and thus dismissed her suit; in the second Mr Daussat was held to be negligent and his suit too was dismissed. Both parties appealed. The consolidated suits were tried before the Court of Appeals of Louisiana, Fourth Circuit, and the main issue was whether the defendant driver was negligent and if so whether the plaintiff was barred from recovery because of his or her contributory negligence.

The accident occurred at about 2.50 a.m. on January 22, 1976, at the intersection of Orleans Avenue and City Park Avenue in the city of New Orleans. The intersection is controlled by an electric semaphore traffic signal, which was operating at the time of the accident. Mrs Putt was driving her car north on Orleans Avenue and Mr Daussat was driving his car east on City Park Avenue. The collision occurred when they were attempting to negotiate the intersection as the front of Mrs Putt's car struck the right rear side of Mr Daussat's vehicle. Since both parties argued that the green light was in their favour, the trial judge did not give reasons for his judgment. J. J. Hood in the Court of Appeals examined the evidence and the testimony of an eyewitness to the accident Bruce N. Johnson, who was travelling in his automobile north on Orleans Avenue less than two car lengths behind the Mrs Putt vehicle, and he said that the traffic light was green in her favour. The court, therefore, concluded that Mr Daussat was negligent in entering the intersection on a red light and his negligence in that respect was a proximate cause of the accident.

As far as Mrs Putt's negligence was concerned, the court reasoned:

> As a general rule, a motorist who approaches and enters an intersection on a green light, where the intersection is controlled by an electric semaphore signal, is not required to observe traffic facing a red or stop signal at that crossing, but he may rely on the assumption that motorists on the intersection street will obey the traffic signal and stop.... There, however, are exceptions to that rule. Although the motorist may assume that an electric semaphore signal will be obeyed by other motorists, he nevertheless must continue to exercise the caution that is commensurate with the circumstances as he approaches and enters the crossing. He is required to maintain a general observation of the controlled intersection, even though he enters with a green light facing him, and he must avoid accidents which can be averted by the exercise of the slightest degree of care.

From the evidence it was clear that Mr Daussat had crossed a substantial part of the intersection before the collision occurred, and Mrs Putt had barely entered it. Also there was nothing to obstruct her view and both vehicles were proceeding at relatively slow speeds, Mrs Putt at 30 miles per hour and Mr Daussat at 35 miles per hour. Mrs Putt testified that until the moment of collision she had not seen the vehicle, whereas Mr Daussat testified that he saw Mrs Putt's vehicle approaching when he was at least half a block from the traffic light.

The Court of Appeals of Louisiana held that:

> We believe that Mrs. Putt could and would have observed the Daussat car as it crossed the south-bound lanes of traffic and the neutral ground of Orleans Avenue if she had been maintaining a general observation of the intersection as she approached it, or if she had been exercising the caution which was commensurate with the circumstances. If she had seen his car in the intersection before she reached it, she could have avoided the accident by merely reducing the speed of her car slightly, and thus allowing the other vehicle to clear her lane of traffic, before she proceeded into the crossing. She thus could have avoided the accident by exercising only the slightest degree of care.

It was argued that since Mrs Putt's negligence in failing to observe the car and avoiding it was a contributory cause of the accident, the court held that she was barred from recovery. So was Mr Daussat. The trial court's verdict was affirmed.

We find that while Mr Daussat was held negligent by the due care approach, Mrs Putt was held negligent by the untaken precaution approach. She had the light in her favour and was driving at slow speed, yet her failure to observe the negligence of Mr Daussat, who was driving on a red light, was seen as negligence. Since she could have avoided the accident by reducing her speed by a little, she was held to have "failed to exercise the slightest degree of care in attempting to avoid the collision." We note that this can be inferred as the "extra care" over and above what she had been taking. The extra precaution of reducing the speed was cost-justified given that the other party was negligent.

4.2 Cases where the reasoning points towards the adoption of the untaken precaution approach in holding the injurer negligent

Levi v Southwest Louisiana Electric Membership Cooperative[16] concerned a case in which an oil field worker was critically injured by an electric shock when the mast of his truck came in contact with a 14,400-volt uninsulated electric distribution line run by Southwest Louisiana Electric Membership Company (Slemco). On February 16, 1982, Giovanni Levi, an employee for Amoco Oil Company as a pumper in an oil production field referred to as Dome Field in St Martin Parish, was working with a co-worker Randy Calais when they encountered an equipment problem – a cable became entangled in the paraffin lubricator. Since they did not have the appropriate instruments to do the repair work, they decided to go to another part of the oilfield. On the main road they came across a group of contract employees whom Levi knew and who had the tools he required. He pulled over his truck next to E. C. Stuart Well # 2. After descending from his truck, he started to raise the mast in order to do the repairs and in the process the mast either came very close to or actually touched the power line closest to the well and the electric shock went through his body. As a result he suffered burns and scarring, as well as muscle and tissue damage to his lower extremities, which necessitated amputation of both legs just below the knees. Levi filed a suit for damages before the 15th Judicial District Court, Parish of Lafayette (Louisiana). At the trial, the jury found that the company's conduct had not fallen below the required standard of care. He appealed to the Court of Appeals of Louisiana, Third Circuit, which affirmed the verdict of the District Court by a majority. Levi appealed to the Supreme Court of Louisiana, which reversed.

Amoco owned the Dome field, which consisted of 22 producing wells that were drilled in the 1940s and 1950s. All the wells were drilled before Slemco constructed electrical distribution lines in the Dome field. In the 1960s, Slemco had constructed an uninsulated electrical distribution line to serve most of the 22 wells producing in the field. They routed it so as to avoid crossing a well driveway or coming in close proximity to the well by placing the line either across the main road from the well or behind the well, with the exception of E. C. Stuart Well # 2, where the accident occurred. Here the line crossed the access road leading to the well 40.5 feet from the well ahead and 25.7 feet overhead. Slemco's failure to avoid a driveway traversal or a close encounter between its line and E. C. Stuart Well # 2 was because that well was omitted from the power company's original construction plan due to oversight or to the fact that no electricity was supplied to that well or both.

On the day of the accident, Levi and Calais were servicing wells in the field when they found it necessary to dismantle the lubricator for repairs. After borrowing the tools they needed, they looked for a dry place to repair the rig and selected the E. C. Stuart Well # 2 site for the purpose. It was necessary for the workers to raise the mast of the truck and lower the lubricator to the ground to make the repairs. Using control levers, on the side of the truck, Levi raised the mast tip up, over the truck and back towards the power line. Levi had noticed the distribution line at that location on previous occasions but failed to pay attention to it on the day of the incident. The jury found that there was no breach of duty on the part of Slemco and that the risk of harm which resulted in the plaintiff's injuries was not encompassed within Slemco's duty.

Levi's contention before the Court of Appeals was that the jury verdict was erroneous in finding that Slemco did not fall below the standard of care to which it was subject and that the trial court erred in refusing to instruct the jury that if a power company knows of an activity in the area of its lines, it is under a duty to protect workers and others from foreseeable danger by making further inquiry into the nature and extent of the activity and by continuing to provide insulation or covering for its wires. Slemco's argument in support of the jury verdict was five-fold: (i) it complied with the safety standards and isolated the wires at least 20 feet above the ground; (ii) Levi was not servicing E. C. Stuart Well #2 at the time of the accident; (iii) Slemco did not provide electrical service to the well; (iv) although Slemco may have been aware of the presence of high masted equipment in the Dome field, it had no knowledge that the equipment was operated near its lines; and (v) Levi raised the boom of his paraffin truck into a clearly visible power line.

The Court of Appeals examined the record and stated:

> "The location of the power line within 40.5 feet of the EC Stuart well would be far too close to the lines considering the relative size of the paraffin lubricator, workover rigs and other high masted equipment used in the oil field. The most important factor . . . is the knowledge that Slemco had of the operations in the dome Field. This knowledge is evidenced by the testimony of Slemco employees that they were aware of the use of high masted equipment including paraffin lubricators in the field. This knowledge of the risk of harm is further evidenced by the conscious effort of Slemco to avoid the various well access roads through a design process of bypassing these various wells. Slemco used this bypass process for all well sites except for the accident site and in one location where the power line was located 150 feet from the well head.

It reached the conclusion that there was no clear error in the jury's verdict on the basis of the following reasoning:

> The construction of Slemco's line in the Dome Field is in compliance with safety standards established by the National Electric Safety Code. All of the wells located in the dome field were drilled and in production before Slemco constructed its lines. There has been no environmental change in the Dome

Field since Slemco's lines were installed some 16 years prior to this accident.... The location of this line poses no danger to high masted equipment servicing this well, such as that operated by appellant, i.e., a truck 19 feet long with a boom 26.5 feet long, because in servicing such well, it was necessary to back down the access road to well and then raise and position the service equipment over the well head. At the time of the accident appellant was not servicing the E.C. Stuart # 2 well.

The Court highlighted the fact that the Stuart well road was a dead end road that intersected the main road through the Dome field and was constructed solely for the purpose of gaining access to the Stuart well, and Slemco could therefore expect that this road would be used exclusively by persons servicing the Stuart well. The court concluded that it was a combination of unusual factors that concurred to cause this accident:

> The entanglement of the cable in the paraffin lubricator while performing work on the St. Martin # 8 well; the lack of tools necessary to disassemble the lubricator at the site of the break-down; the discovery of a crew on the main road across from the Stuart well road with the necessary tools to effect the repairs; the decision of the appellant to pull his truck front end first onto the Stuart road in close proximity to the Slemco line although several other nearby safe locations were available; and, finally, Levi's act of raising the boom into a clearly visible power line of which he was admittedly aware.

The Court concluded that the facts and the circumstances surrounding the unfortunate accident do not support a conclusion that Slemco violated any legal duty to the appellant.

Judge Knoll dissented in part and gave his reasons from the judgment from *Frazee v Gulf States Utilities Co*. 498 So. 2d 47 (La. App. 1st cir. 1986):

> It is well settled that *Louisiana courts require a high duty of care by those dealing in the manufacture and distribution of electricity*. Utility companies which maintain and employ high voltage power lines are required to exercise the utmost care to reduce hazards to life as far as practicable, and are required to protect against reasonably foreseeable situations. (emphasis added)

He went on to argue that:

> The evidence is equally clear that although none of Slemco's employees were designated as inspectors, its service personnel, linemen and meter readers, were aware of the use of paraffin trucks at the various wellhead sites. With wires carrying 14,400 volts of electricity, arcing or direct contact with wires was reasonably foreseeable.

He further argued:

> It is of no moment that Slemco was not providing electricity to the E.C. Stuart well or that Levi was not servicing that well. Slemco knowingly placed these electric distribution lines in close proximity (within 41 feet) to this particular wellhead, and crossed over the access road to the well. Slemco did this even though all other cases in the Dome Field it purposefully did otherwise. Slemco, . . . argues that it does not have to anticipate every accident. In the present case, since Slemco knew that high masted equipment was in regular use in the dome Field it was reasonable for Slemco to expect that the equipment would have to cross under the lines, and because of the size of Mr. Levi's paraffin truck and the short distance between the power lines and the well (the next closest distance in the Dome Field was 73 feet) it was just as likely for the boom to come in close proximity to the lines. Furthermore, since Slemco was aware of the presence of high masted equipment on a regular basis it was likely for that machinery to break down and need repair. The access roads at any of the wellhead sites provided a shelled place to make repairs in an oil field that was described as low lying, swampy, and poorly drained. Such was the case in the present matter: Levi's presence at this wellhead site came after almost one week of rain.

Judge Knoll concluded that since Slemco allowed a dangerous condition to exist it had breached its duty to safeguard the public and was responsible for Levi's injuries.

We note that in the Court of Appeals, both the majority and Judge Knoll adopted the due care approach, but the magnitudes were different. Regarding the contributory negligence question, Judge Guidry had said that Levi chose that site for repairs "although several other nearby safe locations were available," indicating that choosing the other options was cost-justified. Judge Knoll, however, points out that after a week of rain, it was difficult to find a dry place and "the access roads at any of the well head sites provided a shelled place to make repairs in an oilfield that was described as low lying, swampy and poorly drained."

The Supreme Court of Louisiana reversed the verdict stating that the power company should have recognized that its conduct involved risk of harm to oil field workers. It had actual knowledge of previous instances of oil field workers' negligence or inattentiveness in moving erect masts under or near the uninsulated power lines. It elaborated:

> In the present case there is no dispute as to the fact that the power company had actual knowledge of the oil company's regular use of the trucks with erectable high masts around its well. Because this activity had continued on a regular basis over a long period of time the power company should have been aware of the physical characteristics of this equipment and any electrical hazard it might create. An Amoco employee testified that although the E.C. Stuart # 2 Well was not a 'problem paraffin well', the paraffin was removed

from it every two to three weeks. Levi testified that other wells in the field were serviced as frequently as every week. The truck involved in the accident was designed to cut paraffin accumulating in the wells. The truck itself measured 19 feet in length. The mast attached to the rear of the truck with hinges, 7.4 feet above ground level, was 26.5 feet long. Thus, when raised to its full height the mast extended approximately 34 feet above ground level. Since the power company knew that its uninsulated 14,400-volt electric line passed near oil wells at a level of only 25 to 26 feet above ground, the company should have known that electrical hazards would be created if masts were raised near the line.

Further, the argument was that:

> We do not think reasonable minds can disagree with the conclusion that the power company, particularly with its superior knowledge, skill and experience in electrical safety, should have recognized that its conduct under these circumstances involved risk of harm to oil field workers. Aside from the obvious serious possibility that an inattentive worker might raise the mast while parked on the access too near the power line, there were similar chances that a falling mast could pass dangerously close to the line or that a careless roustabout might attempt to drive under the line on his way to another well without fully lowering his mast.

To the complaint of the power company that it should not be charged with recognition of any risk that takes effect through a victim's negligence, the Supreme Court argued:

> But the ordinary reasonable person, and even more so the power company, is required to realize that there will be a certain amount of negligence in the world. When the risk becomes serious, either because the threatened harm is great, or because there is an especial likelihood that it will occur, reasonable care demand precautions against, 'that occasional negligence which is one of the ordinary incidents of human life and therefore to be anticipated. . . . It is not due care to depend on the exercise of care by another when such reliance is accompanied by obvious danger.' Since 'the power company had actual knowledge of previous instances of oil field workers' negligence or inattentiveness in moving erect masts under or near the uninsulated power lines', it should have taken 'utmost care.'

Regarding the question whether the hazard was unreasonable risk of harm, the Court argued:

> The facts of the present controversy and other similar power line cases invite a sharp focus upon the essential balancing process that lies at the heart of

negligence. . . . In such a case, a paraphrase of the hand formula helps to bring the elements of the process into relief: since there are occasions when high voltage electricity will escape from an uninsulated transmission line, and since, if it does, it becomes a menace to those about the point of its escape, the power company's duty, as in similar situations, to provide against resulting injuries is a function of three variables: (1) the possibility that the electricity will escape; (2) the gravity of the resulting injury, if it does; (3) the burden of taking adequate precautions that would alert the mishap. When the product of the possibility of escape multiplied times the gravity of the harm, if it happens, exceeds the burden of precautions, the failure to take those precautions is negligence.

Given the negligence of the other party, extra precaution was justified.

In the context of the present case, the Supreme Court held:

the likelihood that a roustabout's inattentiveness or that a malfunction of a rig would allow a mast to come close enough to the uninsulated power line to cause electricity to escape varied between locations in the oil field. This danger was greatest on the E.C. Stuart # 2 well site at which the accident happened. This was the only location at which the power company suspended its uninsulated line completely across a road used by masted truck operators for access to a well. It was one site where the uninsulated line was located only about two truck lengths from the well, leaving very little room for a high masted truck to maneuver safely. The fact that the power company systematically avoided these hazards elsewhere within the oil field possibly tended to make workers less wary of them at the accident site and thereby increased the likelihood of an accident. Under these circumstances, there was a significant chance that the power company's conduct would cause harm or death to one or more of the class of workers handling masted equipment at the well site.

The plaintiff had alleged several untaken precautions:

(1) The power company could have routed the line differently so as to avoid creating a hazardous driveway crossing and a dangerously small workspace abutting the hot high voltage wires; (2) The company simply could have raised the line to a safer level at the site of the accident; (3) The utility could have replaced the line at the well with factory installed insulation or could have insulated the line temporarily with rubber hose type insulation; (4) The company could have attached one of various forms of warnings, i.e., signs on poles, stakes or on the line itself; or orange balls on the wires; (5) The power utility could have installed the line underground instead of overhead at the accident site.

The defendants did not argue that the precautions were not cost-justified, but held that they did not satisfy the cause-in-fact requirement. The Supreme Court, however, examined each precaution and held that they could have prevented the accident. It was held that rerouting the power line to eliminate the danger at the Stuart well could have been done without creating danger elsewhere as was alleged by the defendant's expert. Also, the court held:

> As for the company's evidence that insulation of the line would have to be replaced from time to time, it is clear that this small additional cost would not cause the burden of precautions to outweigh the gravity of the harm threatened when multiplied by the likelihood that it will happen.

Slemco had argued that no warning would have been effective because the plaintiff knew of the existence of the uninsulated line and nevertheless encountered the danger. The Supreme Court held:

> The purpose of a duty of care or standard of care requiring a warning, however, is to attract and arrest the attention of a potential victim. It assumes both the possibility and probability of his inattention. Although such legal obligation is not imposed to protect the utterly indifferent or foolhardy, at the same time, however, its protection is not restricted to those whose senses are precisely attuned to the prospect of the particular warning called for.

It further held:

> The evidence does not indicate that Levi would have been oblivious to a warning sign or an orange ball warning on the power line at the E.C. Stuart well site. On the contrary, there is every reason to believe that if such a warning had been posted, because of the absence of warnings at other well sites (due to lack of necessity for them there), Levi's attention would have been drawn to the warning, causing him to be more attentive to the danger.

The Supreme Court finally concluded:

> When the components of the evidence are brought into relief and weighed in the light of their interrelationships, reasonable minds must agree that minimal burden of adequate precautions was clearly outweighed by the product of the chance and the gravity of harm. Accordingly, the power company was guilty of negligence that was a legal cause of the plaintiff's injuries, or, in other words, the company breached its duty to take precautions against the risk that took effect as those injuries, and the lower courts committed manifest error in not reaching this conclusion.

J. Marcus, concurring with the verdict held: "I agree that the power company breached its high duty of care to plaintiff under the circumstances, and the risk of plaintiff's accident was within the scope of the duty owed." J. Lemmon, in his dissenting opinion reasoned:

> The problem with plaintiff's theory is that oilfield activity in servicing this well site had nothing to do with this accident, and therefore any fault in defendant's placement of its lines in proximity to foreseeable oilfield activity near the well site was not a cause in fact of this accident. The well site could have been located 200 feet from the power line, and the accident would have occurred exactly as it did when plaintiff pulled off the main road into the spot he chose to perform his repair. Any duty on defendant to place its power lines a reasonable distance from the well site did not extend to a plaintiff who pulled off the main road to perform a job chore that had nothing to do with the well site and could have been performed at any dry location on the entire field.

He went on to specifically elaborate on the options the plaintiff had:

> Plaintiff could have stopped on the roadway, on a shell driveway across the roadway from this particular site, or at any of the numerous other places where there was a shelled area. Because the power lines crossed the main road at least six times, there were at least six points on the main road that posed this exact hazard to an inattentive worker who stopped his truck to repair the crane.

We note that whether the plaintiff was responsible for his own injuries was a crucial point, given that the power company had been negligent in its placement of the wires. While the majority thought that his choice of site for repair was cost-justified given that it had rained during the previous week and a dry level spot was difficult to come by, J. Lemmon argued that such a spot could be found. However, the fact that such danger points existed on six locations only indicates that safe points were indeed very few on the oil field. Perhaps it would be costly to go around the whole field looking for a suitable spot. We note that the essential difference in the conclusions arose from the reasoning adopted. While the jury, the Court of Appeals and Lemmon adopted the due care approach, the Supreme Court adopted the untaken precautions approach to hold the defendants negligent. Since the power company knew that oil field workers were often negligent, the standard required of them was higher. Many cost-justified precautions could be found which, if taken, could have averted the accident.

Pipher v Parsell[17] concerned a case in which one passenger brought an action against the driver of a truck for failing to prevent a second passenger from grabbing the steering wheel and causing an accident. On March 20, 2002, around 6.00 p.m., three 16-year olds – Kristyn Pipher, Johnathan Parsell and Johnene Beisel – were travelling south of Delaware Route 1 near Lewes, Delaware, in Parsell's pick-up truck, all three in the front seat. Parsell was driving, Pipher was sitting in the middle and Beisel was in the passenger seat next to the door. As they were travelling at 55 miles an hour, Beisel unexpectedly "grabbed the steering wheel causing the truck to veer off onto the shoulder of the road." Parsell did not do anything in response. About 30 seconds later, Beisel repeated her action. This time it caused Parsell's truck to leave the roadway, slide down an embankment and strike a tree. Pipher was injured as a result of this and she brought an action against the other two. She alleged that despite the dangerous nature of the conduct, Parsell and Beisel just laughed about it like it was a joke. The trial judge of the Superior Court of Delaware, in and from Kent County, ruled in favour of the defendant driver. The plaintiff appealed to the Supreme Court of Delaware, which reversed the judgment.

At the trial, Pipher testified that the three occupants in the vehicle were engaged in a light hearted conversation as they drove south on Route 1. She said that after Beisel yanked the steering wheel for the first time, Parsell was able to regain control of the truck. She felt Beisel grabbed the steering wheel a second time because Parsell "laughed it off" the first time. Parsell acknowledged that he could have taken different steps to prevent Beisel from grabbing the wheel a second time. He could have admonished her, pulled over to the side of the road and required her to get to the back seat or warned her that he would put her out of the vehicle. Beisel was not traceable before, during or after the trial. The trial judge concluded that Parsell had no duty to do anything after Beisel yanked the wheel for the first time because it would be reasonable for the driver to assume that it would not happen again. Additionally, the trial judge ruled that there was no negligence in failing to discharge the dangerous passenger and that failing to admonish the dangerous passenger was not negligence and could not be considered a proximate cause of Pipher's injuries.

In the Supreme Court of Delaware, the allegations of Pipher were examined. She had argued that after Beisel grabbed the steering wheel initially, "Parsell was on notice that a dangerous situation would reoccur in the truck." She alleged that "once Parsell had notice of a possibly dangerous situation, he had the duty to exercise reasonable care to protect his passengers from harm." Parsell went on driving without attempting to remove, or at least address, that risk. Parsell had testified that Beisel's conduct caused him both shock and surprise. Though he was on guard he did not expect Beisel to grab the wheel again. The Supreme Court observed: "Nevertheless, his recognition of how serious Beisel's conduct was, shows he was aware that he now had someone in his car who had engaged in dangerous behavior." Justice Holland referred to the similar case of *Bessette v Humiston*[18] in which the Supreme Court of Vermont had held a driver liable in damages resulting from the passenger seizing the driver's arm and knowing that the driver was "a playful fellow," he should have forecast the peril. Justice Holland concluded: "In such cases, the driver is expected to make a reasonable attempt to prevent the passenger from taking such actions again."

We find that the trial court decided that the driver was nonnegligent by following the due care approach and held that he was entitled to assume responsible behavior on the part of his passengers. The Supreme Court of Delaware, however, used the untaken precaution approach holding that Parsell, knowing that Beisel was engaging in dangerous conduct, continued as if nothing had happened. Justice Holland argued:

> In general, where the actions of a passenger that cause an accident are not foreseeable, there is no negligence attributable to the driver. But, when actions of a passenger that interfere with the driver's safe operation of the motor vehicle are foreseeable, the failure to prevent such conduct may be a breach of the driver's duty either to other passengers or to the public. Under the circumstances of this case, a reasonable jury could find that Parsell breached his duty to protect Pipher from Beisel by preventing Beisel from grabbing the steering wheel a second time.

The particular untaken precautions that were identified by Pipher: admonishing Beisel, stopping the vehicle and sending her to the back seat or warning her that he would make her leave the vehicle were acknowledged to be actions that would constitute a "reasonable attempt" to prevent Beisel's repeat conduct. We can infer that the Supreme Court thought that they were cost-justified.

4.3 Cases where the reasoning points towards the adoption of both the approaches in holding the injurer negligent

One oft-cited case in the economic analysis of law is *Davis v Consolidated Rail Corp.*[19] The plaintiff, Davis, then 33 years of age, was employed as an inspector by the Trailer Train Co., a lessor of cars to railroads. On the day of the accident in 1983, Davis had come to the marshaling yard of Conrail in East St. Louis in an unmarked van that was the same colour as the Conrail vans used in the yard but without the identifying "C" painted on each of Conrail's vans. He saw a train coming from east to west and noticed that several of its cars were Trailer Train cars that he was required to inspect. The train halted and was decoupled near the front; the locomotive followed by several cars pulled away to the west. Without informing anyone, Davis started his inspection and this required him to crawl underneath the cars to look for cracks. Suddenly the train started moving without any advance warning. In his attempt to scramble to safety, his leg got caught beneath the wheels and his leg was severed below the knee and most of the foot of the other leg was also sliced off. Davis brought a suit for damages in the United States District Court for the Southern District of Illinois, Alton Division, and a jury, which awarded damages amounting to three million dollars, though they reduced the amount going to Davis by one-third on the ground of contributory negligence. The two defendants, Conrail and Trailer Train, appealed to the United States Court of Appeals, Seventh Circuit, which affirmed the verdict of the jury.

From the evidence, it was found that after the decoupling the remainder of the locomotive was stretched out for three-quarters of a mile to the east and because it lay on a curved section of the track, its rear end was not visible from the point of decoupling. The train had a crew of four – two were in the cab of the locomotive and the other two, one of whom was designated as the rear brakeman, were somewhere alongside the train (the record did not show where but they were nowhere near the western end of the train where Davis was). The crew was ordered to move the train because it was blocking a switch. The crew made the movement without blowing the train's horn or ringing its bell. The only warning perceived by Davis of the impending movement was the sudden rush of air as the air brakes were activated. Davis had not given any indication before crawling under the cars; he did not hang a metal blue flag on the train, as longstanding railroad custom and regulation required him to do.

Regarding the negligence of Conrail, Davis presented three theories to the jury each of which consisted of an untaken precaution by the railroad which could have prevented the injury. His first claim was that Lundy, an employee of Conrail, who was equipped with a two-way radio should have notified the crew that an unknown man was sitting in a van parked near the tracks. In the Court of Appeals, Judge Posner argued that Lundy had no reason to think that the man in the van would crawl under the railroad cars on a live track – a track that was not blue-flagged. Judge Posner stated:

> Maybe, since the van resembled the vans used by Conrail employees, it should have occurred to Lundy that the person in the van had business on the tracks. But it is a big jump from recognizing that possibility to thinking that the man was in danger because he might crawl under a car without taking the usual precautions. . . . In sum, the probability that Davis would crawl under a car without first asking that it be blue flagged was too low, as it reasonably appeared to Lundy, to obligate Lundy to warn Davis or alert the train's crew.

Judge Posner was saying in effect that Lundy was entitled to assume that the man in the van would take due care. Given that, the probability of harm was low; thus, the precaution of informing the crew was not cost-justified.[20] In this context, Judge Posner quoted Judge Learned Hand's negligence formula.

Davis's second theory was that before the train was moved a member of the crew should have walked the whole length of the train checking under the cars. This, Judge Posner argued, would have taken an hour since there were 50 cars in all stretching over a total distance of a mile and a half, and since the cars were only 12 inches off the ground, checking would necessitate getting on the ground on all fours. Since the probability that someone was under the cars was so slight, this precaution was not cost-justified. The third theory was that it was negligent for the crew to move the train without first ringing the bell or blowing the horn. Judge Posner argued:

> Although the crew had no reason to think that Davis was under a car, someone – whether an employee of Conrail or some other business invitee to the yard (such as Davis) – might have been standing in or on a car or between cars,

for purposes of making repairs or conducting an inspection; and any such person could be severely, even fatally, injured if the train pulled away without any warning or even just moved a few feet. Regarding the application of the Hand formula to such a theory of negligence, not only was B vanishingly small – for what would it cost to blow the train's horn? – but P was significant, though not large, once all the possible accidents that blowing the horn would have averted are added together. For in determining the benefits of a precaution – the PL, the expected accident costs that the precaution would avert, is a measure of the benefits of the precaution – the trier of fact must consider not only the expected cost of this accident but also the expected cost of any other, similar accidents that the precaution would have prevented.

To the argument that the horn would not have been effective, Judge Posner reasoned that although such a possibility was there in a busy yard in which every movement of train would cause a cacophony and deprive the horn of its efficacy, in the instant case, there was no way to determine its effect without knowledge of the actual circumstances prevailing in the yard. Conrail's argument was that, given the blue-flag rule, the train had no duty to warn the persons who might be near or under the train. To this Judge Posner responds:

> There is in general no duty to anticipate and take precautions against the negligence of another person. Such a requirement would tend to induce potential injurers to take excessive safety precautions relative to those taken by potential victims; the cost of safety would rise.

Thus,

> If the motorist on the through highway had to travel at such a speed that he could stop his car in time to avoid collisions with vehicles which ignore stop signs on intersecting roads, the purpose of having a through highway in the first place would be entirely thwarted.

He went to say:

> It is true that if precautions necessary to prevent an undue risk of injury to persons who are exercising due care are omitted and a careless person is injured as a result, then in a jurisdiction such as Illinois where the complete defense of contributory negligence has given way to the partial defense of comparative negligence the careless victim can recover some damages. But he can do so, in general, only if there was a breach of duty to the careful.

This amounts to saying that even if the other party is negligent, if due care calculated on the assumption that the other party is taking due care is not taken then the party will be found negligent. All he is saying is that if due care is not adhered to, there will be a breach. We know that when the untaken precautions approach is adopted, the due care level would be higher. According to Judge Posner's argument, even if others are negligent the due care level that is applicable is the lower one calculated on the assumption that others are taking due care.

He went on to argue:

> The burden of sounding the horn would have been trivial, and the expected benefits positive, for despite the blue flag rule there was some probability that an employee or invitee was working in or dangerously near the train, reasonably believing that he would receive some warning before the train pulled away.

We note that he was saying that despite the blue-flag rule, Conrail was not supposed to place complete reliance on it. Judge Posner further argued:

> Moreover, we were careful to qualify our statement of the rule that a potential injurer is entitled to assume that potential victims will exercise due care, by saying that this is true 'in general.' A certain amount of negligence is unavoidable, because the standard of care is set with reference to the average person and some people have below-average ability to take care and so can't comply with the standard, and because in any event efforts at being careful produce only a probability, not a certainty, of avoiding careless conduct through momentary inattention. Potential injurers may therefore be required to take *some* care for the protection of the negligent, especially when the probability of negligence is high or the costs of care very low. You cannot close your eyes while driving through an intersection, merely because you have a green light. If, as the jury could have found, Conrail could have avoided this accident by the essentially costless step of blowing the train's horn, it may have been duty-bound to do so even if only a careless person would have been endangered by the sudden movement of the train.

The Court found evidence of Trailer Train's negligence as well. It was held that the nature of the work that Davis did would necessitate that he be told how to protect himself. However, his employers did not tell him that. They "relied on the fact that Davis was an experienced railroad worker who knew all about blue flags and the danger of being under a car when the train started to move." Judge Posner argued that Trailer Train had no safety rule for its employees:

> A reasonable jury could find (if barely) that Trailer train should have made clear to Davis that he was not to inspect any car without insisting on blue flagging and should have prescribed a procedure for implementing this requirement. Since blue flagging takes some time, the absence of a work rule put Davis in a potential dilemma. If he was too meticulous about safety, this might slow down his inspections too much and jeopardize his job. Trailer

Train should have dispelled any doubt that safety must come first. . . . He should have been more careful and if so would have averted this terrible accident. But that just means he was contributorily negligent; *it does not completely excuse Trailer Train for relying on his prudence and caution.* (emphasis added)

It can be inferred that Judge Posner was saying that Trailer Train was not entitled to rely on Davis taking due care, although they knew that he was an experienced worker who had been in their employment for the past six years prior to the accident.

Regarding the negligence of the plaintiff, his failure to blue-flag the train was seen to be negligent. Judge Posner argued:

When he saw the western end of the train pull away he assumed the train would stay put. Yet as an experienced railroad worker he knew perfectly well that the train could be pulled from either end, and since he couldn't see the other end from where he was working, he was taking a grave risk that a locomotive would hook on to that end and pull the train east, crushing him beneath it. He may well have been more negligent than the railroad.

One can infer from here that Davis, being an experienced railroad worker, was not entitled to assume that the train would stay put and would not move without advance warning. We find that the untaken precaution approach is being applied in determining his contributory negligence. Judge Posner argued in the context of assumption of risk:

Davis knew there was a chance that the train would pull away without warning, but reckoned the chance small (perhaps counting on the railroad to be more careful than it was), and decided to take it. Such conduct in the face of obvious danger of negligence is the type of assumption of risk that closely resembles contributory negligence ('secondary' assumption of risk, it is sometimes called) and that has been abolished along with contributory negligence as a complete defense to liability. It does not presuppose the defendant's lack of negligence. It reduces the injurer's liability, but not to zero, if the injurer is negligent.

What Judge Posner was saying can be interpreted as follows: Davis had estimated a lower probability of harm because he relied on the assumption that the crew will blow the horn; thus, he did not think that the precaution of blue-flagging was cost-justified. Judge Posner thought that Davis was wrong in attaching such a low probability, and there is a hint in the argument that had David attached the correct estimate of probability then the precaution would have been cost-justified.

On the whole, we find that Judge Posner has been adopting the untaken precaution approach in his finding of negligence of all three parties. For each party due care required that they take some precaution – for Conrail, blow the horn and whistle; for Trailer Train, give proper safety instructions to their inspectors; and for Davis, blue-flag the train himself or ask the crew of Conrail to do it. Each party was not entitled to assume that the other party would take that precaution due care required, and they were all held negligent. In addition, Conrail and Davis were held negligent by the due care approach as well because by Illinois law, blowing the horn was a statutory duty, and regulation required that the blue-flag rule be followed.

Another important negligence case in this category is *Chicago, Burlington and Quincy Railroad Co. v Leo Krayenbuhl*[21] in which a minor, Leo Krayenbuhl, four years of age, sustained personal injuries while playing on a railroad turntable at Palmer, Nebraska. The incident occurred on Sunday, October 20, 1895, in the village of Palmer, which had 200 inhabitants, through which two lines of the defendant ran in a northwesterly direction. The turntable was located between the branches of the defendant's line. On the day of the incident, Leo's elder brothers and sisters placed him upon the turntable while they were playing, loosened it from its fastenings and revolved it by means of levers at the ends. In the course of the revolution, Leo's right foot was caught between the rails and severed at the ankle joint. The plaintiff's father, Samuel Krayenbuhl, as next friend, brought a suit against the Chicago, Burlington and Quincy Railroad Company in the District Court of Merrick County (Nebraska), and the jury entered a verdict for the plaintiff. The defendants brought error and the Supreme Court of Nebraska reversed the judgment for error in instructions to the jury amounting to improper comment on the evidence. On the question of negligence, the verdict of the jury was affirmed.

From the evidence, it was found that on and prior to the day of the incident, the defendants operated a line of railroad extending through the village of Palmer, at which point it maintained a passenger depot, roundhouse, coalhouse, water-tank and turntable. A path or footway, in common use by the general public and by the plaintiff's family, passed within about 70 feet of the turntable. The turntable had a movable bolt by which it could be held in position and was provided with a padlock. Although the defendant's rules required its employees to keep the turntable locked when not in use, there was evidence that this rule was frequently disregarded and that one of the staples was so loose that the turntable could be unfastened without difficulty. The children from the plaintiff's family and another family living close by often resorted to the coalhouse, roundhouse and turntable and rode on the turntable while it was in motion; this was known to the defendant, who did not object to it.

On the day of the incident, in the absence of his parents, the plaintiff along with his siblings and other children from the neighbourhood were playing in a push car, moving it up and down the railroad track. The agent in charge of the station joined them for a short distance, then left and went to his rooms in the station. The children continued to push the car and then reached the turntable which was alleged to be unlocked and unguarded. The defendants argued that on Saturday evening between 4.00 and 6.00 p.m., the roundhouse foreman, William Young, had assisted the trainmen in turning their engines and starting the trains and left after locking the turntable with the padlock and bolting the table into the frame surrounding it and there were no trains on Sunday. On Sunday, the plaintiff and some other children got on to the turntable, while two of the others set it in motion. While it was in motion, the plaintiff's foot was caught and mangled between the ends of the rails.

The Supreme Court of Nebraska went on to an exhaustive discussion of what is commonly known as the doctrine of turntable cases, which could be summarized as follows:

> where a turntable is so situated that its owner may reasonably expect that children too young to appreciate the danger will resort to it, and amuse themselves by using it, it is guilty of negligence for failure to take reasonable precautions to prevent such use.[22]

The defendant insisted that the doctrine was unsound and asked the court to repudiate it on the grounds that the owner of dangerous premises owes no active duty to trespassing children. In response to this the court quoted from the opinion by Sedgwick in *Tucker v Draper*,[23] where he says:

> There may be, and often are, circumstances under which one owes some active duty to a trespasser upon his premises. If a man willfully lies down upon a railroad track the engineer must not wantonly run his engine over him.... If I know that there is an open well upon my premises and know that children of such tender years as to have no notion of their danger are continually playing around it and can obviate the danger with very little trouble to myself and without injuring the premises or interfering with my own free use thereof, I owe an active duty to those children, and if I neglect that duty and they fall into the well and are killed it is through my negligence. I cannot urge their negligence as a defense, even though I never invited or encouraged them expressly or impliedly to go upon the premises.

We note that the cost of precautions has been mentioned – "obviate the danger with very little trouble" and without interfering with the use of the premises. Essentially, if cost-justified precautions exist, given one's knowledge of the negligence of the other party, one ought to take them.

C. Albert, in the Supreme Court of Nebraska examining Sedgwick's quote, held that:

> The language amounts to a reaffirmance of the doctrine of turntable cases, and, to our minds, suggests the true principle upon which cases of this character rest; that is, that where the owner of dangerous premises knows, or has good reason to believe, that children, so young as to be ignorant of the danger, will resort to such premises he is bound to take such precautions to keep them from such premises, or to protect them from injuries likely to result from the dangerous condition of the premises while there, as a man of ordinary care and prudence, under like circumstances, would take.

He elaborated:

> At first sight, it would seem that the principle, thus stated, is too broad, and that its application would impose unreasonable burdens on owners, and intolerable restrictions on the use and enjoyment of property. But it must be kept in mind that it requires nothing of the owner that a man of ordinary care and prudence would not do, of his own volition, under like circumstances. Such a man would not willingly take up unreasonable burdens, nor vex himself with intolerable restrictions.

The insistence is on cost-justified precautions – not that they have to take *all* precautions – cost-justified or not. This reasoning is consistent with the economic model.

In an oft-quoted passage of the opinion by Albert, we find further explanation:

> The business of life is better carried forward by the use of dangerous machinery; hence the public good demands its use, although occasionally such use results in the loss of life or limb. It does so because the danger is insignificant, when weighed against the benefits resulting from the use of such machinery, and for the same reason demands its reasonable, most effective and unrestricted use, up to the point where the benefits resulting from such use no longer outweigh the danger to be anticipated from it. At that point the public good demands restrictions. For example, a turntable is a dangerous contrivance, which facilitates railroading; the general benefits resulting from its use outweigh the occasional injuries inflicted by it; hence the public good demands its use. We may conceive of means by which it might be rendered absolutely safe, but such means would so interfere with its beneficial use that the danger to be anticipated would not justify their adoption; therefore the public good demands its use without them.

This conforms perfectly with the cost-benefit balancing that is adopted in the economic model.

With respect to the present case, one particular untaken precaution – that of provision of a lock – was pointed out to be cost-justified in the circumstances:

> But the danger incident to its use may be lessened by the use of a lock which would prevent children, attracted to it, from moving it; the interference with the proper use of the turntable occasioned by the use of such lock is so slight that it is outweighed by the danger to be anticipated from an omission to use it; therefore the public good, we think, demands the use of the lock.

He distinguished between situations when certain precautions would not be cost-justified and when they would:

> The public good would not require the owner of a vacant plot on which there is a pond to fill up the pond or enclose it with an impassable wall to

insure the safety of children resorting to it, because the burden of doing so is out of all proportion to the danger to be anticipated from leaving it undone. But where there is an open well on a vacant lot, which is frequented by children, of which the owner of the lot has knowledge, he is liable for the injuries sustained by children falling into the well, because the danger to be anticipated from the open well, under the circumstances, outweighs the slight expense or inconvenience that would be entailed in making it safe.

It is clear that the untaken precaution approach was being used to decide the question of negligence. We note that it is consistent with the due care approach as well. The court explicitly held that when the negligence of the other party is known, there would exist cost-justified precautions that ought to be taken. The Supreme Court stressed that those precautions would also have to be cause-in-fact as well as cost-justified:

> Hence, in all cases of this kind, in the determination of the question of negligence, regard must be had to the character and location of the premises, the purpose for which they are used, the probability of injury therefrom, the precautions necessary to prevent such injury, and the relations such precautions bear to the beneficial use of the premises. The nature of the precautions would depend on the particular facts in each case. In some cases, a warning to the children or the parents might be sufficient; in others, more active measures might be required. But in every case they should be such as a man of ordinary care and prudence would observe under like circumstances. If, under all the circumstances, the owner omits such precautions as a man of ordinary care and prudence, under like circumstances, would observe, he is guilty of negligence.

Although the defendants were found negligent, the Supreme Court reversed the verdict of the District Court on the grounds of error in instructions to the jury and remanded the case for further proceedings according to law.

4.4 Cases where the reasoning points towards the adoption of the due care approach in holding the injurer nonnegligent

Davison v Snohomish County[24] is an oft-cited case in which the plaintiffs were injured when their car disembarked from the road and went over a bridge when they were on their way to Snohomish County. It was about eight in the evening on November 11, 1926, when the plaintiff Edwin F. Davison was driving his Ford automobile towards Snohomish when they had to cross a bridge, known as the "Bascule Bridge," across Ebey slough from east to west at low speed when he lost control and the car skidded, struck the railing on the outer edge of the approach, broke through the railing and fell to the ground. The plaintiffs received severe injuries and the vehicle was wrecked. The plaintiffs filed a suit before the Superior Court for Snohomish County (Washington) alleging negligence in the construction and maintenance of the roadway. The court ruled in favour of the plaintiff. The defendants appealed to the Supreme Court of Washington (Department Two) which reversed the judgment of the trial court.

From the evidence it was found that in the southwesterly approach to this bridge there was a right angle turn towards the south, just easterly of the slough, and at that point the causeway or approach to the bridge was at quite an elevation above the ground level. The bridge itself was approximately 18 feet wide; the approach, leading to the bridge proper, at the curve just to the east of the bridge, increased in width to a maximum of 30.9 feet, narrowing again to 18 feet at the end of the turn. The plaintiffs alleged that at the time of the accident the railing through which their car broke was insufficient to act as a guard, that the posts which supported them were decayed and that the floor or deck of the approach was so constructed as to slope out and down from the centre of the curve to the outer edge. A considerable quantity of dirt had been scattered on and over the approach by the defendants while repairing the road near the west approach to the bridge prior to the accident, and rain had made it slippery; coupled with the other factors it was a menace to motor vehicle traffic.

The Supreme Court of Washington held that:

> It is undoubtedly the law that it is the duty if the municipality to keep bridges in a reasonably safe condition for travel.... On the other hand, a municipality is not an insurer of the safety of every one who uses its thoroughfares; nor is it required to keep the same in such a condition that accidents cannot possibly happen upon them.

The plaintiff had alleged three elements of negligence; first, the insufficiency of the railing or guard to prevent their car from skidding off the approach; second, the construction of the deck of the approach in a manner that it sloped downward towards the outer edge, which had a tendency to cause automobiles to slide in that direction; and third, the collected dirt had not been removed from the deck of the approach and rain had made it slippery.

Regarding the first untaken precaution, the Supreme Court stated:

> The use of the automobile as a means of transportation of passengers and freight has, during recent years, caused certain changes in the law governing the liability of municipalities in respect to the protection of their roads by railings or guards. A few years ago, when people traveled either on foot or by horse-drawn vehicles, a guard rail could, to a considerable extent, actually prevent pedestrians or animals drawing vehicles from accidentally leaving the roadbed; but, as a practical proposition, municipalities cannot be required to protect long stretches of roadway with railings or guards capable of preventing an automobile, moving at a rapid rate, from leaving the road if the car

be in any way deflected from the roadway proper and propelled against the railing.

The argument can be translated as saying that when people travelled by foot or by horse-drawn vehicles, the expected harm was low, and the precaution of guard railings were enough. However, with the use of automobiles the expected harm has risen. Even so, the Supreme Court held that to build and maintain railings strong enough for the new circumstances would be too costly. The Court quoted from *Leber v King County*, 69 Wash. 134, 124 P. 397, 42 L.R.A. (N.S) 267:

> Roads must be built and traveled, and to hold that the public cannot open their highways until they are prepared to fence their roads with barriers strong enough to hold a team and wagon when coming in violent contact with them, the condition being the ordinary condition of the country, would be to put a burden upon the public that it could not bear. It would prohibit the building of new roads and tend to the financial ruin of the counties undertaking to maintain the old ones.

It held that it was especially difficult to build a guard of any desired strength along the side of an elevated frame causeway or viaduct. This precaution was clearly not cost-justified.[25]

The next untaken precaution – that the approach of the deck sloped slightly downward – was not taken to "constitute such negligence on the part of appellant as would render appellant liable to respondents in this action." Regarding the third untaken precaution – that some dirt was scattered over the deck and rain had made it unusually slippery – the Supreme Court held that they were "unable to find any testimony in the record which would justify the submission of the element of alleged negligence to the jury." It was held:

> Appellant would not be liable because of any ordinary accumulation of dirt or similar matter upon the approach, unless a dangerous condition were permitted to exist for such a period of time as would imply, in law, notice to appellant of the fact that its roadway was unsafe, and it should further appear that appellant had been negligent in not remedying the condition within a reasonable time.

We find that the defendants were declared nonnegligent by the due care approach. It was evident that the Supreme Court did not find any cost-justified untaken precaution that could have prevented the accident. The court quoted from the decision in *Zolawenski v Aberdeen*[26]:

> Manifestly, it seems to us, a city cannot be held negligent for suffering to remain in a sidewalk a defect so inconsequential as this one was shown to be. A city is not an insurer of the personal safety of everyone who uses its public

walks. It owes no duty to keep them in such repair that accidents cannot possibly happen upon them. Its duty in this respect is done when it keeps them reasonably safe for use – safe for those who use them in the exercise of ordinary care – and we cannot but conclude that this one was thus reasonably safe.

This meant that the defendants were allowed to assume that people using the roadway would use ordinary care. Also, it was enough that precautions that were cost-justified were taken. There was no requirement that all accidents need to be eliminated. This is consistent with the economic model.

One case in which a domestic servant brought an action against her employer to recover damages for personal injuries sustained in her employment was *Mcdonald v Fryberger*.[27] On July 9, 1948, the defendants employed the plaintiff, who was 65 years old at the time in their home in the city of Duluth. Shortly before, the defendants had remodeled their kitchen and in the process new kitchen cabinets were installed. With the exception of the particular cabinet involved here, all the cabinets were fastened to the kitchen walls when installed. The cabinet in question had not been fastened because the defendant possibly contemplated making further rearrangements to their kitchen fixtures. On the morning of July 29, 1948, the plaintiff opened the bottom drawer and stepped on it to use it as a stepladder to put some bowls on a high shelf on the wall. The unsecured cabinet fell on her and she was injured. The plaintiff filed a suit in the District Court for St Louis County (Minnesota). The jury awarded her damages but the District Court granted judgment notwithstanding the verdict to the employer. The plaintiff sought review in the Supreme Court of Minnesota and on review the Court found no showing of negligence on the part of the employer.

The plaintiff's contention was that the defendants violated their duty as masters to provide a safe place to work and reasonably suitable and safe appliances to work with, and that the jury was justified in finding defendants negligent in the following respects: first, failure to have the cabinet fastened to the wall; second, failure to inform the plaintiff about this fact; and third, failure to furnish the plaintiff a stool or other instrumentality to enable her to reach the top kitchen shelves. Regarding the first precaution, it was on record that the Youngstown steel cabinet base came equipped with two wood screws about one and a half inches long with which it could be fastened to the wall. The manager of the kitchen appliance department of the Duluth store from where the defendants purchased their Youngstown cabinets testified that half of the 40 or 50 such cabinets he had personally installed were not fastened to the wall. It was entirely up to the customer; some installed them permanently, while others wanted them so they could be moved around. A witness called by the plaintiff, on the other hand, testified that out of the 150 cabinets he had installed in the Duluth area he did not recall installing a single one without fastening them to the wall. Both parties conceded that only light objects were kept in the drawers of the cabinet in question and that a weight or pressure in excess of 30 pounds placed upon the front end of the bottom drawer of an empty cabinet, such as the one in question, pulled out practically all the way will cause the cabinet to tip forward. The defendants claimed that the cabinets only became dangerous when it was put to an improper use by the plaintiff for a purpose for which it was neither constructed nor maintained. The defendants could not have anticipated or foreseen that the plaintiff would use it for the purpose to which she was using it at the time of the accident.

In response to the allegations that the defendants did not have a stepladder or step stool for their kitchen, the defendants argued that there were four hardwood kitchen chairs located in the dinette area of the kitchen which the plaintiff had used previously to reach the high shelves in the kitchen. The plaintiff, on her part, argued that the area was slippery and she decided not to use it "any more than (she) had) to." We find that she was trying to show that the expected harm from using the chairs was higher on this occasion because the floor was slippery, so she chose what she thought was the safer option. However, given that the cabinets were known to hold only a weight of 30 pounds, her choosing that option was not cost-justified as the accident proved ex post. The defendants had argued that the plaintiff was guilty of contributory negligence as a matter of law and assumed the risk incidental to her use of the cabinet drawer as a footstool. The Supreme Court quoted from *Christianson v C. St. P. M. & O. Ry. Co.*[28]: "★★★If a person had no reasonable ground to anticipate that a particular act would or might result in any injury to anybody, then, of course, the act would not be negligent at all; ★★★."

The Supreme Court further held:

> It is universally agreed, therefore, that an employer is not liable where the servant's injury was not caused by any defect in the appliance which affected its safety when it was used in the ordinary manner and for the purposes for which it was intended. . . . The mere fact that an appliance happens to be placed where it can be used for the performance of the work which the injured servant undertook to do with it does not warrant the inference that the master intended that he should use it as he did, or the inference that he was in fault in not knowing that he was likely to do so. Any other rule would involve the consequence that every master who leaves any implement upon his premises, which his servants cannot safely use for every purpose which suits their convenience, sets a trap for them.

Applying the principle to the present case, the court held:

> There is nothing in the record here to show that plaintiff or anyone else had previously used the cabinet drawer as a step stool. Such a use was not authorized by the defendants, and at no time did they have reason to expect that plaintiff would attempt so to use it. It appears that there were readily available four wooden chairs of solid construction for such use.

The Court finally quoted from *Blomberg v Trupukka*[29]: "★★★An act which exposes another to risk of injury only by his failure to conform to those rules of conduct for his own safety *with which he might reasonably be expected to comply* does not violate the standards of care" (emphasis added). It went on to state:

> Thus, where, as here, a standard kitchen appliance, reasonably safe for its intended purpose, is put to an improper, unauthorized, and unnecessary use by a domestic servant, and such use is one which the master cannot be expected to have foreseen, the master is not negligent or liable for injuries to the servant resulting from such improper use.

The court concluded that the record fails to establish negligence on the part of the defendants in any of the respects claimed. We note that the Supreme Court held the defendants nonnegligent by the due care approach. They were entitled to assume that the plaintiff would use due care. The court specifically subscribed to the argument: "Ordinary care does not involve forethought of extraordinary peril."

4.5 Cases where the reasoning points towards the adoption of the untaken precaution approach in holding the injurer nonnegligent

Blaak v Davidson[30] was a case in which the Supreme Court of Washington held that there can be no absolute rule with respect to automobiles, and the circumstances will determine whether a party is negligent. This case involved an accident that occurred when a delivery truck driver rearended a car in which the plaintiff was driving in conditions of near zero-visibility due to dust clouds. On September 16, 1971, when the defendant, Mr Davidson, was driving an 18,000-pound gasoline truck on the Pasco-Kahlotus Highway and visibility was poor due to the dust raised by winds from recently ploughed farmlands adjoining the highway. His visibility became completely obscured by a dust cloud in response to which he reduced his speed to 5 to 10 miles per hour. Despite the precaution, his truck hit the rear of the car that Mr Blaak was driving, and in which Mrs Blaak was a passenger. The plaintiff filed a suit in the Superior Court for Franklin County, Washington, which granted his motion for a new trial after the jury rendered a verdict in favour of the defendant driver. The Court of Appeals of Washington affirmed the trial court's entry of judgment notwithstanding the verdict against the truck driver. The defendant driver appealed to the Supreme Court of Washington, which reversed.

When the defendant was proceeding on the highway towards Kahlotus, a wind was blowing moderately with occasional strong and persistent gusts picking up loose soil from the adjoining farmlands and creating dust clouds that significantly reduced visibility. He passed through one such dust cloud that continued for 100 to 150 yards, after which the dust subsided and visibility increased to approximately one-quarter mile, and he observed that there were no cars on the highway ahead of him. Shortly thereafter, another dust cloud engulfed the truck and the highway completely obscuring visibility. On the plaintiff's post-trial motion the court held that when the defendant's visibility "became so obscured, as a matter of law he had a duty to stop his vehicle." Justice Munson took as conclusive evidence the testimony of the driver that he had "no visibility" and that it was necessary for him to look out the driver's door window and follow the centerline in order to sustain his forward movement of 5 to 10 miles per hour. In the order directing a verdict against the defendant, the trial court stated that the plaintiff's negligence, if any, was not a proximate cause of the collision. The defendant assigned on appeal to that and the Court of Appeals held that the verdict stood affirmed. It also affirmed the verdict that the defendant's negligence in failing to stop the truck was the proximate cause of the accident.

The Court of Appeals examined the untaken precaution of "stopping the vehicle when visibility was totally obscured." The defendants argued that visibility was partially obscured. However, the court held:

> Appellant should not drive any faster than that speed which would allow him to also observe the roadway to the front and right side and give such attention to such part of the roadway as will allow him to observe anything thereon in time to take appropriate action, which *would include the duty to stop*.

The defendant's testimony that: "after being engulfed by the dust cloud, he proceeded – 'probably 40, 50 yards, something like that or approximately 75 yards; 50, 75 yards' – at a speed of 5 to 10 m.p.h.," to which the court added: "This shows conclusively he could have stopped his vehicle." The reasoning for this deduction was given as:

> Defendant also testified that he was proceeding, at this slow rate of speed, in an attempt to get through the dust cloud, knowing of a turnoff a short distance ahead of the location of the accident. He had no intention of stopping once the dust cloud engulfed him. Consequently, even if he was "engulfed" by the cloud, he had time to stop his vehicle, but did not; he was negligent as a matter of law for failing to do so.

Justice Munson, however, added:

> This court is sympathetic to defendant's position. We perceive the more common driving practice is to proceed through fog or dust much in the same manner as did the defendant. There is also merit to the defendant's contention that to stop a highly dangerous gasoline truck upon the main traveled portion of the road in a cloud of dust would be extremely dangerous to the driver and to others.

However, the conclusion remained unaltered: "Nevertheless . . . the latest pronouncement by our Supreme Court on the precise question presented affirms the position that when visibility is totally obscured, there is a duty to stop." Here they are adopting a fixed rule as the due care level, irrespective of the burden of precautions.

Justice Green, in his dissenting opinion, emphasized that the cost of precautions ought to be considered in determining the issue of negligence. He reasoned:

> Under the evidence in the instant case, the jury could have found that both plaintiff and defendant were negligent in driving into the dust cloud or, on the other hand, they could have found that the dust suddenly engulfed both parties creating an emergency situation in which neither party should be held negligent – an act of nature over which neither party had any control. Moreover, the shoulder was too narrow to allow defendant to pull off the roadway. For the court to hold that defendant was negligent as a matter of law for not stopping his gasoline loaded truck weighing 18,000 pounds in the main portion of the highway, knowing that large wheat trucks and petroleum tankers regularly used that highway, invades a factual area that is more properly reserved for the jury. The danger contemplated by the defendant driver became a reality when the tanker traveling in the opposite direction struck another car which had stopped at the point of the accident involved in this case.

The reasoning in the Supreme Court of Washington was also along similar lines. It stated:

> The defendant did not stop the truck for three interrelated reasons: (1) large wheat trucks and petroleum tankers regularly traveled the road, and the defendant feared that one might strike his gasoline truck from the rear, thereby causing it to explode; (2) the shoulder of the highway was too narrow to allow the defendant to pull completely out of the line of travel of other vehicles traveling in the same direction; and (3) the defendant knew of a safe and sufficiently wide pull-out a short distance ahead, at which he intended to stop and wait for the dust storm to subside.

He had slowed to 2 to 3 miles per hour – nearly to a stop – on this normally high speed highway. At the time of collision, the defendant's headlights were on. The Supreme Court focussed attention on the crux of the matter: when the visibility of a driver of a vehicle is completely obscured by atmospheric conditions, e.g., a dust storm is the driver negligent as a matter of law for failure to stop the vehicle. Justice Finley held that in Washington, two divergent rules had evolved: one, if dust has been responsible for completely obscuring vision, it was generally held that the driver of the vehicle is under an absolute duty to stop and failure to do so leads to a finding of negligence as a matter of law; second, when the driver was blinded by the lights of an oncoming vehicle, although earlier decisions indicated an absolute duty to stop, more recent decisions indicated that it was a matter for the jury to decide. As regards obstruction of vision by sun, there is an absolute duty to stop. The Supreme Court thought this distinction to be "difficult and unrealistic."

Further, Justice Finley argued:

> A consideration of whether an absolute rule should be formulated must focus upon the subject matter involved and the potential variables as to facts and circumstances. In these respects, the automobile and its use in our mobile society is particularly unique. Seldom, if ever, are the facts and circumstances surrounding a collision the same. Thus, particularly with respect to automobiles, the property of solidifying the law into mechanistic rules for universal application is dubious, and this legal reasoning or philosophy is clearly on the wane.

Referring to the rule laid down by Justice Holmes in *Goodman* and subsequently rejected by Justice Cardozo in *Pokora*, Justice Finley argued that instead of an absolute rule, a growing number of cases prefer the jury to consider all the surrounding circumstances.

In the present case, the learned justice argued:

> The excessive rigidity of an absolute duty to stop is underscored by the facts of the instant case. Since it is the very nature of dust clouds – as well as fog – that their density and the surrounding lack of visibility may vary considerably within a few yards, the defendant herein could not assume that all vehicles behind him would necessarily be stopped. Moreover, the defendant's truck was loaded with gasoline; there was no place to immediately pull off the highway; and the defendant feared being rear ended on this heavily traveled road. That the defendant's fears were not solely the figment of an overactive imagination is well illustrated by the fact that a car which had stopped close to the place of the accident herein was struck by a tanker traveling in the opposite direction. In any event, it is at least debatable whether stopping on the highway for an indeterminate period of time would be safer, with respect to other users of the highway, than slowly proceeding to a known, safe, pull-out a short distance ahead.

A sweeping conclusion was reached:

> On the basis of the foregoing analysis we reject the rule holding a driver of a vehicle negligent as a matter of law for failure to stop when his vision is completely obscured, because such a rule would be too rigid to cope with the numerous situations presenting new or additional factors and variables ... when vision is partially or completely obscured, the jury should determine whether the defendant's failure to stop constitutes negligence under the general test of whether defendant acted as a reasonable man in view of all the facts and circumstances.

The two options that the driver had can be compared: first, stopping, and second, moving slowly with an intention of stopping at an appropriate juncture. Regarding the first option, the probability of being rearended was high if the vehicle stopped since it was a heavily travelled highway, and the magnitude of harm was also high since it was a truck carrying gasoline. It may have prevented this particular accident, but *ex ante* there was a possibility of greater damage. That was borne out by the collision that occurred when a car stopped close to the place of this accident. The precaution of slowly proceeding to a known, safe, pull-out a short distance ahead was cost-justified. There was the possibility that in the manner in which he was driving either he would be rearended or he may hit a car ahead of him, but the probability was lower than if he stopped. He took the risk on the assumed possibility of being able to reach the safe spot soon.

We note that he was adjudged nonnegligent by the untaken precaution approach. It was held that

> since it is the very nature of dust clouds – as well as fog – that their density and the corresponding lack of visibility may vary considerably within a few yards, the defendant herein could not assume that all vehicles behind him would necessarily be stopped.

That the driver was entitled to make the assumption that due care may not be exercised by other highway users under the prevailing conditions is indicative of the untaken precaution approach. Given the two options, the probability of collision appeared higher if he stopped. Thus, stopping was not cost-justified.

4.6 Cases where the reasoning points towards the adoption of both the approaches in holding the injurer nonnegligent

One famous negligence case that has been used to examine the reasoning employed by Justice Cardozo is *Adams v Bullock*.[31] The defendant ran a trolley line in the city of Dunkirk, which was powered by a system of overhead wires. At one point, the trolley line was crossed by a bridge that carried the tracks of the Nicole Plate and Pennsylvania railroads. The bridge was often used as a shortcut between streets, and children often played on it. On April 21, 1916, the plaintiff, a 12-year old boy, while crossing the bridge, was swinging a wire about eight feet long and it came in contact with the defendant's trolley wire, which ran beneath the bridge. The plaintiff received electrical shock and got burned when the wires came together. The trial term awarded a verdict in favour of the plaintiff. The defendants appealed to the Supreme Court of New York, Appellate Division, Fourth Department, on the ground that the evidence was insufficient to support the verdict. The verdict of the trial court was affirmed by a divided Court (J. Foote and J. De Angelis dissented). The defendants appealed to the Court of Appeals of New York, which reversed the judgment.

Justice Cardozo, who read the opinion of the Court of Appeals, recounted: The side of the bridge was protected by a parapet 18 inches wide. Four feet seven and three-quarters inches below the top of the parapet, the trolley wire was strung. He argued that there were no special dangers at this point on the bridge to warn the defendants that greater precaution should be taken. His reasoning is clear from the oft-quoted passage from the judgment:

> The defendant using an overhead trolley was in the lawful exercise of its franchise. Negligence, therefore, cannot be imputed to it because it used a system and not another. There was, of course, a duty to adopt all reasonable precautions to minimize the resulting perils. We think there is no evidence that this duty was ignored. The trolley wire was so placed that no one standing on the bridge or even bending over the parapet could reach it. Only some extraordinary casualty, not fairly within the area of ordinary prevision, could make it a thing of danger.

Justice Cardozo was in effect saying that there was no untaken precaution that was cost-justified. The expected harm at *this* point was low. This he went on to elaborate:

> Reasonable care in the use of destructive agency imports a high degree of vigilance. But no vigilance, however alert, unless fortified by the gift of prophecy, could have predicted the point upon the route where such an accident would occur. It might with equal reason have been expected anywhere else. At any point upon the route, a mischievous or thoughtless boy might touch the wire with a metal pole, or fling another wire across it. If unable to reach it from the walk, he might stand upon a wagon or climb upon a tree. No special danger at this bridge warned the defendant that there was need of special measures of precaution. No like accident had occurred before. No custom had been disregarded. We think that ordinary caution did not involve forethought of this extraordinary peril.

Next, he turned his attention to the burden of precautions. He argued:

> There is, we may add, a distinction, not to be ignored, between electric light and trolley wires. The distinction is that the former may be insulated. Chance of harm, though remote, may betoken negligence, if needless. Facility of protection may impose a duty to protect. With trolley wires, the case is different. Insulation is impossible. Guards here and there are of little value. To avert the possibility of this accident and others like it at one point or another on the route, the defendant must have abandoned the overhead system, and put the wires underground. Neither its power nor its duty to make the change is shown. To hold it liable upon the facts exhibited in this record would be to charge it as an insurer.

The only precaution that would have satisfied the cause-in-fact requirement would be to put the wires underground. However, Justice Cardozo argues that it was not shown that the defendants had the "power" to undertake that precaution. The term "power" could be interpreted as financial strength. He argued that it was not shown through cost calculations that given the low probability of harm, it was cost-justified to have undertaken the precaution of placing the wires underground. We note that Cardozo did not explicitly mention the magnitude of harm, perhaps because it is common knowledge that electrocution poses the gravest of dangers.

We find that the Court of Appeals held the defendants nonnegligent by the due care approach. Not only were they lawfully exercising their franchise they had also placed the wires in a manner so that no one standing on the parapet or even bending over the bridge could reach it. No other cost-justified precaution existed that could have prevented the accident. We can infer that the defendants were held nonnegligent by the untaken precaution approach as well. The court had acknowledged the fact that: "Pedestrians often use the bridge as a short cut between streets and children play on it." Also, there was a possibility of meddling with the wires at other points:

> At any point upon the route, a mischievous or thoughtless boy might touch the wire with a metal pole or fling another wire across it. If unable to reach it from the walk, he might stand upon a wagon or climb upon a tree.

Despite this, the precautions the defendants had taken were held to be sufficient.[32]

Most of the 15 American cases considered are landmark in laying down defining principles in negligence law. These cases have been widely analyzed and used to substantiate theoretical propositions by researchers in law and economics. In fact, the famous statement of Justice Stone in *Dragotis* that it is not due care to depend on the exercise of due care by others, often serves to demonstrate the untaken precaution approach. In *Dragotis*, although the injurer's negligence is determined using the due care approach, the negligence of the plaintiff was determined by the untaken precaution approach. Similarly, in *Baltimore and Ohio Railroad Company v Goodman*, Justice Holmes argued that in the circumstances the plaintiff's husband who was killed in the accident should have taken the extra precaution of "getting out of the vehicle" to check if a train was approaching. This is an instance of strategic manipulation where the defendant's negligence made this extra precaution warranted in the circumstances. Justice Cardozo, in his landmark judgment in *Pokora*, rejected this standard of getting down to look. This chapter also covered the famous case of *Carroll Towing* in which Judge Hand elaborated on the formula of weighing costs and benefits for determining negligence, which became the "Hand Formula" standard in negligence determination.

Notes

1 202 Minn. 425; 281 N.W. 261; 1938 Minn.
2 Barnes and Stout (1992), p. 110. This aspect has been elaborated in Keeton et al. (1984), pp. 198–199. This case is also known for the fact that before comparative negligence came into force, courts were forced to accept the rule of contributory negligence as a bar to

recovery to the plaintiff. Justice Holt had stated: "No one can appreciate more than we the hardship of depriving the plaintiff of his verdict and of all right to collect damages from defendant; but the rule of contributory negligence, through no fault of ours, remains in our law and gives us no alternative other than to hold that defendant is entitled to judgment notwithstanding the verdict. It would be hard to imagine a case more illustrative of the truth that in operation the rule of comparative negligence would serve justice more faithfully than that of contributory negligence. We blind our eyes to obvious reality to the extent that we ignore the fact that in many cases juries apply it in spite of us. But as long as the legislature refuses to substitute the rule of comparative for that of contributory negligence we have no option but to enforce the law in a proper case."

3 190 Minn. 128; 250 N.W. 804; 1933 Minn.
4 275 U.S. 66; 48 S. Ct. 24; 72 L. Ed. 167; 1927 U.S.
5 292 U.S. 98; 54 S. Ct. 580; 78 L. Ed. 1149; 1934 U.S.
6 The Illinois Act provides: "Every railroad corporation shall cause a bell of at least thirty pounds weight, and a steam whistle placed and kept on each locomotive engine, and shall cause the same to be rung or whistled by the engineer or fireman, at the distance of at least eighty rods from the place where the railroad crosses or intersects any public highway, and shall be kept ringing or whistling until such highway is reached."
7 In the tort literature, the *Goodman* case is paired with *Pokora* and have been analyzed extensively, particularly with regard to the questions of choosing between rigid formalistic categories, what are called the "jurisprudence of rules," and a more flexible, open-textured and policy-oriented approach or the "jurisprudence of balancing" [Johnston (1991)], Holmes's "bright line rule" versus Cardozo's "flexible standard" [Schlag (1985)] and as landmarks in influencing tort law in general [For instance, Schwartz (1999) and Cunningham (2010)].
8 See for instance, Terry (1915), Landes and Posner (1987), Wright (2003), Gilles (2001), Lyons (2005) and Cunningham (2010).
9 43 N.Y. 502; 1871 N.Y.
10 Landes and Posner (1987) have given a reasoning in which they say that if the value of the two lives could be said to be equal, then if the probability of saving the child was higher, then expected benefit was higher; thus, his action was cost-justified.
11 Terry (1915) spelled out the elements of reasonableness of the act of rescue as follows: "(1) The magnitude of the risk was the probability that he would be killed or hurt. That was very great. (2) The principal object was his own life, which was very valuable. (3) The collateral object was the child's life, which was also very valuable. (4) The utility of the risk was the probability that he could save the child. That must have been fairly great, since he in fact succeeded. Had there been no fair chance of saving the child, the conduct would have been unreasonable and negligent. (5) The necessity of the risk was the probability that the child would not have saved himself by getting off the track in time. Here, although the magnitude of the risk was very great and the principal object very valuable, yet the value of the collateral object and the great utility and necessity of the risk counterbalanced those considerations, and made the risk reasonable."
12 Wright (2003) argues that this verdict was incorrect even according to the economic model. Regarding Landes and Posner's assumption that Eckert's life and the child's life are equally valuable, he argues: "While this is a fundamental principle of the equal-freedom-based justice theory and most countries' legal systems, it is an implausible assumption under a utilitarian or economic efficiency theory. Under the latter theories the lives will have different values, depending on the total aggregate utility each is expected to generate or on how much the person or others are willing and able to pay for the person's life. For example, the child may have been mentally and physically disabled, with very limited life prospects, while Eckert may have been a person upon whom many were or would be economically, emotionally, or socially dependent. Or vice versa." He further argues that: "On the actual facts, it seems clear that the ex ante probability of Eckert's being hit (P1) was greater than the ex ante probability of his rescuing the child (P2), since the attempt

to rescue the child would necessarily leave Eckert exposed to the oncoming train for a longer time than would be required to rescue the child." Lyons (2005) cites this case as an example to show that "under the law actors will not always be regarded as culpable for causing foreseeable, seriously harmful consequences. Under certain circumstances, intended ends may justify acceptance of significant foreseeable but unintended harm risked by their conduct."

13 159 F.2d 169; 1947 U.S. App.
14 Kelly (2001) in an exhaustive article on the significance of this case holds that the case and the negligence formula occupy a significant place in current casebooks to show how negligence is determined. However, there is an enormous amount of literature criticizing the central role given by law and economics to the Hand Formula. Richard Wright is one of the most vociferous of the critics; see Wright (2002a, 2002b, 2003). Others include England (1991) and Zipursky (2007). Cunningham (2010) argues: "Because Hand rarely used the formula and later abandoned it, perhaps the Hand formula should be renamed the Posner formula" (n.172).
15 381 So. 2d 955; 1980 La. App.
16 542 So. 2d 1081; 1089 La.
17 930 A.2d 890; 2007 Del.
18 121 Vt. 325, 157 A.2d 468 (Vt. 1960). 13 Id. at 470.
19 788 F.2d 1260; 1986 U.S. App.
20 Wright (2003) argues that: "The precaution of using the two-way radio to notify the second locomotive would hardly have been "elaborate" or burdensome. If there had been any foreseeable possibility, no matter how slight, that Davis might crawl under or between the train cars, the great magnitude of potential injury (L) surely would have required taking this minimal precaution to protect him, since he was a business invitee on the railroad's property." We note that it was clearly stated in the judgment that Lundy did not know who the man in the blue van was, nor at the purpose of his visit was.
21 65 Neb. 889; 91 N.W.880; 1902 Neb.
22 In short, railroad turntables constituted "attractive nuisances" to children. The doctrine of turntable cases constituted an exception to the usual no-duty rule with respect to trespassers on the defendant's land.
23 62 Neb. 66; 86 N.W. 917.
24 149 Wash. 109; 270 P. 422. Supreme Court of Washington, 1928.
25 In a later decision of the same court, *Bartlett v Northern Pacific R. Co.*, 74 Wash. 2d 881 P.2d 735 (1968), where the facts were almost identical, the trial court had granted summary judgment to the defendant based on *Davison*. However, the Supreme Court reversed and remanded, saying: "The reasoning in *Davison* ★★★ was based on the impracticability as a matter of engineering and on prohibitive costs. We do not consider the ideas of the court, expressed 40 years ago, as necessarily authoritative on the engineering and financial phases of the same problem today. We are satisfied that the parties should have opportunity of presenting their evidence as to the practicality (cost wise or otherwise) of guardrails or barriers on dangerous or misleading roadways to stop slow-moving vehicles." We note that the essential difference between the two cases was that what was not a cost-justified precaution during a particular period of time may become one later, with improvements in technology. However, the reasoning was the same.
26 72 Wash. 95, 129 P. 1090.
27 233 Minn. 156; 46 N.W. 2d 260; 1951 Minn.
28 67 Minn. 94, 97, 69 N.W. 640, 641.
29 210 Minn. 523, 526, 299 N.W. 11, 13.
30 84 Wn.2d 882; 529 P.2d 1048; 1975 Wash.
31 227 N.Y. 208; 125 N.E. 93; 1919 N.Y. See for instance, Landes and Posner (1987), Grady (1983), Green (1997) and Cunningham (2010).
32 Rabin (1981) argues that the cost of warning signs on the bridge was ignored in the decision. Landes and Posner (1987) respond to this saying: "Courts ordinarily do not

consider technological possibilities not urged by one of the parties, and although this may mean that judicial decisions do not always reach optimal decisions (which in any case is obvious), it does not contradict the positive economic theory of tort law. With the benefit of hindsight it is possible to imagine all sorts of ways in which courts could have made better decisions, but as long as the approach they employ is efficient within the framework of the facts presented to and recited by the court in its opinion, we are entitled to find our theory, which is a theory about judicial behavior rather than global optima, supported."

References

Barnes, David W. and Lynn A. Stout (1992), *Cases and Materials on Law and Economics*, St. Paul, Minnesota, West Publishing Co.
Buckley, Richard A. (2007), *Buckley: The Law of Negligence*, United Kingdom, LexisNexis Butterworths.
Cunningham, Lawrence A. (2010), 'Traditional versus Economic Analysis: Evidence from Cardozo and Posner Torts Opinions', 62 *Florida Law Review*, 667.
Dobbs, Dan B. (2000), *The Law of Torts*, St. Paul, Minnesota, West Publishing Co.
Dworkin, Ronald (1986), *Law's Empire*, Oxford (UK), Hart Publishing.
Englard, Izhak (1991), 'Law and Economics in American Tort Cases: A Critical Assessment of the Theory's Impact on Courts', 41 *University of Toronto Law Journal*, 359.
Farnsworth, Ward and Mark F. Grady (2009), *Torts – Cases and Questions*, 2nd ed., New York, Aspen Publishers.
Gilles, Stephen G. (2001), 'On Determining Negligence: Hand Formula Balancing, the Reasonable Person Standard, and the Jury', 54 *Vanderbilt Law Review*, 813.
Gilles, Stephen G. (2002), 'Symposium on Negligence in Courts: The Actual Practice: The Emergence of Cost-Benefit Balancing in English Negligence Law', 77 *Chicago-Kent Law Review*, 489.
Grady, Mark F. (1983), 'A New Positive Theory of Negligence', 92 *Yale Law Journal*, 799–829.
Grady, Mark F. (1984), 'Proximate Cause and the Law of Negligence', 69 *Iowa Law Review*, 363–449.
Grady, Mark F. (1988), "Discontinuities and Information Burdens: A Review of the Economic Structure of Tort Law by William M. Landes and Richard A. Posner', 56 *George Washington Law Review*, 658–678.
Grady, Mark F. (1989), 'Untaken Precautions', 18 *Journal of Legal Studies*, 139–156.
Grady, Mark F. (1994), *Cases and Materials on Torts*, St. Paul, Minnesota, West Publishing Co.
Green, Michael D. (1997), 'W. Page Keeton Symposium on Tort Law: Negligence = Economic Efficiency: Doubts', 75 *Texas Law Review*, 1605.
Johnston, Jason Scott (1991), 'Uncertainty, Chaos and the Torts Process: An Economic Analysis of Legal Form', 76 *Cornell Law Review*, 341.
Kelly, Patrick J. (2001), 'Teaching Torts: The Carroll Towing Company Case and the Teaching of Tort Law', 45 *Saint Louis University Law Journal*, 731.
Keeton, W. Page et al. (1984), *Prosser and Keeton on the Law of Torts*, 5th ed., St. Paul, Minnesota, West Publishing Co.
Landes, William M. and Richard A. Posner (1987), *The Economic Structure of Tort Law*, Cambridge (MA), Harvard University Press.
Lyons, Edward C. (2005), 'Balancing Acts: Intending Good and Foreseeing Harm – The Principle of Double Effect in the Law of Negligence', 3 *Georgetown Journal of Law and Public Policy*, 453.
Posner, Richard A. (1972), 'A Theory of Negligence', 1 *Journal of Legal Studies*, 29.

Posner, Richard (1995), 'Wealth Maximization and Tort Law: A Philosophical Inquiry', in David G. Owen (ed.), *Philosophical Foundations of Tort Law*, New York, Oxford University Press.
Posner, Richard (2005), 'The Law and Economics Movement: From Bentham to Becker', in Francesco Parisi and Charles K. Rowley (eds.), *The Origins of Law and Economics: Essays by the Founding Fathers*, Cheltenham (UK), Edward Elgar.
Posner, Richard A. (2007), *Economic Analysis of Law*, 7th ed., New York, Aspen Publishers.
Rabin, Robert L. (1981), 'The Historical Development of the Fault Principle: A Reinterpretation', 15 *Georgia Law Review*, 925.
Rabin, Robert L. (2011), 'The Pervasive Role of Uncertainty in Tort Law: Rights and Remedies', 60 *De Paul Law Review*, 431.
Regan, Donald H. (1972), 'The Problem of Social Cost Revisited', 15 *Journal of Law and Economics*, 427–437.
Rogers, W.V.H. (2010), *Winfield and Jolowicz on Tort*, 18th ed., London, Sweet and Maxwell.
Rose-Ackerman, Susan (1986), 'The Simple Economics of Tort Law: An Organizing Framework', 2 *European Journal of Political Economy*, 91–98.
Rowley, Charles K. (1998), 'Law and Economics from the Perspective of Economics', in Peter Newman (ed.), *The New Palgrave Dictionary of Economics and the Law*, Vol. 2, New York, Macmillan.
Schlag, Pierre (1985), 'Rules and Standards', 33 *University of California Law Review*, 379.
Schwartz, Gary T. (1981), 'Tort Law and the Economy in Nineteenth-Century America: A Re-Interpretation', 90 *Yale Law Journal*, 1717.
Schwartz, Gary T. (1999), 'Cardozo as Lawmaker', 49 *DePaul Law Review*, 305.
Schwartz, Victor E., Katherine Kelly and David F. Partlett (2010), *Prosser, Wade and Schwartz's Torts – Cases and Materials*, 12th ed., New York, Thompson Reuters Foundation Press.
Street, Harry (1972), *The Law of Torts*, 5th ed., London, Butterworths.
Terry, Henry T. (1915), 'Negligence', 29 *Harvard Law Review*, 40–54.
Weir, Tony (2004), *A Casebook on Tort*, 10th ed., London, Sweet and Maxwell.
Wright, Richard W. (2002a), 'Symposium on Negligence in Courts: The Actual Practice: The Emergence of Cost-Benefit Balancing in English Negligence Law', 77 *Chicago-Kent Law Review*, 489.
Wright, Richard W. (2002b), 'Just and Reasonable Care in Negligence Law', 47 *American Journal of Jurisprudence*, 143.
Wright, Richard W. (2003), 'Hand, Posner and the Myth of the Hand Formula', 4 *Theoretical Inquiries in Law*, 145–274.
Zipursky, Benjamin C. (2007), 'Law and Morality: Tort Law: Sleigh of Hand', 48 *William and Mary Law Review*, 1999.

APPENDIX 4.A Schematic representation of the 15 cases analyzed

Case type and No.	Approach (s) Used for Negligence Determination	Names of the cases
4.1 [seven]	Defendant held negligent by reasoning pointing towards the due care approach	*Haeg v Sprague* *Dragotis* *Goodman* *Pokora* *Eckert* *CarrollTowing* *Putt v Daussat*
4.2 [two]	Defendant held negligent by reasoning pointing towards the untaken precaution approach	*Levi v Slemco* *Pipher v Parsell*
4.3 [two]	Defendant held negligent by reasoning pointing towards both the approaches	*Davis* *Chicago B & Q co. v Krayenbuhl*
4.4 [two]	Defendant held nonnegligent using the due care approach.	*Davison v Snohomish County* *Mcdonald v Fryberger*
4.5 [one]	Defendant held nonnegligent using untaken precaution approach.	*Blaak v Davidson*
4.6 [one]	Defendant held nonnegligent using both approaches.	*Adams v Bullock*

5
CONCLUSION

In this book an attempt was made to study the efficiency issue arising from determination of negligence by scrutinizing actual court decisions from three common law jurisdictions – Britain, India and the United States of America. An analysis of the cases reveals that the untaken precaution approach to negligence determination is quite widespread.[1] The mainstream law and economics view is that court decisions are efficient whenever the liability rule used is such that it satisfies the condition of negligence liability. However, when the untaken precaution approach is used, even though the liability rule used may be a rule satisfying negligence liability, the decision may not be efficient.

We note that while in general the two approaches of due care and untaken precaution are logically and completely independent, in some cases, when certain assumptions are satisfied, even when the untaken precaution approach is used, we can infer negligence or otherwise with respect to the due care approach.[2] Therefore, in all cases where the untaken precaution approach is used, the question of efficiency may not be indeterminate. In the cases of *Wagon Mound (2)* and *Pipher v Parsell*, the injurers were held negligent by the untaken precaution approach, but as is clear from the analysis of the cases carried out in Chapters 2 and 4 respectively, they would have been negligent by the due care approach as well. Thus, both the verdicts can be described as efficient.

In most instances when one party is negligent by the due care approach and the other party is nonnegligent by the due care approach, then it would be the case that the party that was nonnegligent by the due care approach would be negligent by the untaken precaution approach because one can expect that extraordinary care on the part of the nonnegligent party can often be beneficial from the point of view of averting a greater social loss. In all cases where one party is nonnegligent by the due care approach, and the nonnegligent party is declared negligent by the untaken precaution approach, we can unambiguously say that the court decision would be inefficient. This is illustrated by the American case of *Haeg v Sprague*, where the injurer was held negligent by the due care approach and the plaintiff was held negligent by the untaken precaution approach. From the facts of the case it appears to be the case that the plaintiff was nonnegligent by the due care approach. Thus, although in *Haeg v Sprague* the liability rule used was the rule of negligence with the defense of contributory negligence that satisfies negligence liability, the court decision was clearly inefficient. By the same reasoning, the decision in the American case of *Dragotis v Kennedy* can be said to be inefficient. In both the cases reference is being made to the final verdicts.

In the Indian case of *Krishna Goods Carriers Private Limited, Delhi v Union of India*, the trial court held the injurer negligent by the due care approach and the plaintiff negligent by the untaken precaution approach. Here also from the facts of the case the plaintiff appears to be nonnegligent by the due care approach. The High Court of Delhi indeed found the plaintiff nonnegligent by the due care approach. In another Indian case – *Pramodkumar Rasikbhai Jhaveri v Karmasey Kunvargi Tak and Others* – the Tribunal had held the injurer negligent by the due care approach and the plaintiff nonnegligent by the due care approach. The High Court of Gujarat adopted the untaken precaution approach and held the plaintiff negligent as well. Thus, it is clear that the decision arrived by the High Court was inefficient.

Further, when both the parties are negligent by the due care approach, they would be negligent by the untaken precaution approach as well. The extent of negligence would, however, depend on whether negligence is construed in terms of the due care approach or the untaken precaution approach. Therefore, if the liability shares under a rule like comparative negligence are determined by the extents of negligence, then it becomes important to know whether the due care approach is being used or the untaken precaution approach is being used. Also the approach needs to be employed consistently. For instance, in the case of *Pramodkumar Rasikbhai Jhaveri v Karmasey Kunvargi Tak and Others*, the High Court of Gujarat had used the untaken precaution approach to hold the plaintiff negligent and apportioned the liability as 70 percent to the injurer and 30 percent to the plaintiff. In a few other cases too we find that the rule used was comparative negligence, but one of the parties was held negligent using the untaken precaution approach. These include the trial court decision in the British case of *Qualcast Ltd.v Haynes*, the trial court decision in the Indian case of *Rural Transport Service v Bezlum Bibi*, the Madhya Pradesh High Court decision in *Vidya Devi v MPSRTC*, the Bombay High Court decision in *Municipal Corporation of Greater Bombay v Shri Laxman Iyer and Another* and the final verdict in the American case of *Davies v Consolidated Rail Corp*.

We note that comparative negligence is not a single liability rule; it is rather a class of liability rules depending on how liability is apportioned when both parties are negligent. If sometimes comparative negligence is used along with the due care approach, and sometimes it is used along with the untaken precaution approach, then in effect different versions of comparative negligence are being used. Although all versions of comparative negligence are efficient, if courts sometimes use one version and at other times use another version, then it is not at all clear whether the court judgments will be efficient. For instance, there are two versions of the negligence rule that courts use – the simple negligence rule in which the negligent injurer is liable for the entire harm to the victim, and the incremental negligence version in which a negligent injurer is liable only for that part of the harm that can be attributed to his negligence. Jain (2011) has shown that if there is uncertainty about which of these versions of the negligence rule will be employed by the courts for determining liability of a negligent injurer, inefficiency is possible, even though both versions of the negligence rule are efficient.

Thus, even when courts are using the so-called efficient liability rules, that is to say, the liability rules satisfying negligence liability like the negligence rule, there are at least three potential sources of inefficiency:

First, the determination of negligence may not be done according to the due care approach, and it is this source of inefficiency that was the primary focus of this study.
The second source of inefficiency arises because courts sometimes use the due care approach and at other times the untaken precaution approach; this means that even though formally courts are using the same rule, in fact they are using different rules at different times.
The third source of inefficiency that has not been investigated in this study, but is quite important, is that even when courts use liability rules satisfying negligence liability and determine negligence according to the due care approach, they may be using sometimes one rule and at other times another rule.[3] Uncertainty about which rule the court will use is a potential source of inefficiency.

This study has shown that there is a need to look at actual court decisions, particularly those cases in which both parties' negligence is discussed. This is because it is in these cases that the efficiency question will often hinge on whether the due care approach is being used or the untaken precaution approach is being adopted. More such cases need to be analyzed to see how often inefficiency occurs due to the use of the untaken precaution approach. Also, there is need for theoretical work to determine the conditions under which inefficiency problems will not arise, notwithstanding the use of more than one liability rule in the same jurisdiction.

One can conclude that a thorough analysis of the actual application of the rules is important to arrive at a conclusion about the efficiency of court verdicts. Referring to their landmark work on the economic structure of tort law, Landes and Posner (1987) had pointed out:

> Another possible objection to our empirical procedure is that we use as evidence to test our theory only two features of appellate opinions in tort cases – the outcome of the case and the rule that can be extracted from the opinion – and ignore the language of the opinion. . . . We agree that judicial reasoning is relevant to the economic analysis of law, because it is essential for determining the actual meaning of the rule that can be extracted from the judicial opinion.[4]

It is only from a scrutiny of the reasoning that one can determine whether the liability rule the court is using is being applied in a manner that allows firm conclusions about efficiency to be reached. Of particular value is deciphering the situations in which the efficiency of the court decision becomes suspect. This would not only help in pointing out inefficient decisions that may have long been taken as precedents but also in aiding academic research by pointing out possible sources of inefficiency.

In this chapter, we conclude that the analysis of cases from three common law jurisdictions reveals that the untaken precaution approach is quite widespread. Regarding the implications of determination of negligence according to one conceptualization on that of the other, one can say that under certain conditions, even when the untaken precaution approach is used we can infer negligence or otherwise with respect to the due care approach. Therefore, cases can be identified in which the untaken precaution approach is used; the question of efficiency is not indeterminate. Further, cases have been identified where one party is nonnegligent by the due care approach and the nonnegligent party is declared negligent by the untaken precaution approach; in these cases, we can unambiguously say that the court decision would be inefficient. When both the parties are negligent by the due care approach, they would be negligent by the untaken precaution approach as well. The extent of negligence would, however, depend on whether negligence is construed in terms of the due care approach or the untaken precaution approach. This would be significant in the case of rules that require apportionment of liability, like in cases of comparative negligence.

Notes

1 Barnes and Stout (1992) had argued that the untaken precaution approach was the dominant approach to negligence determination.
2 Jain (2012b).
3 For instance, in *Miller v Jackson*, while the court is saying that the rule of simple negligence is being used, from the reasoning one finds that strict liability actually is being used. In the Court of Appeal, Lord Geoffrey Lane argued: "The risk of injury to persons and property is so great that on each occasion when a ball comes over the fence and causes damage to the plaintiffs, the defendants are guilty of negligence." In *Klaus Mittelbachert v East India Hotels Ltd.*, it is not clear which rule is being used. Although from the initial reasoning it appears that comparative negligence is being used because the negligence of the plaintiff is discussed in great detail; however, from the final reasoning it appears that simple negligence was used.
4 Landes and Posner (1987), p. 22.

References

Barnes, David W. and Lynn A. Stout (1992), *Cases and Materials on Law and Economics*, St. Paul, Minnesota, West Publishing Co.

Jain, Satish (2011), 'Uncertainty Regarding Interpretation of the "Negligence Rule" and Its Implications for the Efficiency of Outcomes', Unpublished Manuscript, Centre for Economic Studies and Planning, Jawaharlal Nehru University, New Delhi.

Jain, Satish (2012a), 'The Coasian Analysis of Externalities: Some Conceptual Difficulties', Unpublished Manuscript, Centre for Economic Studies and Planning, Jawaharlal Nehru University, New Delhi.

Jain, Satish (2012b), 'A Note on the Logical Relationship between Different Notions of Negligence', Unpublished Manuscript, Centre for Economic Studies and Planning, Jawaharlal Nehru University, New Delhi.

Landes, William M. and Richard A. Posner (1987), *The Economic Structure of Tort Law*, Cambridge (MA), Harvard University Press.

BIBLIOGRAPHY

Abraham, Kenneth S. (2001), 'The Trouble with Negligence', 54 *Vanderbilt Law Review*, 1187.
Arlen, J. (1990), 'Re-Examining Liability Rules When Injurers as Well as Victims Suffer Losses', 10 *International Review of Law and Economics*, 233–239.
Arrow, Kenneth J. (1963), *Social Choice and Individual Values*, 2nd ed., New York, Wiley.
Babu, P.G. et al. (2010), *Economic Analysis of Law in India: Theory and Application*, New Delhi, Oxford University Press.
Baird, Douglas G. et al. (1994), *Game Theory and the Law*, Cambridge (MA), Harvard University Press.
Bar-Gill, Oren and Omri Ben-Shahar (2003), 'The Uneasy Case for Comparative Negligence', 5 *American Law and Economic Review*, 433–469.
Barnes, David W. and Lynn A. Stout (1992), *Cases and Materials on Law and Economics*, St. Paul, Minnesota, West Publishing Co.
Becker, G. (1968), 'Crime and Punishment: An Economic Approach', 76 *Journal of Political Economy*, 169.
Becker, Gary (1971), *The Economics of Discrimination*, Chicago, Chicago University Press.
Becker, Gary (1976), *The Economic Approach to Human Behavior*, Chicago, Chicago University Press.
Becker, Gary (1993), 'Nobel Lecture: The Economic Way of Looking at Behaviour', 101 (3), *Journal of Political Economy*, 385–409. [Reprinted in Francesco Parisi and Charles K. Rowley (eds.), *The Origins of Law and Economics: Essays by the Founding Fathers*, Cheltenham (UK), Edward Elgar.]
Bender, Leslie (1988), 'A Lawyers Primer on Feminist Theory and Tort', 38 *Journal of Legal Education*, 3.
Bender, Leslie (1993), 'An Overview of Feminist Torts Scholarship', 78 *Cornell Law Review*, 575.
Bernstein, Anita (2002), 'Symposium on Negligence in the Courts: The Actual Practice: The Communities that Make Standards of Care Possible', 77 *Chicago-Kent Law Review*, 735.
Brown, John P. (1973), 'Towards an Economic Theory of Liability', 2 *Journal of Legal Studies*, 323–350.
Buckley, Richard A. (2007), *Buckley: The Law of Negligence*, United Kingdom, LexisNexis Butterworths.

Burrows, P. (1999), 'A Deferential Role of Efficiency Theory in Analyzing Causation-Based Tort Law', 8 *European Journal of Law and Economics*, 29–49.
Burrows, P. and Cento G. Veljanovski (1981), 'Introduction: Economic Approach to Law', in P. Burrows and Cento G. Veljanovski (eds.), *The Economic Approach to Law*, London, Butterworths, 1–33.
Calabresi, Guido (1961), 'Some Thoughts on Risk Distribution and the Law of Torts', 70 *Yale Law Journal*, 499–553.
Calabresi, Guido (1970), *The Cost of Accidents: A Legal and Economic Analysis*, New Haven, Yale University Press.
Calabresi, Guido (1975), 'Concerning Cause and the Law of Torts', 43 *University of Chicago Law Review*, 69–108.
Calabresi, Guido (1980), 'About Law and Economics: A Letter to Ronald Dworkin', 8 *Hofstra Law Review*, 553–562.
Calabresi, G. and J. Hirshoff (1972), 'Towards a Test for Strict Liability in Tort', 81, *Yale Law Journal*, 1055–1092.
Calabresi, Guido and D. Melamed (1972), 'Property Rules, Liability Rules and Inalienability: One view of the Cathedral', 85 *Harvard Law Review*, 1089.
Calabresi, Guido and Jeffrey Cooper (1996), 'New Directions in Tort Law', 30 *Valparaiso University Law Review*, 859–884.
Calfee, J. and R. Craswell (1984), 'Some Effects of Uncertainty on Compliance with Legal Standards', 70 *Virginia Law Review*, 965–1003.
Chung, Tai-Yeong (1993), 'Efficiency of Comparative Negligence: A Game Theoretic Analysis', 22 *Journal of Legal Studies*, 395–404.
Coase, Ronald H. (1960), 'The Problem of Social Cost', 3 *Journal of Law and Economics*, 1–44.
Coase, Ronald H. (1993), 'Law and Economics at Chicago', 3 *Journal of Law and Economics*, 1–44.
Coleman, Jules L. (1988), *Markets, Morals and the Law*, Cambridge, Cambridge University Press.
Cooter, Robert D. (1982), 'The Cost of Coase', 11 *Journal of Legal Studies*, 1.
Cooter, Robert D. (1985), 'Unity in Torts, Contracts and Property: The Model of Precaution', 73 *California Law Review*, 1–51.
Cooter, Robert D. (1989), 'Punitive Damages for deterrence: When and how much?' 40 *Alabama Law Review*, 1143–1196.
Cooter, Robert D. (1991), 'Economic Theories of Legal Liability', 5 *Journal of Economic Perspectives*, 11–30.
Cooter, Robert D. and Thomas Ulen (2004), *Law and Economics*, 4th ed., Delhi, Pearson.
Craswell, R. and J. Calfee (1986), 'Deterrence and Uncertain Legal Standards', 2 *Journal of Law, Economics and Organization*, 279–303.
Cunningham, Lawrence A. (2010), 'Traditional versus Economic Analysis: Evidence from Cardozo and Posner Torts Opinions', 62 *Florida Law Review*, 667.
Dari Mattiacci, G. (2002), 'Tort Law and Economics', in A. Hatzis (ed.), *Economic Analysis of Law: A European Perspective*, Cheltenham (UK), Edward Elgar.
Demsetz, Harold (1972), 'When does the Rule of Liability Matter?' 1 *Journal of Legal Studies*, 13.
Demsetz, Harold (1997), 'The Primacy of Economics: An Explanation of the Comparative Success of Economics in the Social Sciences', 35 *Economic Inquiry* 1.
Dharmapala, Dhammika and Sandra Hoffman (2005), 'Bilateral Accident with Intrinsically Interdependent Costs of Precaution', 34 *Journal of Legal Studies*, 239–272.
Diamond, P. (1974), 'Single Activity Accidents', 3 *Journal of Legal Studies*, 107–164.
Diamond, P. (2002), 'Integrating Punishment and Efficiency Concerns in Punitive Damages for Reckless Disregard of Risks to Others', 18 *Journal of Law, Economics and Organization*, 117–139.
Dobbs, Dan B. (2000), *The Law of Torts*, St. Paul, Minnesota, West Publishing Co.

Dworkin, Ronald (1980), 'Is Wealth a Value', 9 *Journal of Legal Studies*, 323–356.
Dworkin, Ronald (1986), *Law's Empire*, Oxford (UK), Hart Publishing.
Englard, Izhak (1991), 'Law and Economics in American Tort Cases: A Critical Assessment of the Theory's Impact on Courts', 41 *University of Toronto Law Journal*, 359.
Farnsworth, Ward and Mark F. Grady (2009), *Torts – Cases and Questions*, 2nd ed., New York, Aspen Publishers.
Feldman, Allan M. and John M. Frost (1998), 'A Simple Model of Efficient Tort Liability Rules', 18 *International Review of Law and Economics*, 201–215.
Ferguson, Adam (1767), *An Essay on the History of Civil Society*, edited by L. Schneider, New Brunswick (NJ), Transaction Publishers, 1980.
Galligan, Thomas C., Jr (1993), 'A Primer on the Patterns of Negligence', 53 *Louisiana Law Review*, 1509.
Galligan, Thomas C., Jr (1997a), 'Cats or Gardens: Which Metaphor Explains Negligence? Or, Is Simplicity Simpler than Flexibility?' 58, *Louisiana Law Review*, 35.
Galligan, Thomas C., Jr (1997b), 'Revisiting the Patterns of Negligence: Some Ramblings Inspired by Robertson', 37 *Louisiana Law Review*, 1119.
Gandhi, B.M. (2006), *Law of Torts*, 3rd ed., Lucknow, Eastern Book Company.
Geistfeld, Mark (2001), 'Economics, Moral Philosophy, and the Positive Analysis of Tort Law', in Gerald J. Postema (ed.), *Philosophy and the Law of Torts*, 250–275, Cambridge, Cambridge University Press.
Gilles, Stephen G. (1992), 'Negligence, Strict Liability and the Cheapest Cost: Avoider', 78 *Virginia Law Review*, 1291.
Gilles, Stephen G. (1994), 'The Invisible Hand Formula', 80 *Virginia Law Review*, 1015–1054.
Gilles, Stephen G. (2001), 'On Determining Negligence: Hand Formula Balancing, the Reasonable Person Standard, and the Jury', 54 *Vanderbilt Law Review*, 813.
Gilles, Stephen G. (2002), 'Symposium on Negligence in Courts: The Actual Practice: The Emergence of Cost-Benefit Balancing in English Negligence Law', 77 *Chicago-Kent Law Review*, 489.
Goodman, John C. (1978), 'An Economic Theory of Evolution of the Common Law', *Journal of Legal Studies*, 393–406.
Grady, Mark F. (1983), 'A New Positive Theory of Negligence', 92 *Yale Law Journal*, 799–829.
Grady, Mark F. (1984), 'Proximate Cause and the Law of Negligence', 69 *Iowa Law Review*, 363–449.
Grady, Mark F. (1988), 'Discontinuities and Information Burdens: A Review of the Economic Structure of Tort Law by William M. Landes and Richard A. Posner', 56 *George Washington Law Review*, 658–678.
Grady, Mark F. (1989), 'Untaken Precautions', 18 *Journal of Legal Studies*, 139–156.
Grady, Mark F. (1994), *Cases and Materials on Torts*, St. Paul, Minnesota, West Publishing Co.
Green, J. (1976), 'On the Optimal Structure of Liability Laws', 7 *Bell Journal of Economics*, 553–574.
Green, Michael D. (1997), 'W. Page Keeton Symposium on Tort Law: Negligence = Economic Efficiency: Doubts', 75 *Texas Law Review*, 1605.
Grey, Thomas C. (2001), 'Accidental Torts', 54 *Vanderbilt Law Review*, 1225.
Haddock, D. and C. Curran (1985), 'An Economic Theory of Comparative Negligence', 14 *Journal of Legal Studies*, 49–72.
Harrington, Matthew (1998), 'The Admiralty Origins of Law and Economics', 7 *George Mason Law Review*, 105.
Hart, H.L.A. (1961), *The Concept of Law*, London, Oxford University Press.
Henderson, James A. (2002), 'Why Negligence Dominates Tort', 50 *UCLA Law Review*, 377.
Hepple, B.A. and M.H. Matthews (1974), *Tort: Cases and Materials*, London, Butterworths.

Hetchner, Steven (2001), 'Non-Utilitarian Negligence Norms and the Reasonable Person Standard', 54 *Vanderbilt Law Review*, 863.

Heuston, R.F.V. and R.A. Buckley (1992), *Salmond and Heuston on the Law of Torts*, 20th ed., London, Sweet and Maxwell.

Hume, David (1739), *A Treatise on Human Nature*, edited by P.H. Nidditch, New York, Oxford University Press, 1978.

Hurd, Heidi M. (1996), 'Symposium: The Deontology of Negligence', 76, *Boston University Law Review*, 249.

Jain, Satish (2011), 'Uncertainty Regarding Interpretation of the "Negligence Rule" and Its Implications for the Efficiency of Outcomes', Unpublished Manuscript, Centre for Economic Studies and Planning, Jawaharlal Nehru University, New Delhi.

Jain, Satish (2012a), 'The Coasian Analysis of Externalities: Some Conceptual Difficulties', Unpublished Manuscript, Centre for Economic Studies and Planning, Jawaharlal Nehru University, New Delhi.

Jain, Satish (2012b), 'A Note on the Logical Relationship between Different Notions of Negligence', Unpublished Manuscript, Centre for Economic Studies and Planning, Jawaharlal Nehru University, New Delhi.

Jain, Satish K. (2006), 'Efficiency of Liability Rules: A Reconsideration', 15 *The Journal of International Trade and Economic Development*, 359–373.

Jain, Satish K. (2007), 'Efficiency of Liability Rules with Multiple Victims', 14 *Pacific Economic Review*, 119–134.

Jain, Satish K. (ed.) (2010a), *Law and Economics*, New Delhi, Oxford University Press.

Jain, Satish K. (2010b), 'On the Efficiency of the Negligence Rule', 14, *Journal of Economic Policy Reform*, 343–359.

Jain, Satish K. (2015), *Economic Analysis of Liability Rules*, New Delhi, Springer.

Jain, Satish K. and Ram Singh (2002), 'Efficient Liability Rules: Complete Characterization', 75 *Journal of Economics*, 105–124.

Jain, Satish K. and Rajendra P. Kundu (2006), 'Characterization of Efficient Simple Liability Rules with Multiple Tortfeasors', 26 *International Review of Law and Economics*, 410–427.

Jain, Satish K. and Rajendra P. Kundu (2011), 'Decomposition of Accident Loss and Efficiency of Negligence Rule', in Krishnendu Ghosh Dostidar et al. (eds.), *Dimensions of Economic Theory and Policy: Essays for Anjan Mukherji*, New Delhi, Oxford University Press.

Johnston, Jason Scott (1991), 'Uncertainty, Chaos and the Torts Process: An Economic Analysis of Legal Form', 76 *Cornell Law Review*, 341.

Kahan, Marcel (1989), 'Causation and Incentives to Take Care under the Negligence Rule', 18 *Journal of Legal Studies*, 427–447.

Kaldor, Nicholas (1939), 'Welfare Propositions of Economics and Interpersonal Comparisons of Utility', 49 *Economic Journal*, 549–552.

Kaplow, Louis and Steven Shavell (1996), 'Property Rules versus Liability Rules', 109 *Harvard Law Review*, 713–790.

Kaplow, Louis and Steven Shavell (1999), 'The Conflict between Notions of Fairness and the Pareto Principle', 1 *American Law and Economics Review*, 63–77.

Keating, Gregory C. (1996), 'Reasonableness and Rationality in Negligence Theory', 48 *Stanford Law Review*, 311.

Keeton, W. Page et al. (1984), *Prosser and Keeton on the Law of Torts*, 5th ed., St. Paul, Minnesota, West Publishing Co.

Kelly, Patrick J. (2001), 'Teaching Torts: The Carroll Towing Company Case and the Teaching of Tort Law', 45 *Saint Louis University Law Journal*, 731.

Kelly, Patrick J. and Laurel A. Wendt (2002), 'Symposium on Negligence in the Courts: The Actual Practice: What Judges Tell Juries About Negligence: A Review of Pattern Jury Instructions', 77 *Chicago-Kent Law Review*, 587.

Kidner, Richard (2002), *Casebook on Torts*, 7th ed., New Delhi, Oxford University Press.

Kornhauser, L. and R. Revesz (1989), 'Sharing Damages among Multiple Tortfeasors', 98 *Yale Law Journal*, 831–890.

Kronman, A. (1995), 'Remarks at the Second Driker Forum for Excellence in the Law', 42 *Wayne Law Review*, 115.

Lakshminath, A. and M. Sridhar (2007), *Ramaswamy Iyer's: The Law of Torts*, 10th ed., Nagpur, LexisNexis Butterworths Wadhwa.

Landes, William M. and Richard A. Posner (1980), 'Joint and Multiple Tortfeasors: An Economic Analysis', 9, *Journal of Legal Studies*, 517–556.

Landes, William M. and Richard A. Posner (1981), 'The Positive Economic Theory of Tort Law', 15 *Georgia Law Review*, 851.

Landes, William M. and Richard A. Posner (1987), *The Economic Structure of Tort Law*, Cambridge (MA), Harvard University Press.

Leong, A.K. (1989), 'Liability Rules When Injurers as Well as Victims Suffer Losses', 9 *International Review of Law and Economics*, 105–111.

Lyons, Edward C. (2005), 'Balancing Acts: Intending Good and Foreseeing Harm: The Principle of Double Effect in the Law of Negligence', 3 *Georgetown Journal of Law and Public Policy*, 453.

Marshall, Jared (2010), 'Note: On the Idea of Understanding Weinrib: Weinrib and Keating on Bipolarity, Duty and the Nature of Negligence', 19, *Southern California Interdisciplinary Law Journal*, 385.

Medema, Steven G. (1999), 'The Place of the Coase Theorem in Law and Economics', 15 *Law and Philosophy*, 209–233.

Miceli, Thomas J. (1997), *Economics of the Law: Torts, Contracts, Property, Litigation*, New York, Oxford University Press.

Miceli, Thomas J. (2004), *The Economic Approach to Law*, California, Stanford University Press.

More, Daniel (2003), 'The Boundaries of Negligence', 4 *Theoretical Inquiries in Law*, 339.

Mumey, Glen A. (1971), 'The "Coase Theorem": A Re-Examination', 85 *Quarterly Journal of Economics*, 718–723.

Noah, Lars (2000), 'General Tort Principles: The Role of Statutes in Common Law Adjudication: Statutes and Regulations: If Noncompliance Establishes Negligence per se, Shouldn't Compliance Count for Something?' 10 *Kansas Journal of Law and Public Policy*, 162.

Owen, David G. (2007), 'The Five Elements of Negligence', 35 *Hofstra Law Review*, 1671.

Perry, Stephen (2001), 'Symposium: Cost – Benefit Analysis and the Negligence Standard', 54 *Vanderbilt Law Review*, 893.

Polinsky, A. Mitchell (2003), *An Introduction to Law and Economics*, 3rd ed., New York, Aspen Publishers.

Polinsky, A. Mitchell and Steven Shavell (1998), 'Punitive Damages: An Economic Analysis', 111 *Harvard Law Review*, 869–962.

Porat, Ariel (2003), 'The Many Faces of Negligence', 4 *Theoretical Inquiries in Law*, 105.

Posner, Richard A. (1972), 'A Theory of Negligence', 1 *Journal of Legal Studies*, 29.

Posner, Richard (1995), 'Wealth Maximization and Tort Law: A Philosophical Inquiry', in David G. Owen (ed.), *Philosophical Foundations of Tort Law*, New York, Oxford University Press.

Posner, Richard (2005), 'The Law and Economics Movement: From Bentham to Becker', in Francesco Parisi and Charles K. Rowley (eds.), *The Origins of Law and Economics: Essays by the Founding Fathers*, Cheltenham (UK), Edward Elgar.

Posner, Richard A. (2007), *Economic Analysis of Law*, 7th ed., New York: Aspen Publishers.
Priest, George L. (1977), 'The Common Law Process and the Selection of Efficient Rules', 6 *Journal of Legal Studies*, 65.
Priest, George L. (1985), 'The Invention of Enterprise Liability: A Critical History of the Intellectual Foundations of Modern Tort Law', 15 *Journal of Legal Studies*, 461.
Priest, George L. (2005), 'The Rise of Law and Economics: A Memoir of the Early Years', in Francesco Parisi and Charles K. Rowley (eds.), *The Origins of Law and Economics: Essays by the Founding Fathers*, Cheltenham (UK), Edward Elgar.
Rabin, Robert L. (1981), 'The Historical Development of the Fault Principle: A Reinterpretation', 15 *Georgia Law Review*, 925.
Rabin, Robert L. (2011), 'The Pervasive Role of Uncertainty in Tort Law: Rights and Remedies', 60 *DePaul Law Review*, 431.
Regan, Donald H. (1972), 'The Problem of Social Cost Revisited', 15 *Journal of Law and Economics*, 427–437.
Rogers, W.V.H. (2010), *Winfield and Jolowicz on Tort*, 18th ed., London, Sweet and Maxwell.
Rose-Ackerman, Susan (1986), 'The Simple Economics of Tort Law: An Organizing Framework', 2 *European Journal of Political Economy*, 91–98.
Rowley, Charles K. (1998), 'Law and Economics from the Perspective of Economics', in Peter Newman (ed.), *The New Palgrave Dictionary of Economics and the Law*, Vol. 2, New York, Macmillan.
Schlag, Pierre (1985), 'Rules and Standards', 33 *University of California Law Review*, 379.
Schwartz, Gary T. (1978), 'Contributory and Comparative Negligence: A Reappraisal', 87 *Yale Law Journal*, 697–727.
Schwartz, Gary T. (1981), 'Tort Law and the Economy in Nineteenth-Century America: A Re-Interpretation', 90 *Yale Law Journal*, 1717.
Schwartz, Warren F. (1989), 'Objective and Subjective Standards of Negligence: Defining the Reasonable Person to Induce Optimal Care and Optimal Populations of Injurers and Victims', 78 *Georgetown Law Journal*, 241.
Schwartz, Gary T. (1992), 'The Beginning and the Possible End of the Rise of Modern Tort Law', 26 *Georgia Law Review*, 601.
Schwartz, Gary T. (1999), 'Cardozo as Lawmaker', 49 *DePaul Law Review*, 305.
Schwartz, Victor E., Katherine Kelly and David F. Partlett (2010), *Prosser, Wade and Schwartz's Torts – Cases and Materials*, 12th ed., New York, Thompson Reuters Foundation Press.
Scitovsky, Tibor (1941), 'A Note on Welfare Propositions in Economics', 9 *Review of Economic Studies*, 77–88.
Sen, Amarya K. (1970), *Collective Choice and Social Welfare*, San Francisco, Holden-Day.
Shavell, Steven (1980a), 'Strict Liability versus Negligence', 9 *Journal of Legal Studies*, 1–25.
Shavell, Steven (1980b), 'An Analysis of Causation and the Scope of Liability in the Law of Torts', 9 *Journal of Legal Studies*, 463–516.
Shavell, Steven (1981), 'A Note on Efficiency v Distributional Equity In Legal Rulemaking: Should Distributional Equity Matter Given Optimal Income Taxation?' 71 *American Economic Review*, 414–418.
Shavell, Steven (1986), 'The Judgment Proof Problem', 6 *International Review of Law and Economics*, 45–58.
Shavell, Steven (1987), *Economic Analysis of Accident Law*, Cambridge (MA), Harvard University Press.
Shavell, Steven (2004), *Foundations of Economic Analysis of Law*, Cambridge (MA), Harvard University Press.
Shavell, Steven (2007), 'Liability for Accidents', in A. Mitchell Polinsky and Steven Shavell (eds.), *Handbook of Law and Economics*, Vol. 1, Oxford (UK), North-Holland.

Singh, Ram (2003), 'Efficiency of "Simple" Liability Rules When Courts Make Erroneous Estimation of the Damage', 16 *European Journal of Law and Economics*, 39–58.

Singh, Ram (2004), 'Economics of Judicial Decision-Making in Indian Tort Law. Motor Accident Cases', *Economic and Political Weekly*, June 19, 2613–2616.

Singh, Ram (2007), 'Causation-Consistent Liability, Economic Efficiency and the Law of Torts', 27 *International Review of Law and Economics*, 179–203.

Singh, G.P. (2010), *Ratanlal and Dhirajlal The Law of Torts*, 26th ed., Nagpur, LexisNexis Butterworths Wadhwa.

Smith, Adam (1776), *The Wealth of Nations*, Vol. 2, edited by E. Cannan, London: Metheun and Co, 1904; repr. 1961.

Street, Harry (1972), *The Law of Torts*, 5th ed., London, Butterworths.

Summers, J. (1983), 'The Case of the Disappearing Defendant: An Economic Analysis', 132 *University of Pennsylvania Law Review*, 145–185.

Terry, Henry T. (1915), 'Negligence', 29 *Harvard Law Review*, 40–54.

Weinrib, Ernest J. (1980), 'The Case for a Duty to Rescue', 90 *Yale Law Journal*, 247.

Weinrib, Ernest J. (2007), 'Can Law Survive Legal Education', 60 *Vanderbilt Law Review*, 401.

Weir, Tony (2004), *A Casebook on Tort*, 10th ed., London, Sweet and Maxwell.

Wright, Richard W. (1987), 'The Efficiency Theory of Causation and Responsibility: Unscientific Formalism and False Semantics', 63 *Chicago-Kent Law Review*, 553.

Wright, Richard W. (1995a), 'Right, Justice and Tort Law', in David G. Owen (ed.), *Philosophical Foundations of Tort Law*, New York, Oxford University Press.

Wright, Richard W. (1995b), 'The Standards of Care in Negligence Law', in David G. Owen (ed.), *Philosophical Foundations of Tort Law*, New York, Oxford University Press.

Wright, Richard W. (2002a), 'Symposium on Negligence in Courts: The Actual Practice: The Emergence of Cost-Benefit Balancing in English Negligence Law', 77 *Chicago-Kent Law Review*, 489.

Wright, Richard W. (2002b), 'Justice and Reasonable Care in Negligence Law', 47 *American Journal of Jurisprudence*, 143.

Wright, Richard W. (2003), 'Hand, Posner and the Myth of the Hand Formula', 4 *Theoretical Inquiries in Law*, 145–274.

Zipursky, Benjamin C. (2007), 'Law and Morality: Tort Law: Sleigh of Hand', 48 *William and Mary Law Review*, 1999.

INDEX

Abraham, Kenneth S. 29
accidental injuries 8
actual court judgments 19
Adams v Bullock 199
Ahlawat, Avnish 127
Albert, C. 188, 189
Allen, Judge 167
altruistic reasonable person standard 22
American Institute's First Restatement of Torts 25
American tort law 2; principle 1
Anglo-American tort law 24
Anglo-Newfoundland Development Co v Pacific Steam Navigation Co. 74
apportionment of damage 61
Arlen, J. 13, 14
Arrow, Kenneth J. 7
Article 36 of Limitation Act, 1908 123
Article 120 of Limitation Act 124
Asquith, L. J. 65, 69, 71, 90, 92
Atkin, Lord 121
Atkinson, J. 116
Australia 3
auto-guest statutes 2
average-man rule 21
average value functions 22

Balakrishnan, Justice 118, 119
Baltimore and Ohio Railroad Company v Goodman 159, 162, 163, 201
Barber v British Road Services 76
Barnes, David W. 157

Becker, Gary 4
Belka v Prosperini 60
Bender, Leslie 26, 27
Bentham, Jeremy 3, 4
Bessette v Humiston 181
bilateral care 18, 20
Birkenhead, Lord 77
Blaak v Davidson 195
Blomberg v Trupukka 194
Bloor, Kenneth Charles 98
Blyth v Birmingham Waterworks Co. 33n1
Bolton v Stone 49, 85, 100
Bombay High Court 132, 139, 140, 146, 149
Bombay Police Act 147
breach of duty 9, 88, 169
Britain 3; selection of cases 31–33, 43–103
Brown, John P. 11, 18
Browne v Central SMT Co. 59, 60
Brown v Kendall 1
Bucknill, L. J. 73, 74
but-for test of causation 72, 169
Butterfield v Forrester 1

Cairns, L. J. 76
Calabresi, Guido 5, 13
Calfee, J. 12
Cardozo, Justice 162–165, 198–201
Carmont, Lord 82
causation 10, 13, 72
cause-in-fact 15, 17, 169, 171, 190; of harm 10

Charlesworth 73, 131
Chicago, Burlington and Quincy Railroad Co. v Leo Krayenbuhl 187
Christianson v C. St. P. M. & O. Ry. Co. 194
Christopher Clarke, Lord 63
Circuit Court of Appeals 159, 162
Clause (f) of Rule 100, Motor Vehicles Act (1939) 142
Clauson, Lord 84
Clerk, Lord 107, 120, 126, 135
Coase, Ronald H. 3, 4, 7, 8, 33, 54, 55
Coase theorem 5, 8
Cohen, L. J. 69
Coleman, Jules L. 5
collective negligence liability 13
common law 5, 8, 143
Common Law, The 15
common law jurisdictions 2
community norm 22, 29
comparative negligence 3
contributory negligence 2, 13, 29, 73, 78, 116, 118, 138
Corporation of Glasgow v Muir and Others 81
cost-benefit analysis 16, 17, 22, 24, 26
cost-benefit balancing 24, 25
cost-justified precaution 20, 201
cost-justified untaken precaution 19, 89, 159
Cost of Accidents, The 5
court decisions 20
Court of Appeals 44, 50, 51, 56, 58, 61–69, 71, 73, 78, 81, 86, 88, 90, 91, 93–96, 98, 99, 144, 160, 162, 163, 165, 166, 171, 172, 174, 176, 180, 182, 183, 196, 201; of Louisiana 171, 172; of New York 166, 199; of Washington 195
Craswell, R. 12
Cumming-Bruce, Lord 50, 53, 55

Davies v Mann 2, 74
Davies v Swan Motor Company (Swansea) Limited 73
Davison v Snohomish County 190
Davis v Consolidated Rail Corporation 72, 182
degree of blameworthiness 61
degree of competence 94
Delhi High Court, India 109, 111, 112, 127
Demetrius Dragotis v Vincent Kennedy and Another 157
Denning, L. J. 44, 50, 52, 55, 73, 74, 78–81, 91, 98, 100
Desai, Justice 124
Diamond, P. 12
Diplock, Lord 46–47
Director, Aaron 4
Director-Coase type of work 5
disproportionate cost approach 24, 25

Divan, Justice 124
Donoghue v Stevenson 44, 120, 121
Dragotis v Kennedy 30, 208
due care approach 9, 14, 207; holding injurer negligent 155–173, 182–190; holding injurer nonnegligent 190–195, 199–201; injurer declared negligent 43–58, 64–81, 104–126, 129–152; injurer declared nonnegligent 81–100
Dunedin, Lord 60, 70, 148
Du Parcq, Lord 60, 70–72, 134, 151
Dworkin, Ronald 5

Eckert v Long Island Railroad 165
economic analysis of law 3–8
Economic Analysis of Law, The 5
economic analysis of tort law 8–14, 31
Economic Approach to Human Behavior, The 4
Economic Structure of Tort Law, The 6
economic theory of crime 4
efficient levels of care 11, 14
efficient liability rules 209
Elias, Justice 64
Ellerman Lines, Ltd. V Grayson 101n32
equal freedom theory 28, 29
Eurymedon, The 74, 77
Evershed, L. J. 74
Evershed, M. R. 96, 97
expected accident loss 11
expected liability 11, 18
externalities 7, 34n22
extraordinary precautions 58, 60, 63, 64, 70, 72, 118, 120, 148

Fardon v Harcourt-Rivington 70, 148
Fatal Injuries Acts 1846–59 75
fault concept 1
Feldman, Heidi 26
"feminine" ethic of care 26
Finley, Justice 197, 198
Flanelly v Delaware and Hudson Co. 225 U.S. 597, 603 161
Frazee v Gulf States Utilities Co. 498 So. 2d 47 175

Gavigan, Nicholas Joseph 63
Geddis v Proprietors of Barn Reservoir 46
General Cleaning Contractors Limited and Others v Christmas 78
General Cleaning Contractors v Christmas 103
Geoffrey Lane, Lord 50–53, 55
Gilles, Stephen G. 21–26, 32
Glasgow Corp v Muir 103
Gobald Motor Service Ltd. v Veeraswami Chettiar 134
Goddard, C. J. 65

Index

Government of NCT of Delhi and Others v Sudha Devi and Another 127
Grady, Mark F. 14–18, 22, 30
Green, J. 12, 197
Greene, M. R. 70–72
Greer, L. J. 74
Grey, Thomas C. 24
Grover, Judge 166, 167
Guidry, Judge 176
Gwalior Tribunal 116

Haeg v Sprague, Warner and Co. Inc. 111, 155, 208
Hailsham, Lord 119
Halsbury 138, 144
Hand, Judge 169–171, 201
Hand Formula 21–25, 168
Harvey v Road Haulage Executive 76
Havers, Lord 60
Hedley Bryne 120
Hendricks v Peabody Coal Co. 16
High Court, India 105–108, 114, 117, 118, 120, 122, 124–129, 131, 133–135, 138, 141, 143, 144, 146
Hodson, L. J. 79, 80, 91
Holland, Justice 182
Holmes, Justice 159, 161, 162, 198, 201
Holmes, Oliver Wendall 15, 16
Holt, Justice 156, 157
Home Office v Dorset Yacht Company Limited 43, 100, 120
Hood, J. J. 171
Hooper, Justice 61
House of Lords 66, 68, 72, 78, 80–82, 85–93, 96, 98, 99, 131
Hughes, Justice 62
Humphreys, Judge 68–70

idem for idem case 54
India: selection of cases 31–33, 104–154
individualized due care 80, 88, 93, 123, 151
Introduction to the Principles of Morals and Legislation 3
invisible Hand Formula 23
Ishwardas Paulsrao Ingle v General Manager, Maharashtra State Road Transport Corporation, Bombay and Others 139
Iyer, Venkatarama (Justice) 134

Jain, Satish K. 6, 12–14, 17–20, 209
Jay Laxmi Salt Works Pvt. Ltd. v State of Gujarat 123
Jenkins, L. J. 86, 94
Jones, J. 78
Jones v Livox Quarries Ltd. 74

Journal of Law and Economics 4
Jowitt, Earl 80
judgment-proof problem 13
Jung Bahadur Singh v Sundarlal Mandal and Others 106

Kahan, Marcel 18
Kaldor criterion 7
Kaldor-Hicks criterion 6
Kaldor-Hicks efficiency 6
Kaldor principle 6
Kantian-Aristotelian theory of legal responsibility 27
Karnataka High Court 134
Keeton, W. Page 8, 21, 29, 30, 32
Keith, Lord 98, 99
Kelly, Patrick J. and Wendt, Laurel A. 26
Kerala High Court 149–151
Klaus Mittelbachert v The East India Hotels Ltd. 111
Knightley v Johns and others 55
Knoll, Judge 175, 176
Krishna Goods Carriers Private Limited, Delhi v Union of India 109, 208
Kronman, A. 5
Kundu, Rajendra P. 12, 14

Lahoti, Justice 112, 113
Landes, William M. 5, 8, 12, 13, 15, 16, 20, 21, 24, 25, 209
Lang v London Transport Executive and Another 58, 63, 64
last clear chance 1
Latimer v Aec Limited 51, 90
Law of Negligence, The 73
Law of Torts 124
Law Reform (Contributory Negligence) Act, 1945 2
Laws of England 138, 144
Leber v King County, 69 Wash. 134, 124 P. 397, 42 L.R.A. (N.S) 267 192
legal liability 82
Lemmon, J. 180
Leong, A.K. 40
Levi v Southwest Louisiana Electric Membership Cooperative 173
liability assignments 8
liability rules 8, 9, 11–13, 17, 207
Lindsell, Lord 107, 120, 126, 135
litigation 139
Lloyd-Jacob, J. 79, 80
Llyods Bank Limited and Another v Railway Executive 144
London Passenger Transport Board v Upson and Another 59, 68, 76, 131, 134, 135
Lynskey, J. 64–67

222 Index

Macdermott, Lord 66, 67
Mackay, Lord 59
Mackenna, J. 76, 77
Macmillan, Lord 82, 85, 120
Madhya Pradesh High Court 130, 136
Madhya Pradesh State Road Transport Corporation and another v Ms. Basantibai and Others 120
Madras High Court 134
mainstream conceptualization of negligence 14
Maritime Conventions Act, 1911 2
"masculine" ethic 26
Mcdonald v Fryberger 193
Menon, Balakrishna 149
Merton, Lord 71, 72
Miller v Jackson 50, 100
Minor Veeran and another v Krishnamoorthy and Another 149
momentary physical faintness 85
Moncrieff, Lord 83
Montgomery, Edmond A. (Judge) 157
Morton, Lord 66, 68, 97
Motor Accidents Claims Tribunal 118, 130, 131, 133, 139, 141
Motor Vehicles Accident Claims Tribunal 104, 105
multiple tortfeasors 75, 135
Municipal Corporation of Delhi v Subhagwanti and Others 114
Municipal Corporation of Delhi v Sushila Devi Smt. And Others 125
Municipal Corporation of Greater Bombay v Shri Laxman Iyer and Another 131
Munson, Justice 196

Nair, M. Madhavan (Justice) 150, 151
Nandrajog, Pradeep (Justice) 127, 128
Negligence 131
negligence concept 1, 3, 9–11, 17–19, 22, 23, 29, 31, 59, 66, 114, 137, 142, 150, 159, 166, 200, 210; in Anglo-American law 24; conceptualizations, economic analysis of law 14–20; defined 23; legal literature, competing conceptualizations of 20–31; vitality of 2
negligence determination 3, 13, 14, 17, 18, 20, 21, 24, 25, 31, 32, 55, 68, 72, 74, 78, 99, 100, 100n12, 122, 141, 145, 162, 168, 201, 207, 210n1
negligence liability 12, 13, 19, 20, 26, 207–209
Normand, Lord 66, 67
Norris, Judge 96, 98, 99

novus actus interveniens 63
nuisance 8, 50, 52–55, 85, 86, 116, 203n22

Oaksey, Lord 67, 80, 81, 91
Oliver, L. J. 86
optimal care 13, 16, 23
optimal loss 14
Ordinary, Lord 82, 85
ordinary care concept 26
Owen, David G. 9

Pareto-criterion 6
Pareto efficiency 6
Paris v Stepney Borough Council 64, 97
Parker, L.J. 97
proximate cause 9, 10, 171, 181, 196
Parmasivan v Wicks 61
Pasayat, Arijit (Justice) 132
Patel, Justice 146–148
Patna High Court, India 106–108
Pearce, Lord 120
Pearson, Lord 44–46
Pedestrian Crossing Places (Traffic) Regulations, 1941 69, 71
Peterson, Justice 156, 157
Pigou's solution of state intervention 7
Pilcher, Judge 90, 93
Pipher v Parsell 180, 207
Pokora v Wabash Railway Co. 162
Porter, Lord 71, 148
Posner, Judge 72, 183–186
Posner, Richard A. 3–6, 8, 11–13, 15, 16, 20, 21, 23–25, 209
practical legal theory 23
Pramodkumar Rasikbhai Jhaveri v Karmasey Kunvargi Tak and Others 118, 208
Prasad, Justice Raj Kishore 107
President, Lord 85
Priest, George L. 5
"The Problem of Social Cost" 3, 4, 7
property rights 8
Prosser, Wade and Schwartz's Torts – Cases and Materials 32
Prosser and Keeton on the Law of Torts 32
Pushpabai Purshottam Udeshi and Others v Ranjit Ginning and Pressing Company Private Limited and Another 122
Putt v Daussat 171

Qualcast (Wolverhampton) Limited v Haynes 81, 96
Queen's Bench Division 59, 90

Radcliffe, Lord 88, 89, 99
Railway Accident Enquiry Committee 109

Raina, Justice 137, 138
Ratanlal and Dhirajlal The Law of Torts 32
reasonable care 22
reasonable foreseeability 10, 128
reasonable foreseeable risk 24, 25, 87
reasonable man 21
reasonableness 27
reasonable person 22
reasonable person standard 30, 31
Reed, Frank E. (Judge) 155
Reeve, J. 50, 51, 53, 55
Reid, Lord 49, 55, 80, 81, 87, 89, 90, 120
Re Polemis 48
res ipsa loquitur 115
Restatement (Third) of Torts (2005) 1, 23, 24
Richards, Norman 75
right, supreme principle 28
Rix, Lord 61
Rogers, W.V.H. 31
Rohtagi, Justice 109, 110
Romer, Lord 84
Rouse v Squires and others 75
Rural Transport Corporation v Bezlum Biwi 152
Rural Transport Service v Bezlum Bibi and Others 104

Sahai, Justice 124
Santharama Rao, K. 133, 134
Sarla Dixit v Balwant Yadav 154
Schwartz, Gary T. 2, 32, 33
Scitovsky, Tibor 7
Scott v Gavigan 63
Section 13 of Railways Act, 1890 143, 144
Section 78 of Motor Vehicles Act 130
select American cases: due care approach, holding injurer negligent 155–173, 182–190; due care approach, holding injurer nonnegligent 190–195, 199–201; economic analysis of 155–204; untaken precaution approach, holding injurer negligent 173–190; untaken precaution approach, holding injurer nonnegligent 195–201
select British cases: due care approach, injurer declared negligent 43–58, 64–81; due care approach, injurer declared nonnegligent 81–100; economic analysis of 43–103; untaken precaution approach, injurer declared negligent 58–81
select Indian cases: due care approach, injurer declared negligent 104–126, 129–152; economic analysis of 104–154; untaken precaution approach, injurer declared negligent 127–152

Sellers, L. J. 97
Shavell, Steven 12, 13
Shaw, Chief Justice 1
Shaw, Lord 74
Sheth, Justice 124
Simon, Justice 64
Simonds, Lord 66, 68
Singh, G. P. (Justice) 32, 120, 121, 124, 130, 131, 136–138
Singh, Ram 12
single-owner instructions 23
Singleton, L. J. 86, 91
Smith v Leurs 46
Smt. Sarla Dixit and Another v Balwant Yadav and Others 116
social costs 11, 12, 17–20
socially efficient levels of care 11
Somervell, L. J. 86, 88–90
S. S. Wagon Mound 47
standard man 21
standards of care 27, 28
Stanley Burnton, Lord 61
State v Bhalchandra Waman Pethe 145, 152
Stephenson, L. J. 56, 57
Stepney Borough Council 64
Stone, Justice 158, 201
Stout, Lynn A. 157
Stovin v Wise 144, 145
strict liability 1, 2, 9, 11, 12, 13, 14, 33n2, 50, 93, 114, 210n3
Sturges v Bridgman 52, 53
substantial risk 24–26, 49, 88
Summers, J. 13
Sundara Shetty v K. Sanjeeva Rao (Deceased by L. Rs.) and Others 133
Supreme Court: of Delaware 181; of Louisiana 173, 176; of Minnesota 155–158, 193; of Nebraska 187, 188; of New South Wales 48; of New York 166, 199; of United States 159, 162, 163; of Vermont 181; of Washington 191, 195, 197
Supreme Court, India 114–117, 122–126, 141–145, 147, 149; Regulation (6) of Tenth Schedule of Motor Vehicles Act, 1939 118; Regulation (7) of Tenth Schedule of Motor Vehicles Act, 1939 117
Sushma Mitra v Madhya Pradesh State Road Transport Corporation 135, 140
Sutherland Shire Council v Heyman 144
Swadling v Cooper 119

Tarasoff v Regents of University of California 2
Terry, Henry T. 21

Thankerton, Lord 83–85
"Theory of Negligence, A" 11
Thesiger, Lord Justice 44, 53, 54
Thompson, Lord 59
total social cost 11, 12, 14, 17, 18, 19, 20, 34n28
Tucker, Lord 92
Tucker v Draper 188
turntable cases 188, 189

unilateral care 19, 20
unintentional torts 1
Union of India v United India Insurance Company Limited and Others 141
United States 2; selection of cases 31–33, 155–204
United States v Carroll Towing 168
untaken precaution 14–20, 22, 30–32, 36n58, 43, 47, 48, 50, 52, 53, 56, 58, 60–63, 67, 68, 71–74, 78–81, 85–91, 93, 95, 99, 100, 103, 106, 107, 108, 110, 111, 116, 118, 120, 123, 126, 127–129, 131, 133, 135, 139, 142, 144, 145, 151, 152, 154, 157, 159, 161, 164, 165, 167, 170–173, 178, 180–183, 185, 186, 189, 190–192, 195–199, 200, 201, 206–210, 210n1
untaken precaution approach 14, 15, 17, 18, 20, 30–32, 36n58, 43, 50, 58, 60, 61, 67, 68, 71–74, 78, 80, 81, 85, 90, 93, 99, 100, 103, 106, 111, 120, 127–129, 131, 133, 135, 139, 152, 154, 157, 159, 162, 167, 171, 172, 173–182, 186, 190, 195–199, 201, 206–210, 210n1
Uthwatt, Lord 70, 72, 76, 135
utilitarian calculus 15
utilitarian-efficiency theory 27

vicarious liability 122
Vidya Devi and Another v Madhya Pradesh State Road Transport Corporation and Another 129
virtue ethics theory 26
visible Hand Formula 23
Volute, The 77

Wagon Mound 100
Wagon Mound (1) 47–48, 128
Wagon Mound (2) 47, 48, 55, 128, 207
Wahane, W. U. (Justice) 140
Walton, H. H. J. 61
wealth maximization theory 6
Weinrib, Ernest J. 5, 24, 26, 28, 55
Wells, Catherine 26
Wells v Cooper 93
Winfield and Jolowicz – Torts 31
Wright, Richard W. 24, 26–29, 84, 85
Wringe v Cohen 116

Zolawenski v Aberdeen 192